OBJECTIVE PERSONALITY ASSESSMENT
Changing Perspectives

PERSONALITY AND PSYCHOPATHOLOGY
A Series of Monographs, Texts, and Treatises

1. The Anatomy of Achievement Motivation, *Heinz Heckhausen.* 1966
2. Cues, Decisions, and Diagnoses: A Systems-Analytic Approach to the Diagnosis of Psychopathology, *Peter E. Nathan.* 1967
3. Human Adaptation and Its Failures, *Leslie Phillips.* 1968
4. Schizophrenia: Research and Theory, *William E. Broen, Jr.* 1968
5. Fears and Phobias, *I. M. Marks.* 1969
6. Language of Emotion, *Joel R. Davitz.* 1969
7. Feelings and Emotions, *Magda Arnold.* 1970
8. Rhythms of Dialogue, *Joseph Jaffe* and *Stanley Feldstein.* 1970
9. Character Structure and Impulsiveness, *David Kipnis.* 1971
10. The Control of Aggression and Violence: Cognitive and Physiological Factors, *Jerome L. Singer* (ed.). 1971
11. The Attraction Paradigm, *Donn Byrne.* 1971
12. Objective Personality Assessment: Changing Perspectives, *James N. Butcher* (ed.). 1972

In Preparation

Schizophrenia and Genetics, *Irving I. Gottesman* and *James Shields*

OBJECTIVE PERSONALITY ASSESSMENT

Changing Perspectives

Edited by JAMES N. BUTCHER
Department of Psychology
University of Minnesota
Minneapolis, Minnesota

ACADEMIC PRESS   New York and London   1972

Copyright © 1972, by Academic Press, Inc.
ALL RIGHTS RESERVED
NO PART OF THIS BOOK MAY BE REPRODUCED IN ANY FORM,
BY PHOTOSTAT, MICROFILM, RETRIEVAL SYSTEM, OR ANY
OTHER MEANS, WITHOUT WRITTEN PERMISSION FROM
THE PUBLISHERS.

ACADEMIC PRESS, INC.
111 Fifth Avenue, New York, New York 10003

United Kingdom Edition published by
ACADEMIC PRESS, INC. (LONDON) LTD.
24/28 Oval Road, London NW1

LIBRARY OF CONGRESS CATALOG CARD NUMBER: 73-182655

PRINTED IN THE UNITED STATES OF AMERICA

CONTENTS

List of Contributors   vii
Preface   ix

Chapter 1   **Personality Assessment: Problems and Perspectives**
     James N. Butcher

Sources of Criticism of Personality Assessment	4
Objective Personality Assessment	12
References	17

Chapter 2   **Where Have We Gone Wrong?**
     The Mystery of the Missing Progress
     Starke R. Hathaway

The Clue of the Elusive Construct	24
The Clue of the Complex Origin	26
The Clue of the Missing Criteria	30
The Clue of the Unproductive Strategy	35
The Solution?	39
References	42

Chapter 3   **Some Limitations of Objective Personality Tests**   45
     Jane Loevinger

References	57

v

Chapter 4 **Psychometric Considerations for a Revision of the MMPI** 59
Warren T. Norman

Diagnosis 64
Psychophysics and Scale Development 72
Personality Assessment and Conclusion 81
References 83

Chapter 5 **Whither the MMPI?** 85
W. Grant Dahlstrom

References 114

Chapter 6 **The Practical Problems of Revising an Established Psychological Test** 117
David P. Campbell

Technical Ignorance 118
User Acceptance 120
The Administrative Arrangements 124
References 130

Chapter 7 **Reactions, Reflections, Projections** 131
Paul E. Meehl

References 184

Author Index 191
Subject Index 197

LIST OF CONTRIBUTORS

Numbers in parentheses indicate the pages on which the authors' contributions begin

JAMES N. BUTCHER (1), Department of Psychology, University of Minnesota, Minneapolis, Minnesota

DAVID P. CAMPBELL (117), Department of Psychology, University of Minnesota, Minneapolis, Minnesota

W. GRANT DAHLSTROM (85), Department of Psychology, University of North Carolina, Chapel Hill, North Carolina

STARKE R. HATHAWAY (21), Department of Psychology, Univeristy of Minnesota, Minneapolis, Minnesota

JANE LOEVINGER (45), Department of Psychology, Washington University, St. Louis, Missouri

WARREN T. NORMAN (59), Department of Psychology, University of Michigan, Ann Arbor, Michigan

PAUL E. MEEHL (131), Department of Psychology, University of Minnesota Minneapolis, Minnesota

PREFACE

The field of personality assessment is presently undergoing a great deal of scrutiny and change. Recent research is marked by advances in test construction methodology, developments of "new" instruments to assess well-defined personality dimensions and clinical problems, and elaborate, novel applications of existing "tried" assessment devices. Many assessment procedures such as the projective techniques and some personality inventories, which have received the lion's share of attention, have more recently been succumbing to wide criticism due to their inherent limitations.

Progress in personality assessment is reflected in the process by which a given approach or procedure has come into being as an innovating focus on generating and/or examining behavior or by using a novel way of analyzing or categorizing the test data. The resulting procedure, if the product is useful and offers some validity, will find many uses and misuses until its natural limitations (e.g., narrow response format, low reproducibility, inherent invalidity for some situations, etc.) are reached. It is by examining the drawbacks and limitations of these instruments or the assumptions upon which they are based that the field of personality measurement is able to progress.

This volume is devoted to an examination of issues surrounding personality assessment with objective personality inventories, particularly the most widely used and researched instrument, the Minnesota Multiphasic Personality inventory (MMPI). Five of the papers published in this volume (those by Hathaway, Norman, Loevinger, Campbell, and Dahlstrom) are based on invited addresses at the *Fifth Annual Symposium on Recent Developments in the Use of the MMPI*. This Symposium, honoring the long and distinguished contribution of Starke Hathaway to the field of personality assessment, focused upon the question of whether the MMPI was in need of revision and what problems would surround such an enterprise. In Chapter 2, Professor Hathaway presents his views on the present state of personality assessment and issues some challenges to psychologists who would study the elusive construct, personality. In Chapter 3, Professor Loevinger, who has contributed substantially to the area of personality measurement in the past, gives perspectives and boundaries to the subject matter of this volume. Professor Norman's chapter brings under scrutiny the questionable need for an "omnibus" type of personality inventory and clearly describes the psychometric problem which this entails. In Chapter 5, Professor Dahlstrom, taking the position that an instrument like the MMPI will be needed for some time to come, makes a strong case for revising the MMPI within its present format. Dahlstrom presents some ideas for modifying the MMPI in such a way as to make the information that is contained in the existing MMPI item pool more available to the clinical interpreter in the form of several "experimental" scales. In Chapter 6, Professor Campbell, fresh from revising a major psychological instrument (the Strong Vocational Interest Blank), cautions the "would-be reviser" of the MMPI about the problems that would be encountered. In Chapter 7, Professor Meehl brings a great perspective to the issues under consideration. Having been instrumental in the early development of the empirical method and contributed substantially to personality assessment for over 25 years, Paul Meehl is unusually well qualified to provide this perspective.

A number of other people have contributed to the production of this volume. I would like to express my appreciation to the staff of the Nolte Center for Continuing Education at the University of Minnesota for their continued support of the *Objective Personality Assessment Symposium Series*. I would like to thank Beverly Kaemmer for her editorial assistance and Mary Anne Larson and Carol Glewwe for their help in typing and indexing the volume. The contribution of my family, Nancy, Sherry, Jay, and Neal, always merits acknowledgment.

1

PERSONALITY ASSESSMENT:
Problems and Perspectives

James N. Butcher

Individual differences in personality have long been recognized. In the last hundred years, psychologists have made a great deal of progress in developing procedures for assessing personality. A large number of assessment methods, tests, and gadgets have been used to assay man's behavior, attitudes, thoughts, aspirations, and deviations.

All of these approaches to assessing, categorizing, or measuring personality have involved collecting responses from, or making observations about, the subject which could be used to infer more general personality traits or status characteristics. These methods (listed in Table 1) range from examining relatively superficial physical characteristics, such as head size, to taking complex and highly sensitive physiological measures, such as EEG recordings. Some of these approaches involve a greater inferential leap from the assessment index to the generalization than others do (e.g., heavily shaded drawings versus a response of "true" to the item "I feel anxious much of the time" as indices of anxiety). Some of the assessment approaches involve

TABLE 1

Personality Assessment Methods

Psychological attributes being assessed	Illustrative assessment techniques
Physical characteristics	Measurement of head size and shape; somatotype
Psychomotor performance	Various dexterity measures, finger tapping; memory for digits
Perceptual skills	Perceiving incongruity of situations, spiral after-image; differential development of perceptual skills, e.g., size constancy
Physiological processes	Galvanic skin response; electroencephalographic recording; rapid eye movements (REM); various operative techniques
Performance in specified tasks	Small group interaction; psychodrama
Informant report	Behavioral descriptions; Q-sort technique; rating scales; behavioral inventories
Verbal self-report	Interview; autobiographies; self-report questionnaire; free association; paired association
Nonverbal self-report	Expressive movements, gestures, etc.; gait, posture, attire, etc.
Projection-apperception	The Rorschach; various constructive, thematic, completion tasks which encourage individual responding to ambiguous stimulus situations

extremely weak and unsupported connections of test sign to behavior; for example, the "draw-a-person" technique has an interpretative "lore" which is, at best, weak (Chapman & Chapman, 1969; Swenson, 1957; Wanderer, 1969), whereas others, such as the MMPI and TAT, are substantiated by intricate networks of empirical data.

Almost every conceivable way in which individuals have been observed to differ consistently (and many ways in which it is doubtful) have been utilized as means or procedures for assessing personality differences. Any "search" for novel methods of personality appraisal would probably be futile,

1. Personality Assessment: Problems and Perspectives

since we have tried, or have access to, *most* likely approaches or procedures for evaluating or measuring personality at the present time. New tests or techniques may be "invented," but these will merely be variations of the same themes and will not produce a revolution in the field of personality assessment. There are no foreseeable new horizons for personality assessment.

In view of this pessimistic outlook for new developments in personality assessment, where do we now stand? On the one hand, we know that personality appraisal as a scientific enterprise is frail and beset with many problems. The use of clinical assessment devices is, at best, subject to many sources of error, most of which we are aware of at present: response sets, "halo" and other rating effects, situational variables, examiner influences, method variance, and so on.

On the other hand, interest in and the need for personality assessment will probably not diminish greatly in the foreseeable future. Rather, it appears that the use of personality assessment procedures has increased in many settings despite their limitations. We must point out that there has been a diminution of interest in "psychodiagnosis" in clinical settings in recent years (Carson, 1958; Holt, 1967; Rosenwald, 1963). Although there has been a rapid decline in research activity and practical applicability regarding some assessment procedures such as projective techniques (Ames, 1970; Zubin, Eron, & Schumer, 1965), there is, however, a flurry of new developments in other areas of assessment (Buros, 1970; Butcher, 1969; Cattell, 1970; Loevinger & Wessler, 1970; McReynolds, 1968; Webb, Campbell, Schwartz, & Sechrest, 1966).

This book presents an in-depth look at one approach to personality assessment—the objective personality inventory. More specifically, the focus will be on problems and perspectives of objective personality assessment using the most successful and most widely used inventory, the Minnesota Multiphasic Personality Inventory (MMPI), as a starting point. How has the MMPI withstood the tests of time and wide exposure? What forces has it encountered and what are some of its limitations? We will consider possible modifications of the MMPI and some of the problems posed by a potential revision of this major personality instrument.

In this chapter, we will examine some of the important issues that generally surround the field of personality assessment, from which we hope to provide the proper background for viewing the current status of objective measures of personality, in particular the MMPI.

Sources of Criticism of Personality Assessment

The Questionable Utility of Assessment Devices for Contemporary Decisions

One general source of criticism which, I think, lies at the core of current disillusionment with testing is the question of the *nonutility* of assessment devices for practical decision making. A growing number of contemporary clinical psychologists consider the use of personality assessment devices to be relatively unimportant for making many types of significant decisions. In fact, several approaches to treatment or therapeutic intervention have specifically discarded or warned against pretreatment personality assessment. The following three divergent views illustrate this.

Almost thirty years ago, Rogers (1942) cautioned against the biasing efforts of personality testing toward treatment. He reiterated his concern in 1951:

> Our experience has led to the tentative conclusion that a diagnosis of the psychological dynamics is not only unnecessary but in some ways is detrimental or unwise. The reasons for this conclusion are primarily two. In the first place, the very process of psychological diagnosis places the locus of evaluation so definitely in the expert that it may increase any dependent tendencies in the client, and cause him to feel that the responsibility for understanding and improving his situation lies in the hands of another. When the client perceives the locus of judgment and responsibility as clearly resting in the hands of the clinician, he is, in our judgment, further from therapeutic progress than when he came in. Also, if the results of the evaluation are made known to him it appears to lead to a basic loss of confidence by the person himself, a discouraging realization that "I cannot know myself." There is a degree of loss of personhood as the individual acquires the belief that only the expert can accurately evaluate him, and that therefore the measure of his personal worth lies in the hands of another. The more he acquires this attitude, the further he would appear to be from any sound therapeutic outcome, any real achievement of psychological growth.
>
> The second basic objection to psychological diagnosis, and its accompanying evaluation to the client by the therapist, is that it has certain social and philosophical implications which need to be carefully considered and which, to the writer, are undesirable. When the locus of evaluation is seen as residing in the expert, it would appear that the long-range social implications are in the direction of the social control of the many by the few . . . when the clinician diagnoses a client's vocational aims or marital relationships or religious views as, let us say, immature and works toward changing these conditions in the direction of what he regards as maturity, then this situation has many social implications [pp. 223–224].

More recently these concerns have been expressed by Meehl (1960) who has reported some findings indicating that these views are widespread among psychotherapists, generally. Meehl found that only 17 percent of 168 therapists surveyed endorsed the statement that "It greatly speeds therapy if the therapist has prior knowledge of the clients' dynamics and content from such devices as the Rorschach and TAT."

Community mental health approaches to psychological intervention have little or no use for personality tests of the traditional variety, since the "treatment" is brief, often nondirect (i.e., frequently involves the professional working through nonprofessionals) and crisis-oriented. Assessment devices which were developed in and for the psychiatric hospital are too time consuming to administer and interpret for the typical community consultant. In addition, most psychiatric assessment devices, mainly used for broad, global personality description, are not useful in crisis-oriented work in which the decisions and treatment typically are short-range and based on information available in the problem context.

Some abbreviated assessment devices such as the Mooney Problem Checklist (1950) and, more recently, the Psychological Screening Inventory, (Lanyon, 1970, and reviewed by Butcher, 1971) have been developed explicitly for use in situations in which time is limited. It is likely that more focused, brief assessment devices, for example, Endler-Hunt S-R Inventories, will be developed for these purposes. Whether or not they will be useful and valid is an empirical question to be answered in the next few years.

The "nonutility" criticism of personality assessment finds further support from behavioral modifiers. The increased use of behavior modification techniques has contributed to the waning interest in "traditional" clinical assessment procedures, that is, personality tests. This position is forcefully stated by Eysenck (1959):

> ...the unsatisfactory position of clinical psychology and of diagnostic measurement in general on which so many contributors to the *Annual Review of Psychology* have commented during the past five years is almost entirely due to the fact that so much stress has been laid on notional and empirical tests of the projective and questionnaire type. The present writer does not feel optimistic that the current approaches which attempt to improve the botched up edifice of pseudometrics and psychomagic which constitutes modern clinical practice in personality assessment are radical enough to improve the situation. The only realistic hope he would suggest is a return to the long-neglected principles of scientific work with its stress on the hypothetico-deductive procedure, objective measurement, appropriate techniques of statistical analysis and the realistic restriction of the effort of measurement to something less nebulous and less grandiose than the "total personality" [pp. 122–123].

In recent years, behavioral modifiers have shown a great deal of interest in assessment. The use of behavioral modification or behavioral analytic techniques has been described by Goldfried and D'Zurilla (1969), Goldfried and Kent (1971), Goldfried and Pomeranz (1968), Kanfer and Saslow (1965), Peterson (1968), and Wallace (1966). Behavioral modifiers maintain that behavioral processes are "understood" by the specification of the stimulus control of responding. Thus, according to Kanfer and Saslow (1965),

> An effective diagnostic procedure would be one in which the eventual therapeutic methods can be directly related to the information obtained from a continuing assessment of the patient's current behaviors and their controlling stimuli [p. 533].

Kanfer and Saslow (1965) consider the proper role of assessment to be performing a behavioral analysis and providing a method for analysis.

Unlike "traditional" assessment which suffers from conceptual flaws because the wrong kinds of data have been collected (Peterson, 1968), this approach to assessment focuses on analysis of the environment as well as on the individual, that is, on breaking down "global" personality concepts into more specific characteristics and being more aware of the context in which the behavior to be assessed is expected to occur.

The Criticism That Personality Assessment Devices Do Not Assess Relevant Dimensions

A second criticism of personality assessment, somewhat related to the first, is that many personality tests do not assess relevant personality dimensions. This criticism has taken many forms and may emphasize "weaknesses" in tests caused by focusing on the wrong "level" of personality. For example, personality questionnaires are referred to as "superficial, nondynamic, purely descriptive," and so forth, the implication being that they do not tap behaviors, attitudes, and so on, which are appropriate and necessary to understanding "real" aspects of personality. Cattell (1957), who uses personality questionnaires in his work, believes that a person cannot reveal his major dispositions or long-term motives through consciously verbalizing his opinions in an inventory. He prefers to use more indirect and objective tests to measure motives at both the overt and covert levels.

The Criticism That Personality Assessment Approaches Are Outmoded

This criticism has been raised in many forms. Peterson (1968) noted:

1. Personality Assessment: Problems and Perspectives

> It is increasingly clear that the flaws in clinical assessment are not only procedural but conceptual. Not only have we been using faulty methods, we have been trying to get the wrong kinds of data ... [p. 4].

The criticism of procedural inadequacies has been noted by Mischel (1968) who pointed out that personality assessment approaches have not kept abreast of developments in other areas, particularly experimental personality research.

These views point to the necessity of "modernizing" our assessment methods either by changing the focus of our assessment or by making greater use of procedural developments from other areas of psychology. In my estimation, the search for "new" kinds of data which are more narrowly focused or specific to a particular assessment situation is important and fruitful.

Regarding the latter suggestion, I am not aware of any "new" procedural developments from other areas of psychological investigation that would add significally to contemporary assessment. The general criticism is that personality assessment and personality theorizing have developed more or less independently and, it might be said, in spite of each other. Many psychologists consider this general state of affairs to be undesirable and believe that there "should" be a meeting ground between theoretical and practical (assessment) areas within the personality domain. Buros (1970) seems to place the responsibility on the "assessment" branch of personality. He pointed out that "The vast literature on personality testing has failed to produce a body of knowledge generally acceptable to psychologists [p. xxv]."

Although it is generally true that many assessment instruments have developed in a rather random, blind, empirical fashion, a few assessment procedures have followed from predictions based on a theory, for example, the Blackie Pictures (Blum, 1950). The most recent and extensive effort to tie these two areas together has been made by Loevinger and Wessler (1970).

*The Credibility of Many Assessment Approaches
Has Been Questioned*

These criticisms of assessment, usually thought of as questions of validity, take two forms: The method or approach is invalid as a predictor of behavior or the method is quite susceptible to invalidating conditions, for example, response sets, situational influences, and halo effect.

The first and more general issue—the method is invalid and, therefore, observations or generalizations based on it are likewise invalid—is usually stated in the form of validity coefficients. Various methods can be compared and selected on the basis of their power for predicting in various circumstances. The external validity of an assessment device is perhaps the most important characteristic of a test. Because of the great complexity and changeability of personality, assessment devices typically range from disappointing to modest in validity correlations. Even in the most objectively valid personality devices, such as personality inventories, the .50 "barrier" for validity coefficients seems unbreakable. Regarding projective techniques, the picture is even gloomier—"at best, when the correlation coefficients do reach statistical significance, they tend to be in the .20 to .40 range" (Mischel, 1968).

The credibility of assessment devices is improved when invalidating conditions can be accounted for and precisely measured. In the research literature of projective techniques, the role of situational influences upon test protocols is well documented (e.g., Masling, 1960). However, to my knowledge, no effective means of measuring possible invalidating influences to make protocols more comparable and understandable have been initiated.

In the use of personality inventories, a number of procedures have been designed to provide the test interpreter with an evaluation of possible invalidating conditions, such as defensiveness, faking, dissimulation, and so forth. With the MMPI, Hathaway and McKinley (1940) and Hathaway and Meehl (1947) developed various procedures for assessing deviant response attitudes. The MMPI validity scales and indices L, F and K, $F - K$, and so forth have an extensive literature supporting their validity and utility. The most recent "confirmation" was done by Anthony (1971). Despite these efforts, a large portion of the MMPI literature in recent years has been devoted to issues of the credibility of self-report that require discussion since they questioned the very foundations of the MMPI and other objective inventory approaches. The notion that response sets account for most of the variance in personality inventories like the MMPI took two major forms: (1) the social desirability formulation (Edwards, 1957)—in responding to item content, people choose to give responses which are socially desirable; and (2) the acquiescence response set formulation (Jackson & Messick, 1961)—Jackson and Messick stated that people respond to items as "yea-sayers" or "nay-sayers" with little regard for the content of the item. The response set formulations produced a great deal of controversy in the research literature for more than ten years (telling us about as much about the behavior of psychologists as it did of response sets).

With the publication of Block's monograph (1965), in which the response set formulations were shown to be quite untenable, the controversy subsided. Indeed, most psychologists today would concur with Bock, Dicken, and Van Pelt (1969) who concluded that acquiescence accounts for a relatively small portion of the variance when compared with content.

*The Criticism That Assessment Procedures
Adversely Influence Subsequent Study of Variables*

The problem of *reactivity of personality assessment* devices has been discussed by several investigators (Campbell, 1957; Campbell & Stanley, 1963; Sechrest, 1968; Webb *et al.,* 1966). (A reactive measure is one which is considered to affect subsequent relevant responses of the subject.) According to this view, most currently used personality assessment devices fall short of desired effectiveness because of their reactive characteristics. Thus, it is considered desirable to develop nonreactive and unobtrusive measures of personality, particularly if repeated measurement of psychological variables is intended. Sechrest (1968) points out that:

> In order to achieve nonreactivity of measurement it will probably be necessary to get beyond the standard "test" kind of operation into the observation of behavior in situ and by means which conceal not only the nature of the measurement being conducted but the fact that measurement is occurring at all [p. 574].

In recent years, the use of ingenious nonreactive measures, such as archival and observational techniques, have contributed greatly to attempts to understand behavior in a variety of settings (Webb *et al.,* 1966; Schachter, 1971). The number and quality of assessment tasks seem limited only by the imagination of the researcher.

The development of nonreactive measures for the description of *individual* personality or for making valid predictions about an individual's behavior in *novel* situations has not been adequately pursued. No effective, unobtrusive measuring system for use with individuals has been developed—probably because the necessary cataloging of relevant behaviors, scaling, and then validating against "extra test" criteria would prove an unmanageable task. No doubt the lack of effectiveness of similar "situational tasks" in earlier work (OSS Assessment Staff, 1948) does not strongly encourage efforts in this direction. Consequently, the continued need for individual evaluation will necessitate the use of personality assessment devices that are marred, to some extent, by factors such as reactivity.

The Criticism That Personality Assessment Devices Constitute an Invasion of Privacy

The criticism that men's minds are being tampered with by psychological specialists was popularized by Whyte (1956) and Gross (1962). Whyte, in his discussion of tests in industry, gave tips on how to "beat" personality tests. Gross considered the use of psychological tests invalid and immoral and proposed that they be banned. Great objection to the use of personality tests in government agencies ensued, and in 1965 congressional hearings were held to investigate the use of psychological tests, particularly the use of the MMPI in selecting Peace Corps candidates. This controversy is described in the *American Psychologist* (1965). At the time of the hearings, no empirical investigations of test objections had yet been published.

In recent years, a number of investigations have been devoted to clarifying the invasion of privacy issue. Butcher and Tellegen (1966) found that subjects in a personnel selection situation had considerably more objections to MMPI items than subjects in a general psychiatric situation. In addition, certain types of item contents were found to be most objectionable (items dealing with sex, religion, bladder and bowel functioning, and family relationships). Deletion of these items from the inventory would reduce several scales by about 20 percent without appreciably reducing the overall objections. Consequently, purging the MMPI of objectionable item contents was not viewed as the best solution and a modification in test usage was recommended. Most of the objections to the MMPI concerned its use in personnel selection rather than in psychiatric or counseling settings for which the inventory was designed and which represent the areas of its greatest usage. Several studies aimed at reducing MMPI item objections have been reported. Walker (1967) and Walker and Ward (1969) also found that certain MMPI item contents were objectionable and examined the possibility that modifying the instructions to allow the individual to delete objectionable items would alleviate the problem. Allowing the subjects to omit items tends to lower the reliability of the inventory, but does not, according to the authors, reduce the test validity, since mean profiles are the same.

An alternative suggestion for reducing objections to personality inventories was proposed by Hathaway (1964) in response to a layman's question as to why there were numerous religious items on the MMPI. This approach is essentially an educative one in which the subject is told how the test was constructed, how test-taking attitudes are measured, and how the scales are used. In a study which informed subjects about the MMPI in advance (Fink & Butcher, 1971), the efficacy of this educative approach in reducing MMPI objections was examined. The MMPI and Personality Research Form were administered to two groups of subjects under different conditions—one group under standard conditions, and the other group under instructions which provided detailed information on the rationale of the test, how the inventory was designed, and how scoring was done (namely, that the scorer does not look at individual items). After the testing, subjects in both groups were asked to rate the degree to which they thought the test constituted an invasion of privacy. The results indicated that there were no appreciable differences in the mean profiles between the standard and modified instruction conditions. However, the subjects in the modified instruction group (according to the posttesting questionnaire) considered the test situation to be *less* of an invasion of privacy than subjects in the standard test administration.

It is apparent that particular test usage rather than the personality tests themselves produces objections. Clinical applications or similar situations in which an individual seeks counseling, therapy, and so forth do not normally produce objections. Situations in which the individual takes a personality test for someone else's benefit (employment selection, research, etc.) require special precautions and more carefully planned instructions and debriefings.

The Criticism That Personality Tests
Contain Racially Sensitive Content

This criticism results from a number of studies which have shown that there generally are differences between blacks and whites on various personality tests. Gynther (1971), in an excellent discussion of subcultural differences on the MMPI, points out that discriminatory practices could enter into decision processes which are in part based on personality tests which contain racially sensitive items. Gynther recommends the development of black norms which would provide for a more relevant comparison group, if personality tests are to be administered to blacks.

Subcultural group differences may occur on many personality assessment devices. Whether or not these normative differences actually result in practices, such as employment discrimination, needs to be determined and, if necessary, corrected. Even if personality tests do provide biased test results, they probably yield more "objective" results than alternative methods of collecting data for decisions (such as interviewing).

The sources of criticism we have considered thus far have been raised against "traditional" approaches to personality assessment. There are other issues that could be discussed. The relationship of personality assessment to "diagnosis" has created some disillusionment because of the difficulties involved in psychiatric diagnosis, such as the imprecision (unreliability and invalidity) of current nosology. We must keep in mind that psychiatric diagnosis is only one form of personality assessment. There are other kinds of criticism regarding specific personality assessment procedures, but we will not discuss these issues unless they pertain to objective personality questionnaires.

Objective Personality Assessment

The assessment of personality through objective paper–pencil questionnaires got its initial impetus with the Personal Data Sheet (Woodworth, 1920) when the authors, Woodworth and Poffenberger, responded to the need for developing a method of evaluating large numbers of draftees during World War I. The initial success of the inventory produced a flurry of new test developments after the war. Numerous personality inventories were published for a variety of purposes—to provide an index for measuring "neurosis" or global characteristics, such as "will" or "temperament." Most of these devices suffered from limitations in scope, normative characteristics, and lack of psychometric necessities, such as validity and reliability (Hathaway, 1965). Conceptual and technological advances in test construction methodology were made, and in the early 1940s the most successful personality inventory to date was published. The Minnesota Multiphasic Personality Inventory (MMPI) was designed to avoid most of the pitfalls and problems that had beset previous efforts (Hathaway, 1965; Hathaway & McKinley, 1940), and, specifically, to serve as an aid in the diagnosis of psychiatric cases. Consequently, the content emphasis in the item pool and the structure of the basic scales reflect this bias. The basic scale construction was careful, empirical, and followed the then current, sound, standardization, and methodological procedures. The ease of administration, objectivity of scoring, and high test validity enhanced the use of the MMPI in psychological research and clinical utilization. The interpretation procedures for the MMPI have evolved in a fashion different from the original plan of the test authors. It soon became apparent that scale elevation alone was not sufficient information for profile interpretation. The relationships between MMPI scales or the configural aspects of the profile were noted to be of great importance. Subsequently, a great deal of work has been done with delineating and validating various profile configurations or "code" types. The fact that the MMPI lends itself to clinical individual use, group research, personnel screening, actuarial-computer analysis, and so on, has contributed to its applicability in many different assessment situations.

The success of the MMPI in applied psychology is well known. Over the past thirty years, MMPI usage has expanded and is used in settings and for populations quite different from the normative sample. How extensive MMPI usage is can only be estimated. Most clinical use of the MMPI probably involves in-house scoring and interpretation with psychiatric and correctional populations. Currently, there are at least three automated interpretation systems (two of which are computerized) commercially available. Presently, over one-third of the psychiatrists in practice in the United States and about one thousand institutions subscribe to one system, Roche Laboratories. The Roche service interprets about 1,600 MMPI profiles per week.[1] Extensive use is also being made of the MMPI in industrial screening and over thirty foreign language translations of the MMPI have been done. This ever-increasing utilization of the MMPI is reflected in the growing rate of publication as shown in Buros' *Personality Tests and Reviews* (1970):

> The Rorschach leads with a staggering total of 3,747 references followed by the ever-gaining MMPI with 2,474 references. Together the Rorschach and MMPI account for 6,221 references—33.9 per cent of all references in this volume....
>
> The rate at which references are being currently published is also presented... The MMPI leads with 900 references over the five years ending with 1968. Since very few references published in November and December 1968 are reported in this volume, it is safe to say that over 200 articles, books, and theses are currently being published each year on the MMPI alone. The output for the Rorschach is approximately 120 references per year [p. xxiv].

From the beginning, the MMPI has had a succession of vocal critics. A number of them have been generally condemnatory, taking issue with the inventory approach to assessment and providing little constructive impetus to the field. Since these criticisms are generally well known and have been discussed elsewhere (Block, 1965; Dahlstrom, 1969), we will not elaborate on them here.

Recently, Buros (1970) presented some reflections about the current state of personality assessment:

> In this era of remarkable progress in science and technology, it is sobering to think that our most widely used instruments for personality assessment were published 20, 30, 40, and even more years ago. Despite the tremendous amount of research devoted to these old, widely used tests, they have not been replaced by instruments more acceptable to the profession. Nor has the research resulted in a

---

[1] Personal communication with Raymond Fowler (1971).

consensus among psychologists concerning the validities of a particular test... [p. xxv].

It seems incredible, for example, that the MMPI—now being researched at the rate of 200 articles, books and theses per year—is still the same instrument published 27 years ago. The 2,474 references (over 400 are doctoral dissertations) reported in this monograph apparently have not generated enough new knowledge to bring about a revision or replacement of the test [p. xxvi].

This viewpoint is somewhat of an overstatement since the idea that the MMPI is in need of revision or modification has been the *zeitgeist* for some time. A number of psychologists have pointed out deficits in the MMPI and have made positive recommendations for change. For example, Block (1965), in the context of defending it against response set criticisms, noted a number of problems with the MMPI and suggested some ways of improving it. He considered four kinds of change needed for improving the MMPI and related personality inventories: (1) the use of broader item pools; (2) the use of more sophisticated and more conceptual models for scale development; (3) the use of more intensive and extensive empirical analyses; and, (4) the strengthening of the criteria for scale validation. The reader is referred to Block (1965, pp. 117-129) for discussion of several other related factors.

Many additional factors point to the need for revision or modification of the MMPI format and the need for continued development in the objective personality assessment domain. Some of these shortcomings of the present MMPI will briefly be described here as background for subsequent chapters in this book.

Problems at the Item Level

The length of the MMPI is a topic about which many people have strong and contrary opinions. If you ask most research subjects, obsessional patients, or computer data analysts who work with limited-memory-capacity computers, they will indicate that the MMPI is much *too long* and should be abbreviated. On the other hand, many researchers who are looking for "order and truth" in the world look askance at the deficits in the current MMPI item pool, and many times a harried clinician has turned away from his patient's MMPI profile with his questions unanswered. Both of these views are correct as a brief examination of the item pool clearly shows. In its present form, the MMPI is *too long* for practical purposes. There are about 150 items that are not scored on any of the most widely used clinical scales, and the Form R published by The Psychological Corporation a few years ago reshuffles the items in such a way that all of the "scored" items appear within the first 399 items. How many times for routine use is a patient or job applicant required to fill out *all* 566 items? Also, the 16 repeated items that appear in the booklet form (lore has it that these items are repeated because the scoring machines a few years ago could not score items that appeared on more than one scale unless they were repeated) are unnecessary and could be deleted. It has also been pointed out that the MMPI is too long and cumbersome to use in some community health, or crisis-oriented, settings and efforts are being made to construct abbreviated, MMPI-like instruments that give a briefer sketch of perhaps fewer personality dimensions (Hugo, 1971; Kincannon, 1968; Lanyon, 1970).

However, it is also true that some find the MMPI *too short*. It should be expanded because the item pool is not broad enough; that is, it does not tap behavior that is relevant for many decisions or purposes for which the MMPI is being used. Some examples of these uses are: understanding adolescent personality; selection of personnel for various positions or training programs; rehabilitation counseling; determining suitability of adoptive parents. The problem here is obvious—architects would experience similar, but perhaps more spectacular, problems if they tried to erect an 800 story building without due consideration of the necessary ground-level dimensions. The extensive use of the MMPI for populations and in settings greatly different from its original and quite humble intent has resulted in problems.

Another problem with the MMPI item pool is that some of the items are clearly outdated. Any psychological measuring instrument which contains content from a particular cultural context has the problem of evolved obsolescence. Intelligence tests such as the Binet and interests tests such as the Strong (see Chapter 6) reflect the need to modify test contents with time. Some of the MMPI items suffer from this obsolescence—subjects frequently ask: "What is 'drop the handkerchief'?"

The problem of ambiguous item wording has often been noted. The item "I loved my mother" will often produce the comment "I still do," and the double negatives or "leading questions" often puzzle the subject.

The direction of keying, which Hathaway and McKinley tried to balance by having deviant responding occur for both true and false answers, has resulted in some criticism because the empirical scales were not balanced themselves. This was not, and could not, have been provided on an equal 50–50 (true-false) basis for each empirical scale. Consequently, this imbalance led to criticisms, such as acquiescence interpretation of the MMPI by Jackson and Messick. Block (1965) has subsequently shown that when scales are balanced for T–F responses, the main MMPI dimensions (alpha and beta) emerge and an acquiescence interpretation is untenable. However, no information is available on the loss of validity in balanced (but necessarily shorter) scales. I do not think this is a major problem, although a future revision could attempt this.

Some Problems at the Scale Level

Two issues which most effectively highlight the need to reexamine the current MMPI scale structure are: recent advances in scale construction methodology and the fact that some of the clinical "entities" (on which the original MMPI empirical scales were built) have either changed or are not relevant to current MMPI usage.

I do not mean to imply that we need more MMPI scales (since there are already well over 400), but merely to point out some of the factors that should be examined closely in current MMPI usage.

In recent years, a number of factor, or cluster, analytic studies using the MMPI have been reported. These studies have produced a fairly useful picture of the internal structure of the MMPI item pool (Barker, Fowler, & Peterson, 1971; Block, 1965; Eichman, 1959; Stein, 1968; Welsh, 1956) which should be given due consideration in the development of interpretative systems. This view finds support in the work of Hase and Goldberg (1967) who note that with regard to external validity, the three methods of scale construction (empirical, rational, and factor analytic) were equally effective.

A second issue deals with the possible need for redefinition or restandardization of several of the empirical scales. Some uses of the MMPI at present suggest that traits or dimensions are being assessed rather than the diagnostic "entities." New scale development might well focus, at least in part, on defining traits, or groups of traits, differently in setting up criterion groups. This approach has some precedence in Gough's use of folk concepts (Gough, 1965). For several of the current clinical scales, some of the scale "concepts" defined by the original criterion group may have changed considerably. Chodoff (1954) suggests that some of the reduced interest in conversion hysteria in recent years comes from a reduction in the incidence of the syndrome due to changes in the culture, for example, increased psychological sophistication, decreased sexual prudery, and better education.

The meanings, or correlates, of some scales, particularly the Masculinity—Femininity Scale, are not well understood. Changes in sexual attitudes and practices have been great since the M—F scale was constructed. At the time the scale was constructed and included in the MMPI, it was difficult to study sexual behavioral patterns. Times have certainly changed, and it would now be possible to develop quite different and better self-report measures of masculinity–femininity.

Scale development generally could be on a much firmer footing at the present time than when the MMPI was originally constructed. The greater availability of normative subjects, access to a greater variety of personality "types" or differing populations, and advanced computer technology now make it possible to develop scales which take into account the complexity of human personality and the strengths of the self-report approach to assessment.

Despite the problems inherent in personality inventory methodology and any shortcomings in the MMPI, it is unlikely that its use will diminish in the near future. Rather, with the present growth patterns in personality test usage and because there are no hearty competitors to the MMPI, it seems quite likely that it will enjoy a highly protracted demise.

We seem to be at a point where a number of questions require attention. Is the MMPI adequately functioning as the major assessment device of its type? Is the MMPI in need of major revision? If so, is it desirable to develop improved personality questionnaires along the present lines or are there quite different methodological requirements? What problems might surround any attempts to revise a major psychological instrument, such as the MMPI? The chapters in this book bring these questions and some related issues into clear focus to provide perspective for some chores that appear to be ahead.

REFERENCES

American Psychologist: Special Issue. Testing and public policy. November 1965, p. 20.
Ames, L. B. Projecting the future of a projective technique. *Journal of Projective Techniques and Personality Assessment,* 1970, **34**, 359-365.
Anthony, N. Comparison of clients' standard, exaggerated and matching MMPI profiles. *Journal of Consulting Psychology,* 1971, **36**, 100-103.
Barker, H., Fowler, R., & Peterson, L. Item factor scales for the MMPI. Paper presented at the meeting of the 6th Annual Symposium on Recent Developments in the Use of the MMPI, Minneapolis, April 1971.
Block, J. *The challenge of response sets.* New York: Appleton-Century-Crofts, 1965.
Blum, G. S. *The Blackie Pictures: A technique for the exploration of personality dynamics.* Ann Arbor, Michigan: Psychodynamic Instruments, 1950.
Bock, R. D., Dicken, C., & Van Pelt, J. Method implications of content acquiescence correlation in the MMPI. *Psychological Bulletin,* 1969, **71**, 127-139.
Buros, O. K. *Personality tests and reviews.* New Jersey: Gryphon Press, 1970.
Butcher, J. N. Psychological Screening Inventory: A review. *Professional Psychology,* in press. 1971.

Butcher, J. N. *MMPI: Research developments and clinical applications.* New York: McGraw-Hill, 1969.

Butcher, J. N., & Tellegen, A. Objections to MMPI items. *Journal of Consulting Psychology,* 1966, **30,** 527-534.

Campbell, D. T. Factors relevant to the validity of experiments in social settings. *Psychological Bulletin,* 1957, **54,** 297-312.

Campbell, D. T., & Stanley, J. C. Experimental and quasi-experimental designs for research on teaching. In N. L. Gage (Ed.), *Handbook of research on teaching.* Chicago: Rand McNally, 1963.

Carson, R. C. The status of diagnostic testing. *American Psychologist,* 1958, **13,** 79.

Cattell, R. B. *Personality and motivation structure and measurement.* New York: Harcourt, 1957.

Cattell, R. B., Eber, H. W., & Tatsuoka, M. M. *Handbook for the Sixteen Personality Factor Questionnaire (16 PF).* Champaign, Ill: Institute for Personality and Ability Testing, 1970.

Chapman, L. J., & Chapman, J. P. Illusory correlations as an obstacle to the use of valid psychodiagnostic signs. *Journal of Abnormal Psychology,* 1969, **74,** 271-280.

Chodoff, P. A reexamination of some aspects of conversion hysteria. *Psychiatry,* 1954, **17,** 75-81.

Dahlstrom, W. G. Recurrent issues in the development of the MMPI. In J. N. Butcher (Ed.), *MMPI: Research developments and clinical applications.* New York: McGraw-Hill, 1969.

Edwards, A. *The social desirability in personality assessment research.* New York: Holt, 1957.

Eichman, W. J. Factorial composition of MMPI scales based on female psychiatric samples. Unpublished manuscript, 1959.

Eysenck, H. J. *The structure of human personality.* (2nd ed.) London: Methuen, 1959.

Fink, A., & Butcher, J. N. Reducing objections to personality inventories with special instructions. *Education and Psychological Measurement,* in press. 1921.

Goldfried, M. R., & D'Zurilla, T. J. A behavioral-analytic model for assessing competence. In C. D. Spielberger (Ed.), *Current topics in clinical and community psychology.* Vol. 1. New York: Academic Press, 1969.

Goldfried, M. R., & Kent, R. N. Traditional versus behavioral personality assessment: A comparison of methodological and theoretical assumptions. *Psychological Bulletin,* in press. 1971.

Goldfried, M. R., & Pomeranz, D. M. Role of assessment in behavior modification. *Psychological Reports,* 1968, **23,** 75-87.

Gordon, L. V., & Mooney, R. L. *The Mooney Problem Checklist.* New York: The Psychological Corporation, 1950.

Gough, H. G. Conceptual analysis of psychological test scores and other diagnostic variables. *Journal of Abnormal Psychology,* 1965, **70,** 294-302.

Gross, M. J. *The brain watchers.* New York: Random House, 1962.

Gynther, M. Different cultures—different norms? Paper presented at the 1971 Symposium on Recent Developments in the Use of the MMPI, Minneapolis, April 1971.

Hase, H. D., & Goldberg, L. R. Comparative validity of different strategies of constructing personality inventory scales. *Psychological Bulletin,* 1967, **67,** 231-248.

Hathaway, S. R. MMPI: Professional use by professional people. *American Psychologist,* 1964, **19,** 204-211.

Hathaway, S. R. Personality inventories. In B. B. Wolman (Ed.), *Handbook of clinical psychology.* New York: McGraw-Hill, 1965.

Hathaway, S. R., & McKinley, J. C. A multiphasic personality schedule (Minnesota): Construction of the schedule. *Journal of Psychology,* 1940, **10,** 249-254.

Hathaway, S. R., & Meehl, P. E. *The K scale for the MMPI.* New York: Psychological Corporation, 1947.

Holt, R. R. Diagnostic testing: Present status and future prospects. *Journal of Nervous and Mental Disease,* 1967, **44,** 444-465.

Hugo, J. A. Abbreviation of the Minnesota Multiphasic Personality Inventory through multiple regression. Unpublished doctoral dissertation, Univ. of Alabama, 1971.

Jackson, D., & Messick, S. Acquiescence and desirability determinants on the MMPI. *Educational and Psychological Measurement,* 1961, **22,** 771-790.

Kanfer, F. K., & Saslow, G. Behavioral analysis: An alternate to diagnostic classification. *Archives of General Psychiatry,* 1965, **12,** 529-538.

Kincannon, J. C. Prediction of the standard MMPI scale scores from 71 items: The mini-mult. *Journal of Consulting Psychology,* 1968, **32,** 319-325.

Lanyon, R. I. Development and validation of a psychological screening inventory. *Journal of Consulting and Clinical Psychology,* 1970, **35** (1, Pt. 2).

Loevinger, J., & Wessler, R. *Measuring ego development.* Vol. 1. *Construction and use of a sentence completion test.* San Francisco: Jossey-Bass, 1970.

Masling, J. M. The influence of situational and interpersonal variables in projective testing. *Psychological Bulletin,* 1960, **57,** 65-85.

McReynolds, R. (Ed.) *Advances in psychological assessment, 1.* Palo Alto, Calif.: Science and Behavior Books, 1968.

Meehl, P. E. The cognitive activity of the clinician. *American Psychologist,* 1960, **15,** 19-27.

Mischel, W. *Personality and assessment.* New York: Wiley, 1968.

OSS Assessment Staff. *Assessment of men.* New York: Rinehart, 1948.

Peterson, D. R. *The clinical study of social behavior.* New York: Appleton-Century-Crofts, 1968.

Rogers, C. R. *Counseling and psychotherapy.* Boston: Houghton-Mifflin, 1942.

Rogers, C. R. *Client-centered therapy.* Boston: Houghton-Mifflin, 1951.

Rosenwald, G. C. Psychodiagnostics and its discontents. *Psychiatry,* 1963, **26,** 222-240.

Schachter, S. Some extraordinary facts about obese humans and rats. *American Psychologist,* 1971, **26,** 129-144.

Sechrest, L. Testing, measuring and assessing people. In E. F. Borgatta & W. W. Lambert (Eds.), *Handbook of personality theory and research.* Chicago: Rand McNally, 1968.

Stein, K. B. The TSC scales: The outcome of a cluster analysis of the 550 MMPI items. In P. McReynolds (Ed.), *Advances in psychological assessment.* Palo Alto, Calif.: Science and Behavior Books, 1968.

Swenson, C. H., Jr. Empirical evaluations of human figure drawings. *Psychological Bulletin,* 1957, **54,** 431-466.

Walker, C. E. The effect of eliminating offensive items on the reliability and validity of the MMPI. *Journal of Clinical Psychology,* 1967, **23,** 263-266.

Walker, C. E., & Ward, J. Identification and elimination of offensive items from the MMPI. *Journal of Projective Techniques and Personality Assessment*, 1969, **33**, 385-388.

Wallace, J. An abilities conception of personality: Some implications for personality measurement. *American Psychologist*, 1966, **21**, 132-138.

Wanderer, Z. W. Validity of clinical judgments based on human figure drawings. *Journal of Consulting and Clinical Psychology*, 1969, **33**, 143-150.

Webb, E. J., Campbell, D. T., Schwartz, R. D., & Sechrest, L. *Unobtrusive measures: Nonreactive research in the social sciences.* Chicago: Rand McNally, 1966.

Welsh, G. S. Factor dimensions A and R. In G. S. Welsh, & W. G. Dahlstrom (Eds.), *Basic readings on the MMPI in psychology and medicine.* Minneapolis: Univ. of Minnesota Press, 1956.

Whyte, W. H., Jr. *The organization man.* New York: Simon & Schuster, 1956.

Woodworth, R. S. *Personal Data Sheet.* Chicago: Stoelting, 1920.

Zubin, J., Eron, L. D., & Schumer, F. *An experimental approach to projective techniques.* New York: Wiley, 1965.

2
WHERE HAVE WE GONE WRONG?
The Mystery of the Missing Progress

Starke R. Hathaway

Possibly the title and subtitle of this chapter should be reversed, and I should first establish the argument that we have not made convincing progress in personality tests and inventories. However, if the reader defends the thesis that some forty years of effort have produced convincingly effective personality tests or inventories, I leave the burden of proof to him. I will make a few introductory points that are intended to show the connotation of my thesis that there is a mystery manifest in the history and present status of personality tests.

Our most widely known and used personality inventory is still not included as course, or practicum, teaching in some accredited clinical training programs. One still hears statements by well-known psychologists that personality tests, especially the objective inventories, are of little value. Similarly, the use of projective tests has fallen off, and experimental support for their validities has been disappointing. Finally, many psychologists in clinical and private practice use no personality tests. Although I believe that these psychologists are both limited in their effectiveness and disloyal to a fundamental identity with their profession, I must confess that I can only make a weak argument for the practical value of the tests. The MMPI, for example, needs much "clinical interpretation" despite statistically significant validities for many diagnostic and predictive applications. My chief defense of the MMPI would be the large amount of information provided at a low cost in professional time. Were I asked to give convincing evidence that a given interviewer cannot do as well or better with an hour of his time, I would hesitate to accept the challenge. Surely, therefore, one is justified in taking a modest view of the MMPI as a convincing exhibit of solid progress.

I must digress, at this point, to say that I do not mean to give aid and comfort to those who say that the MMPI, or even the Rorschach, are simply no good and should be abandoned. One who makes such assertions should be vigorously challenged to be explicit about what he would substitute for the tests and to give his evidence for the validities of these better procedures. As nearly as I can determine, those who challenge the tests, saying that they are of little or no value or that they make unfair discriminations, do not deny that personality judgments must in some way be made. There is a constant demand for personality evaluations to improve the basis on which we choose employees, select diagnosis, plan therapy, make decisions about the disposition of offenders, and many similar applications in which assessment of differences in personality affect personal or social action.

Personal judgment from interviews or from hearsay seems to be the nontest user's alternative to testing. Although our best personality tests may fall far short of the validity we desire, a review of the data on validity will show that they are at least as valid and more free of prejudice in nearly every application than are the usual substitutes—interviews or hearsay. The original demand for personality tests grew out of disillusionment with personal judgment and with arbitrary subjectivism in employment selection, counseling, and clinical diagnosis. Psychologists a generation ago collected data on the defects of personal judgment that should make it difficult for us to reject the relative advantages of deriving decisions from objective test profiles. At least the profiles are a common stimulus source for judgments, and the subjects supply them by responding to relatively standard items instead of the uncontrolled nature of interviews, personal appearance, and confidential references. Prejudice or other dangers sometimes attributed to tests are not a property or defect of objective tests. If these threats are meaningful, they originate in the person who provides the interpretation and in those who

2. Where Have We Gone Wrong? The Mystery of the Missing Progress

accept prejudicial interpretation. The only reasonable control lies in the assurance that the test and its interpretation are conducted by a trained professional worker who is bound by a code of professional ethics.

Similarly, I intend no agreement with Dr. Goldberg (1968) who, after a futile search for what he would accept as evidence that patterned predictions such as those made from profile code classes can have more validity than simple linear functions of contributing scales, said:

> I don't wish to accuse Minnesotans of perpetrating the Rorschachian practices of the dying projectivists' cult, but I am beginning to fear that I have been through all this before. I am frankly not convinced that there *should* be a workshop on the MMPI any more than there should be one on the Rorschach, or on the applied use of astrological charts. Historically, the MMPI is of the greatest importance to those of us committed to personality assessment. At present, my own belief is that soon it will be little more than an historically interesting instrument. Let us not run *all* the risks of rapture.

This statement was based on work with a dichotomous criterion of even less than usual clinical meaning and reliability—the discrimination of psychosis from neurosis. I am not denying a place in history for the MMPI, but Dr. Goldberg's time schedule suggests that it will become historical sooner than I think is likely. Even if it has little more to offer us in research, I fear that the aged MMPI will be tolerated for some time by those concerned with practical problems in psychological evaluation. The mystery, then, that seems apparent to me lies in the question: With so many competent efforts, over so many years, why have we not yet developed better personality tests? I could extend the question to a more arbitrary one: Why are we today unable to confidently undertake the development of significantly more valid and useful tests?

In the sections to follow, I will review some salient points about the concept of personality, its development, and the problem of criteria for personality test development. With more hope of being constructive, I will make some remarks about the strategy of our research effort. I do not intend to present theory or a review of personality research. My talents do not lie in that direction. I merely hope to develop ideas that seem important to me about the problems that may have delayed personality test research and development. To remind you that my points are merely undeveloped leads about some of these problem characteristics of personality and personality test development, I will refer to the sections of my chapter as clues. Perhaps they relate to the mystery of the missing progress.

The Clue of the Elusive Construct

Since we have made so little progress toward the construction of satisfactory personality tests, it may be profitable to consider some of the characteristics of the concept we are trying to measure. The word "personality" and its multitude of connotations are hopelessly embedded in the vernacular. Whether or not man is a communal animal, he certainly lives a communal life and his wellbeing, his existence, derives from this context. In a way, it seems ludicrous to expect that a satisfactory analog of this pervasive concept will emerge from a test, even one with 550 items. And some psychologists seriously seem to expect something satisfactory from fewer items or from ten ink blots! If, in routine usage, a considerable list of personal, descriptive words and statements can be applied to a given person, it may be that no test can satisfy us with its limited depiction of a conglomerate of characteristics that we loosely identify as the person's personality.

Everyone knows the word "ghost" and we can use it for communication; but most of us would not seriously expect to devise a ghost-measuring or analyzing test. By analogy I often have serious doubts about whether it is meaningful to expect that we can develop tests to measure or analyze personality.

The severe definition problems peculiar to personality assessment are common to all highly abstract, verbally involved concepts. One has only to open a text dealing with personality to find a myriad of speculations and assertions about the nature of something which we not only fail to see, touch, smell, taste, or hear but also which most of us have an extremely difficult time even thinking about or communicating clearly.

To develop this definitional idea relative to testing personality, consider the paradigm of progress with tests of intelligence, another complex construct. It will probably not be disputed that the psychometric problems in the development of intelligence tests have been more satisfactorily solved than those of personality tests.

As a prescientific concept, intelligence seems to suggest a complex of abilities, both general and specific. Usage of the word suggests about as many different definitions as there are observers who offer definitions. But for intelligence, in contrast to personality, there are more immediate and face-valid criteria. Even before we became sophisticated, there could be little debate that higher achievement in school, quicker and more appropriate adjustment to daily problems, and other similar examples represented more intelligence. Note that we do not readily form even a concept of more personality.

2. Where Have We Gone Wrong? The Mystery of the Missing Progress

One way of viewing the history of intelligence measurement is that the construct and tests of it have already passed through, or by-passed, the period of controversy over the definitions both as construct and as test variables.

Perhaps an operational illustration will aid in the contrast of the personality and intelligence constructs. Let us imagine an experiment to demonstrate the degree to which "intelligence" has an immediate meaning. Suppose we first choose five subjects distributed widely over the range of scores on any reasonably well-established intelligence test. These five subjects will be placed in living quarters that require competitive problem solving in order for them to remain comfortable. If we now select some unsophisticated observers and ask them without elaboration to observe and rank the five on "intelligence," I assume with considerable confidence that the observers will show good interpersonal reliability in ranking.

But now imagine this experiment for a similar naive ranking on "personality." First, which test would one use for selection of Ss? What convincing variable, or variables, would permit selection of Ss comparably distributed. And, finally, I believe you cannot doubt that when the Os have made their rankings, they would show very poor interobserver agreement.

With this imaginary experiment, I am trying to demonstrate the incoherence of our concepts of personality and to suggest that our tests cannot be valid or converge upon evolved criteria by the bootstraps effect from which the intelligence tests have gained so much. In intelligence testing, the construct "IQ," originally validated against the criterion of teachers' judgments, has long since taken on a robustness and a richness in terms of connections with observable behavior and with other psychological concepts that were never approached by the original criterion for validating the construct. The physical and biological sciences offer many examples of the bootstraps effect—the development of a concept, originally meagre in its relations with observables and other constructs and narrowly criterion-oriented, into an indispensable, highly elaborated construct, occupying a prominent position in the further development of theory.

It is hard for us to agree to limit our concept of a person's personality to any descriptive criterion that may be offered by another observer. Most of the criteria we accept, in compromise, have nearly as loose connotational standings as the word "personality" does. I think that most will agree that this is especially true for frequently used nosological categories like sociopath and schizophrenic. We cannot defend research usage of criteria such as "diagnosis of schizophrenia," "dishonest," "attractive," when our several descriptions of those to whom we would apply these terms show such large interpersonal variability.

Like the word "ghost," we use the word "personality" and related words as if there were a substantive entity recognized by others. We carelessly say, "He has a good personality"; "He has an alcoholic personality"; "He is dishonest." Conventionally, such remarks are not challenged. We psychologists know that a challenge would lead to basic disagreement. We have abundant evidence of this in failures to discover an experimental definition of dishonest or a defining personality for the alcoholic; few would agree on the specification of what a "good" personality is. One man's friend is another's enemy and, perhaps fortunately, one man's beloved often has the wrong personality for another. We may, unwittingly, have been asking the interpretations from the personality test to agree with some personal shadow of a reality that is not shared by our friends or colleagues. Personality is a ghost!

In the next section, I will consider further the construct of personality and its developmental origins.

The Clue of the Complex Origin

Personality can be thought of as being constantly in formation by projection and introjection. In the personal pronoun form, suggested by MMPI statements, personalities can be described as inextricable mixtures of "I am" and "he is" systems. The "I am" system is the indeterminately large number of informative items which one may use to describe the kind of person he is. "I am truthful," "I am trustworthy," and "I feel inferior" are examples of "I am" statements. Obviously, "I am not" has a similar descriptive power. A person who expresses himself well can produce a great many of these self-descriptive sentences. An MMPI answer sheet contains 550 such statements. "I am" statements made by a person in similar contexts tend to be intrapersonally reliable. But the context in which the "I am" statements are produced is in constant flux, which is why so many "I am" items have low reliability. "I am" statements cannot be tested for interpersonal reliability.

Another indeterminately large universe of items is provided by observers who describe the person with items of the form "he is"—"He is truthful," "He is reliable," and the like. Unless standard forms are used, each observer will choose a different list of items and observers can disagree. "He is" items have relatively low interpersonal reliability. Adjective checklists are examples of commonly used devices for objective collection of both "I am" and "he is" data. Interpretation of personality test profiles is based on a "he is" system.

2. Where Have We Gone Wrong? The Mystery of the Missing Progress

It should be obvious that "I am" and "he is" items can also be communicated nonverbally by expressive movements, facial expressions, clothing, and the like. Observers can report a personality of the "he is" sort even when the subject is uncooperative or unconscious; but personal verbal or nonverbal reporting is essential for us to gain access to the "I am" personality. It is common that "I am" and "he is" personality systems gradually change with time, environment, and communication context. "I am honest," expressed in socially visible contexts, can be modified to permit one to slip into a theater, if one feels immune from detection. The "I am" and "he is" systems are different with a friend and an enemy, with an employer and a spouse.

"He is" personality judgments and the tests that codify them must be validated against predictive accuracy. We make some judgments of nearly every person we meet, even if there is no significant likelihood of future encounter. To permit social living, we must predict with reasonable accuracy what others will do. When we want to communicate generalities about a person, indicating the consistencies of his behavior, we classify our experiences or judgments into associated groups that become the person's reputed personality. "He is dependable" and "He has a friendly disposition" could be examples. The relative stability for such "he is" generalities permit us to plan our own behavior. We depend on what others will do. We can usually assume that the driver of a car will stop before hitting us. We assume with more certainty that the pilot will follow the flight schedule (unless we are heading for Miami); we do not expect the man who parks our car to keep on going in it.

"I am" systems must also be stable. Their stability wards off the fearful anxiety that we may become insane. To be insane really means loss of continuity of self, a threat to personal life that is even more primitive than the threat of physical death.

In the present context, I am equating self-concept with the "I am" system. As Holtzman (1961) points out, our tendency to preserve self-concepts assures some validity for tests like the MMPI. In a discussion of test validities, he states:

> In fairness to the self-inventory approach, it should be pointed out that scales from these tests usually have fairly high reliability and often correlate with socially observable behavior to a higher degree than any projective technique. Such correlations, however, can frequently be traced directly to the fact that the individual has a conscious self-concept that dominates his test responses and is not unrelated to his social behavior as judged by others [p. 180].

Despite the freedom that Ss (and we ourselves) seem to have to lie, or otherwise distort themselves (responses to the "I am" items of the MMPI, for example), it is fortunately observed that unrationalized lying is not common.

When someone does not behave in a manner appropriate to the situation, we are alerted that he may be threateningly deviant. He may be some kind of enemy, "crazy or something," and I suspect that the source of the "something" is a nameless, primitive nerve network or engram which alerts us to be wary. This fear is a stabilizing force on our own behavior and is expressed, as I suggested above, in the fear of insanity. It motivates the patient's fearful: "Doctor, what makes me do that?" behind which is the recognition that his behavior does not fit into his "I am" system.

It is only when a person behaves in unpopular or unusual ways or when he expresses distinctive ideas that we can describe him as a personality. The existential psychologists state that authenticity derives from the personal sense of choice. One is aware if one chooses and aware of choice when one deviates from the norm. If a person engages in unlawful behavior, associates may call him a criminal; if he is unusually reliable or kind, he can be described as such; if he has no infrequent or particularly acceptable or unacceptable behavior characteristics, he is almost indescribable, except to say that he is colorless in personality. We expect our tests to identify and measure the unique personality potential or characterizing behavior in subjects who would never be distinguished by the vast bulk of personality data about them.

Personality is expressed in transient, complex, and arbitrary ways that seem, nevertheless, to provide enough constancy to enable us to recognize that we have existed for some time and that we will continue to exist for some time. What is the task of our tests? Do we want to capture the enduring but normal and uncharacteristic constancy of the fleeting present or the coming tomorrow? Or do we want to depict the threatening reality or promise of being different in some aspect of personality? This problem in personality measurement reminds me of the problem of the electron that is everywhere when we measure its mass and nowhere when we would locate it. The words we use about personality are common in our speech; but, when we try to define them, the meaning becomes more unsatisfactory as the definition becomes more precise.

I am trying to establish some boundaries or ways of limiting personality. Like the "purloined letter" that could not be found because it was too obvious, the personality characteristics of conventional and predictable behavior are a major part of our behavior from which our tests cannot, as we do, abstract the individual aspects. Once one's attention is called to the fact, the most insane or asocial person still behaves rather normally in the main.

This discussion has not developed much hope for constructive conceptualizations on which we might found a better test instrument. There are further problems.

When the problems of criteria for personality are considered in the next section, a stumbling block will be the lack of disease syndromes, convincingly cohesive clusters of behavioral items, or any other determining framework in which we might fit our concepts of variables or types. One hopeful idea occurs to me. It is possible that personality is not formed fortuitously, being shaped from accidental cultural contexts modifying intraindividual peculiarities. Recent considerations are making us aware that visual perception and the structure of language have primordial foreshadowings from nervous organizations or engrams that emerge from our genetic evolution and earliest ontogenic experience. I have already mentioned my conviction that there is such a source for our anxiety over insanity. There is a growing body of evidence that the child, beginning to separate table and chair, father and mother out of the incredible mass of available sensory stimulus material, comes to perceive meaningful units under the guidance of formative *gestalten* that, although they do not constrain man as much as they do other animals, nevertheless, do provide a head start, facilitating the differentiations that are most significant in the social world and that can be conceived to represent archetypal survival aptitudes.

We may recall that personality breeds true in many lower species of animals. Different breeds of dogs are recognizable by their physical characteristics, but they are also recognizable by their species personality modes. Some breeds of dogs are more man-oriented, infrequently hostile, and poor hunters. Some breeds are nervously active, whereas others are calm. We have to conceive of a genetically determined nervous network that assures that the species-related personality, like the physical characteristics, will occur as the mode. If man has such a genetic heritage, it is hidden by his social learning and remains only as substrata beneath daily behavior that expresses personality.

A more meaningful statement about hypothetical genetic structural entities in personality formation is that social stimuli are patterned by the innate sensitivity to mould personality by behavior shaping. Babies watch faces rather than other parts of the body. There are unmistakably human rewards and punishments from social experience, if one may infer for the baby a disposition to perceive personality classes, such as friendly, threatening, and the like. This disposition would assure early exposure to the primary locus of the nonverbal and, later, verbal display of behavioral intents and would establish effective reinforcing stimuli in the evolution of the personality qualities in social behavior.

The significance of this inductive fancy about genetic *gestalten* lies in the possibility that there are complexes of behavior units which, if we could identify them, would be more cohesive than the pseudonosological classification we now use. For example, if there is a primordial personality perception of "enemy" which disposes the child to the perception of danger from other persons, its behavioral correlates might be foci for the evolution of a less arbitrary paranoia scale.

The Clue of the Missing Criteria

To this point I have denied the substantive reality of personality. With obvious irrationality, I will now develop some thoughts about the personality criteria we consider essential in the routine strategy of test development. I can discuss criteria for personality variables with at least as much sense as there is in our inner conviction that, when all is said and done, we and others do have personalities.

Deliberately omitting the ephemeral promises of the personality theory devotees, we do not know how tests can be developed except to base them upon cogent criteria that have practical interest. The standard system for classification of functional mental disorders is not soundly based in theory or anything else, but it is widely used, and some of its core descriptive content is a part of all training programs of the mental health specialties.

Somewhat as an aside, I believe that today an attempt to use the standard nosology as a base for revalidation of the MMPI would show that we have lost rather than gained in clinical coherence among members of the criterion groups we might now label schizophrenic, depressed, and the like. Training used to stress arbitrary symptomatic items listed in a few dominant texts of psychiatry and studied by most students. Now we have relaxed from this uniformity, and some psychologists even make it a virtue to depreciate training in the diagnostic process. I cannot suppress a sentence of even greater digression at this point. It distresses me that there should be so much agreement on the elusiveness and unreliability of the nosology, yet there is no diminution in the number of conferences on schizophrenics and in the steady flow of research reports using "schizophrenics" as subjects or subject matter. Rarely do participants in these nosology-based activities provide pathognomic or differential symptoms to make sense of the word. Often the same person who inveighs against the nosology in one context accepts it in another.

Certain patterns of MMPI and other personality profile codes are emerging to show intragroup behavioral and predictive power superior to the diagnostic classes of the original criteria. There appear to be some elements of a bootstraps effect. But implications from the foregoing sections that have described the basic unclarity of the concepts of personality suggest that we are not converging upon appreciably more meaningful classes, or, if we are, we have so far no good way of knowing it.

The MMPI workshops have encouraged studies in this code class line of development. Specifically, it seems that such emergent profile code characteristics as the "Conversion V," the "27," the "Spike 4" and a few other familiar categories are already empirically established as more satisfactory than the classical system, and some of their new classifications will, in time, become accepted as standard. Although the several MMPI atlases are disappointing in their failure to classify as many profiles in cross validation of the frequencies, they still do well on cross validation with code type methods. In summary, this is a promising area of research activity, but I judge that the long-term outcome will be of more value as a contribution to the development of methods and an understanding of the problems than as a satisfactory step toward appreciably greater validity of personality tests.

In a recent report on staff perceptions of psychiatric patients, Elstein and Van Pelt (1968) related their experiences in attempting to arrive at consensus in staff ratings of patients. They first found that variables intended to describe the constructs of overt behavior and inferred interpersonal characteristics were substantially related to each other in spite of the a priori dissimilarity.

> Specifically, loadings on a behavioral factor identified as Manageability were closely associated with loadings on an interpersonal characteristics factor called Anxious Intropunitiveness, while level of Psychopathology and Treatability were the second pair of highly correlated factors.

But coupled with this evidence of contamination of superficially independent rating concepts, "the authors found that the level of global agreement between pairs of staff Q sorts about a particular patient rarely exceeded an r of 50." To understand these discrepancies, the authors went back to an argument by Cronbach (1958) who came to the conclusion, ". . .that much of the variance in descriptions of patients might be understood in terms of as yet unexplored individual styles or organizing observations and cognitions about others." Cronbach called the networks of personal categories that form our appraisals of others "implicit personality theories."

Allport long ago discussed the problems of personal assessment with a warning against the normative view of personality. Drawing from Allport's argument, what I am calling the "he is" personality aspect that we import to subjects is inevitably in timebound "frames of reference." These frames of reference which overlap with Cronbach's "implicit personality theories" include any context whatever that exerts a demonstrable influence upon the individual's perceptions, judgments, feelings or actions. Often the frame of reference is not explicit. I have emphasized that observers make ratings with various and unspecified frames of reference. The subject himself is also usually unaware of determining items of the context, and he may entirely overlook the significance of context. Some frames are impersonal and neutral, perhaps merely orienting the judgments in place and time; others are personal and ego involving. Applying these considerations to our present problem, the task of the personality test, as we usually carelessly perceive it, involves the largely incompatible properties of expressing a personality profile for the subject that will agree both with the contextual "he is" reference frame of the observer who tests and the personal "I am" frame that the subject has imperceptively built as his self image.

I have been speaking mainly about the discouraging state of the criterion problem when we attempt to assess a personality at a given time. One might expect that assessment of change over time could suggest conceptualization of better criteria. The most ubiquitous example of the problem of personality change measurement lies with the measurement of progress presumed to result from psychotherapy.

Like many other of the problems with personality, changes with psychotherapy often seem so obvious that one is led to expect the easy development of criteria. A first discouraging point is that our present tests have failed to exhibit much apparent power as criteria. Nearly every familiar personality test and many innovative tests have been applied to the measurement of therapeutic progress with indifferent success. Like our introspective feeling that we mean something explicit when we use the word "personality," we feel convinced that there are personality changes brought about by psychotherapy. But often personality changes that appear to be clearly related to psychotherapy do not become manifest as a convincing difference in test scores or in any other objective fashion. As was true for the rating criteria simply aimed at describing personality, change sensitive criteria in the form of ratings by observers or self-ratings have proved unreliable and semantically arbitrary.

2. Where Have We Gone Wrong? The Mystery of the Missing Progress

Writing of the trouble with criteria for psychotherapeutic change, Carr and Whittenbaugh (1969) summarize:

> This study attempts to identify variables contributing to differences in perceived outcome among psychiatric patients and both experienced and inexperienced therapists. The little or no agreement found between patients, student therapists or their supervisors with regard to outcome judgments and related measures appeared to be a function of (1) selective perception of pertinent source data, (2) differential interpretation of the same source data, and (3) inferential bias.

Muench (1968) makes similar points:

> Unlike the data on normal subjects, as investigated by the experimental psychologist, the data utilized by the research psychotherapist are provided by subjects desperately seeking help in alleviating their distress. The variables to be confronted in psychotherapeutic assessment are exceedingly personal, complex, and difficult to define and measure. The problem of assessing counseling and psychotherapy centers in large part is the fact that important aspects of the therapeutic interaction are covert rather than overt, nonverbal rather than verbal, internal rather than external, and subtle rather than obvious. Many of the data believed to be significant in therapy involve private nuances of phenomenological experience that tend to defy normal modes of communication and investigation [P. 206].

I quote these differently worded views to give force to the position I am stressing. It is not so much that the message is new, it is more that the consequences seem to go unheeded and research efforts pile up in spite of insignificant progress.

Ellsworth, Foster, Childers, and Krocker (1968), discussing behavioral consistency, expressed the difficulty in still another way which reminds me of the trouble we are having with our MMPI atlases.

> When the situation shifted from hospital to community, behavioral consistency was reduced markedly, even when identical scales and raters were used to evaluate behavioral consistency. It was concluded from this that behavior and adjustment are greatly affected by situational changes, suggesting that behavioral determinants are more situationally than personally related phenomena.

The foregoing has mostly been concerned with dyadic judgments for which observers individually assess personality qualities of a subject. Unfortunately, as bad as the dyadic rating problem is, we often put our tests in the still more difficult role of observing and judging both the subject who has the personality and the person or situation on which the S's personality will impinge. An employee is to be matched to an employer or a job role; children are to be identified as predelinquent against a special milieu and value system; one person is to be matched to another as a potential marital partner; a patient is to be evaluated against how maladjusted he will be at home. Note that these examples permit at least three primary sources of error: the third party rater (comprising a mixture of the test and its interpretation); the rated person; and the person or situation to be matched.

Tests, like their interpreters, the subjects, have separate frames of reference. Our early personality tests had narrow reference frames. Woodworth set his inventory in the frame of the current need for evaluation of the emotional fitness of the soldier. Other tests used the frame of a classical clinical description, that is, the use of Adler's description of the inferiority feeling as the source of items. A new war redefined emotional fitness. The students of Adler redefined the inferiority feeling. The corresponding test frames no longer enclosed the originally appropriate material.

I have asserted that observers are variable, and that the criteria we derive from their ratings are based upon elusive and never-repeating frames of reference. These and other factors make for unreliability across observers. Tests have narrow, more stable frames of reference so that interpretative statements based on them are more reliable than are the ratings and descriptions made by observers. But tests lose reliability across subjects because the personal and situational frames of the subject and the testing change, and the test is limited by its item content.

Protests about the MMPI are often directed at the nosologic, "abnormal" frame of reference. In defense, it has seemed that the experimental data support the hypothesis that the clinically derived MMPI scales are more generally meaningful when applied to assessment of normal personalities than are scales so far suggested from nonclinical, counseling experience.

Obviously, a test with no built-in bias or with universal inclusiveness would escape some problems. Unfortunately, the construction of such a test is not possible because we cannot conceive of the separation of context from meaning of any significant personality criterion. This argument does not deny that the instructions and situational context of giving a personality test can stabilize its reference frame. This is a ubiquitous problem for the makers of atlases and for the cross validation of all test interpretation. Our tests and atlases might make a better showing if we took these considerations more seriously and devoted more effort to standardization of the stage setting for the test.

As a summary, Block (1968) has provided an excellent review of some basic reasons for our problems with personality criteria. He identifies four rating flaws:

2. Where Have We Gone Wrong? The Mystery of the Missing Progress

1. The mixing of behaviors of different levels of salience
2. The failure to recognize the effect of environmental factors
3. The comparison of behaviors mediated by different underlying variables
4. The failure to specify or to recognize the bounds within which the posited relationship may be expected to exist.

I take seriously the points of the foregoing sections that argue against our present ability to develop definitive criteria for developing personality tests or even for evaluating the validity of a test. This situation should not be ignored. I do not mean that we should abandon the field, but I do think that we should direct our research efforts toward the search for new strategies rather than continuing to employ research designs that have been and will be unproductive. Therefore, in the next section I will suggest more specifically that we should try to identify flaws in our present personality research strategies and encourage the search for new strategies.

The Clue of the Unproductive Strategy

With all the foregoing arguments there remains the possibility that the models for theory construction and measurement provided by classical natural science are inappropriate for the study of personality. It may be that our scientific prejudice has led to an overzealous application of methods highly successful in one domain to the task of personality measurement which may require a rather different interpretation of the traditional conceptions of measurement, explanation, and understanding.

In view of this suspicion, I feel that we should challenge every aspect of the research methods and concepts that have characterized our past efforts. In particular, we should critically examine the tactics used in the development of the MMPI and related tests as well as the various theoretical and clinical intuitive bases of other personality tests.

Particularly, I would draw attention to possibly bad research tactics involving the application of some seductive features of mathematical order to the analysis of man's personality. Possible trouble exists in the unchallenged assumption that correlations and significance tests are applicable to the kind of data we have for analysis of personality organization. Factor analysis, the regression equation, analysis of variance, and other idols are standard procedures for personality analysis. Literally bales of tests have been produced from the application of these statistical strategies. To me the lack of progress toward greater validity for the projective and objective personality tests is no more dramatic than the failure of the personality tests based more closely on factor analysis, internal consistency, item weighting, and other data treatment procedures. Two or three dominant statistically rational factors account for most of the meaningful variance in tests like the MMPI. These factors are not new to the clinician and their emergence is anticlimactic. Most of the remaining factors that have emerged from the data were more or less consciously put into the data as they were produced. The analyses of ratings by Lorr and by Wittenborn have developed the same clusters of items that the clinician observers have put into their charts and ratings. Without impugning the heuristic value of work with popular statistical tools, I cannot find much relief for my pessimism about the status of our personality instruments in the results evaluated either as criteria or as tests.

I suspect a similar anthropomorphism in carrying over the organization of natural physical science to crack the personality problem (organization of psyche) against the paradigm of the laws of physical nature. This is a "scientism" that leads us to assume that the psyche can be dissected into variables and units for combination and interaction as one might use energy units in natural science.

Certainly, it is a misconception to view the scales of personality inventories as dimensions amenable to all of the procedures and concepts that apply in physical measurement. One aspect of that particular misconception is at least nearly always avoided. It is obvious, given this example, that inventory scales are not of ratio character (Stevens, 1951, Chapter 1). However, the difficulties may go much deeper than that. Scriven (1956, pp. 330-339) makes some good points that are quite relevant to the problems faced by personality and assessment theory in distinguishing the disciplines of natural science from those whose object of study is human behavior.

In preceeding sections, I have tried to convey that the problem of the missing progress may become less of a mystery when we compare the enormity of the complexity of predicting the most simple human behaviors with the task faced by Gallileo and Newton. Even at the level of description of the basic subject matter, the situation with the psychology of personality is far more troublesome. The phenomena to be described are at a conceptual level far removed from simple observation, and we do not have centuries of accumulated observational tradition behind us. If the prediction and explanation of behavior are our tasks, then we are faced with many additional problems which are only compounded by the difficulties of description.

2. Where Have We Gone Wrong? The Mystery of the Missing Progress

Scriven suggests that there is reason to doubt even that it is, in principle, possible to explain adequately some of the phenomena of human behavior; we are only too aware of the practical problems in doing so. Furthermore, the proliferation of research findings that is not explained by or predicted from current theory may increase the difficulties involved in developing a theoretical framework to account for the phenomena of the field.

If we consider simultaneously the difficulties contributed by the problems of definition, measurement, predictive criteria, complexity, and so forth, and if we accept the fact that the results of the last twenty years of research have not simplified our task—they may even have made it more difficult, then it would seem that one of the most important prerequisites for progress in the area of personality assessment is the identification of more fruitful foci of inquiry, more fundamental characteristics of human personality. Our devotion to traditional nosological schemes as a source of criteria and the mechanical application of statistical procedures which have proved fruitful in natural science have not given us enough. While inveighing against scientism and dependence on traditional, but apparently weak, tools, I admit that I am attempting to make progress by induction. It is not enough to say that we could seek new interpretations of the traditional conceptions of measurement, explanation, and understanding. If one even conceives the need, one is challenged to give an illustration or to describe some characteristics of a new interpretation. I am not able to do this. Yet it is not improper to ask that we should, from time to time, be receptive to new interpretations. The progress of natural science abounds in examples where growing dissatisfaction with problems has preceded inspiration and sudden invention. It is obvious that Newton's fabled apple and Archimedes' bath experience refer to a culmination and were not explanatory of the reassortment of factors in the problem.

I have suggested in a previous paper that the study of man's most primitive and universal personality judgments might afford clues (Hathaway, 1961, pp. 144-160). In commenting above on the origins of personality, I have argued for a hypothesis that there are genetically prepotent conglomerates of behavior units. These would be derived from archetypal survival aptitudes that could be conceived of as forming adult personality from the raw material of the current culture and events to insure the character of man as a species yet allowing freedom for man's individual differences.

I have reserved more extended discussion of the possibility and implications of genetic framework for personality to this section on research tactics, since I do not consider these speculations firm enough to merit more than a mention in speaking of the origins of personality. Their place here lies in the exhortation to those who are engaged in research to consider what tactics might lead to the discovery of these heuristically meaningful slices of personality or, at least, to evidence of their existence.

If our characters are formed by these archetypal aptitudes, the search for them is hampered by the thick veil of seemingly chance, formative events that contribute to our reputations. Possibly, we should search more among the normal, invisible personalities than in our usual hunting ground, the more visible and interesting abnormalities.

The notion of character, a basic structure of personality, is not new. It was expressed by Schopenhauer (1968):

> Everyone, during the course of his lifetime, becomes aware of certain events that, on the one hand, bear the mark of a moral or inner necessity, because of their especially decisive importance to him, and yet, on the other hand, have clearly the character of outward, wholly accidental chance. The frequent occurrence of such events may lead gradually to the notion, which often becomes a conviction, that the life course of the individual, confused as it may seem, is an essential whole, having within itself a certain self-consistency, definite direction, and a certain instructive meaning—no less than the best thoughtout of epics [Campbell, p. 193].

It may be too strong an analogy, but my thought is illustrated in certain recent experimental data. Man has throughout history been impressed with the marvelous migration of birds and salmon. The tender complexities of mother love have seemed to be a microcosm of the complexity of personality. Yet suddenly, it is known that the baby salmon samples the water of his native stream and as a mature adult, remembering, cruises the ocean until he is led again to the native source. The black-legged goose mother's affectionate offspring are now manipulated at the imprinting moment to be equally affectionate to a nongoose, motherly human experimenter. Harlow's monkey children and mothers are being modified by simple procedures into most unfilial behavior. My intent has been to remind you of the incomprehensible complexities of some animal behaviors that have yielded to a new approach and have been reduced to startlingly simpler units.

The rhetorical question is: Could it be that the complexities of man's personality, that I hope I have compellingly depicted, will yield to some such inspired slicing? To the tender-minded, such a solution would offend as a kind of analogy to Alexander simply cutting the Gordian knot. I hope we are not overlooking leads because of conscious or unconscious wishes to preserve the mystique of the human psyche.

In summary of this section, I challenge the methodology of science applied to psyche, even advocating an iconoclastic skepticism; yet, I give no

2. Where Have We Gone Wrong? The Mystery of the Missing Progress

convincing lead about the nature of something new. Reading this, a colleague protested that "...much progress in the knowledge of schizophrenia is being made by establishing or observing correlations and going on to discover the parameters that seem to relate to the r's going up or down." But another colleague said that, at my age, I should be permitted to say most anything. With that privilege, I answer my first colleague by saying that I feel I've been here before. I have seen so many schizophrenic correlations and parameters come and go that his faith seems to be based more upon youthful scientific enthusiasm than upon the likelihood that there will be progress this time around.

The Solution?

My presentation has been directed toward a few points that may be clues to where we have gone wrong and I have provided some indications of what I believe could be accomplished by a new MMPI or some alternative personality device.

Faced with the complexities I have outlined, what new items or forms of items could be used for personality tests? So far no one has discovered a way to specify and use the information items we depend upon for the personality judgments of daily life. Our tests cannot yet objectify and use as modifiers the contingency data that we get in face, clothes, and expressive movements. Our tests are also not able to take into account the personal and social frames of reference in which we make our personality judgments and predictions. These limitations are less threatening in view of the fact that our routine judgments of personality have not been found to be inspiringly accurate, and one can argue that, for all we know, the tests do as well as we do or even as well as can ever be done. Even if we do find better criteria, the problem of frames of reference seems insoluble. At this time, I cannot imagine how we can either establish a constant frame of reference or build tests that will have the fluidity we must allow for.

I suppose that it is apparent that I doubt that we can greatly improve the criteria for deriving better MMPI scales until the old types are supplanted by something new and, perhaps, radically different. I am familiar with the work leading toward new classification systems but I don't see much to suggest that any one will be enough better to induce wide adoption. And I fear that even if a genius produced new and more heuristic constructs or types, we would not accept them because, despite the protests, we are too tied to the old ones. It strikes me that we are still not pessimistic or critical enough, and are too likely to persevere in the unprofitable patterns of the last twenty years. So, in summary, we are stuck, I think, with the MMPI (and Rorschach and even the Bernreuter), for a dreary while longer, although a prophet may even now be wandering in the psychological wilderness. Do the MMPI over and you may be able to increase the proportion of items that are valid and reliable, if you can agree on what such items are like. You would get a little less overlap of experimental and control groups and somewhat higher predictive accuracy.

When considering the reasons for the lack of success of psychometric instruments in adequately assessing any given personality, it is not enough to say something like the above and let it go at that. I have made the suggestion that the problem of developing a useful concept of personality amenable to measurement may not, in principle, be solvable with the same mathematical and design tools that have solved problems in other fields of science.

For further example, if a plausible conceptualization of personality or even an aspect of personality, and indirectly predictable behavior concomitants, were tentatively proposed (as in intelligence testing), it might well be that the "bootstraps phenomenon" would contribute to the development of a refined concept of personality and a highly developed psychometric methodology. However, it is conceivable that faced with the complexity of the criterion problem, the incomparabilities between current statistical strategies, and the involved and arbitrary verbal conceptualizations and behavior syndromes, we should give our main energies to the critical scrutiny of our methods and concepts, even to their most fundamental epistemological characteristics: for example, (1) Are the questions we ask in personality assessment "meaningful" with regard to their relation to the criterion? (2) Is it even possible that there is an empirically testable hypothesis concerning the organization of the individual personality?

I can understand that many psychologists will take a more sanguine view than my negative analysis of the problems in developing more heuristic and compelling constructs of personality; but my evaluation of progress in personality appraisal leads me to this position for the moment. I have avoided getting involved here with attempts to document and extend the logic of my points. What motivates me is that I feel too little attention has been paid to the complexities of the concepts of personality in the techniques of personality appraisal. It appears to me that many investigators, apparently unsatisfied with "understanding" derived from available only slightly successful predictions of behavior mostly from class membership, have turned prematurely to quasi-theoretical exposition for explanation and understanding, put in terms of the writer's internally consistent principles of the dynamics and structure of psyche. I cannot comprehend how any psychologist can believe that we are sufficiently advanced in our knowledge about human beings to warrant such descriptions. So far, I hang on to the first-order need for observational data, collected outside such systems, that could reasonably confirm or deny the inferences.

Recalling the analogy of the "black box" in scientific theorizing, it may be that recourse to man-made constructs concerning internal processes is necessary as a sort of mnemonic device to maximize the predictive efficiency of a system. But for us to accept one and another black box "understanding" of the "inner workings" as opposed to the admittedly more prosaic empirical recourse to predicting behavioral outcomes seems to me to be absurd at our present level of sophistication. As a final attempt to state this, I also do not like the comfortable relaxation that lulls many investigators to scientific reverberation. If we cannot reliably say what a man will do in response to a set of stimulus conditions, how can we hope to say *why* he will do it? I have referred above to Scriven's article which *should* have a sobering effect on over-zealous theorists.

I obviously do not think that the issue of personality needs a "new theory of personality." For one reason that would be a "theory" to define a nonexistent construct. If the criteria do not offer a way to tell when we have a "good theory of personality," any more than they define personality, then it seems rather meaningless to call for a theory.

One crucial aspect of the problem which is obviously largely responsible for perpetuating the lack of communication in the area of personality assessment is the apparently unavoidable effect of one's general orientation toward personality upon what he deems appropriate, regarding methods, criteria, and so forth, in approaching the problem of personality appraisal. Each of us possesses some notion of what it is we are about in the task of appraising a given individual's personality—the extreme positions represent the classic controversy between the projective and the objective self-report inventory methods of personality evaluation. The controversy concerning the relative merits of the two approaches is too much based in fundamental experimenter differences reaching all the way to the definition of the concept of personality and to specific emphases dictated by the theoretical orientation. It occurs to me that there may be some reason to doubt even that it is possible to establish a practical reconciliation (for purposes of expedient, day-to-day clinical work) between these two fundamentally different approaches to personality appraisal.

Preparing for this presentation, I have found that nearly every contributor to the current thinking about personality has made points similar to those I have made. What I also learned from my reading is that there is little diminution in the flood of research reports which provide little proof that knowledge of these problems makes much impression on research designs. Recent APA studies of scientific literature communication showed that we are prolific in publication and comparatively illiterate in reading and acting upon the writings of others. If we are content to merely play the old games, another twenty years could lead only to an iteration of my message.

I do not quarrel with some current trends. We can do much more in studying and developing the data we have. Pessimistic as I may be about making a forward step, we have some important spade work to do. My favorite among leads happens to be the exploration, with computer facility, of emerging classifications among the "profile types." We can greatly improve the contingency correlates of some of these new classes. I would be less concerned about the attempt to find enough classes so that every routine profile could be included and in favor of more intensive study of the few more clearly emerging classes. Without expecting dramatic advances, we may be approaching an empirical system of classification that will have more interim value to counselors and clinicians than the current one.

Within the same context, I think that we should try to identify and understand the characteristics that are behind the emergence of these psychometric classes. For example, more fundamental dynamics may be determining the MMPI "27" class than the clinical intuitions and pseudo-theories that are the basis of the standard nomenclature. I think I rest my case on the plea for innovation. We need new approaches in method and conception. I would ask that we dedicate ourselves to giving pellets to those students who think differently and who stage sit-ins against wornout designs and tactics. We need not be overly concerned about this prospect since unconventional thinking will be rare and reinforcement intermittent.

REFERENCES

Allport, G. W. *Personality.* New York: Holt and Company, 1937.
Block, J. Some reasons for the apparent inconsistency of personality. *Psychological Bulletin,* 1968, **70,** 210-212.
Carr, J. E., & Whittenbaugh, J. Sources of disagreement in the perception of psychotherapy outcomes. *Journal of Clinical Psychology,* 1969. **25,** 16-20.

Ellsworth, R. B., Foster, L., Childers, B., Arthur, G., & Kroeker, D. Hospital and community adjustment as perceived by psychiatric patients, their families, and staff. *Journal of Consulting and Clinical Psychology Monograph Supplement,* 1968, **32,** 1-41.

Ellsworth, R. B., Foster, L., Childers, B., & Kroeker, D. Hospital and community adjustment as perceived by psychiatric patients, their families, and staff. *Journal of Consulting and Clinical Psychology Monograph Supplement,* 1968, **32,** (5, P. 2).

Elstein, A. S., & Van Pelt, J. D. Structure of staff perceptions of psychiatric patients. *Journal of Consulting and Clinical Psychology,* 1968, **32,** 550-559.

Goldberg, L. R. The diagnosis of psychosis versus neurosis from the MMPI. Address delivered at the Third Annual Symposium in the use of the MMPI. Univ. of Minnesota, 1968.

Hathaway, S. R. Problems of personality assessment. In Proceedings of XIV International Congress of Applied Psychology. Copenhagen, 1961.

Holtzman, W. H., Thorpe, J. S., Swartz, J. D., & Herron, E. W. *Inkblot Perception and Personality.* Univ. of Texas Press, 1961.

Muench, G. A. The assessment of counseling and psychotherapy: Some problems and trends. In P. Reynolds (Ed.), *Advances in Psychological Assessment.* Vol. 1. Palo Alto, Calif.: Science and Behavior Books, 1968.

Schopenhauer, A. Cited by J. Campbell, *The Masks of God: Creative Mythology.* New York: Viking Press, 1968.

Scriven, M. A possible distinction between traditional scientific disciplines and the study of human behavior. *Minnesota Studies in the Philosophy of Science.* Vol. 1. *The Foundations of Science and the Concepts of Psychology and Psychoanalysis.* Minneapolis: Univ. of Minnesota Press, 1956.

Stevens, S. S. Mathematics, measurement and psychophysics. In S. S. Stevens (Ed.), *Handbook of Experimental Psychology.* New York: Wiley, 1951.

3
SOME LIMITATIONS OF OBJECTIVE PERSONALITY TESTS[1]

Jane Loevinger

Although it is time to reexamine the MMPI from as many perspectives as possible, with a view to its radical revision and updating, surely all will agree that in its time and of its kind it was the best. If we can do better now or in the future, and we do not know yet that we can, it will be to a large extent because of the impetus given to personality research by this major and foresighted endeavor.

If memory serves, a prevailing, though perhaps unspoken, assumption at the time the item pool was being assembled was that the questionnaire form could substitute for a psychiatric diagnostic interview. Many of the questions seem to have been lifted verbatim from the standard anamnestic interviews of that time. Probably no one today believes that the MMPI is a direct,

---

[1] Preparation of this paper was supported by Research Grant MH-05115 and Research Scientist Award K5 MH-657 from the National Institute of Mental Health, Public Health Service.

question-for-question, substitute for an interview. Meehl (1945) made that point clear. Therefore, the whole matter of the content of the item pool should be reopened. The amazing thing is that the MMPI items went on being reassembled into new tests by other psychologists for many years after the original assumption became outdated.

The original purpose, to take the place of a diagnostic interview, was not, however, translated into relevant statistical techniques. I do not know of any attempt to create scoring procedures that would sort subjects into one of a set of diagnostic categories. Curiously, Lazarsfeld's latent structure analysis (not available at the time of the original MMPI work), which does attempt to sort persons into categories, was applied to the problem of soldier' attitudes toward the Army. A priori, favorableness of attitude is a quantitative rather than a categorical variable, whereas diagnosis is a categorical more than a quantitative problem. I have discussed this point before (Loevinger, 1957). Here is a basic issue. If a diagnostic decision is the aim, why devise a series of quantitative scales? If a series of quantitative measures is the aim, why take diagnostic groups as the basis for scoring keys? If a truly radical revision is attempted, this is one place to start.

The issue of response bias and the related issue of item format are the best known and most hackneyed ones. I would like to discuss them in terms of my own research experiences. Hathaway, of course, was not at all naive with respect to this problem. In fact, contrary to popular impression, which credits Cronbach and Edwards as the discoverers, some of the earliest work on response bias was done here at Minnesota by Rundquist and Sletto (1936), probably more or less under the direction of Donald Paterson. Rundquist and Sletto not only noticed the effects of response bias but also that social desirability was an element of it. There were sophisticated validity scales in the MMPI from the start. The subtler defensiveness variable measured by the K scale was not originally programmed for, however.

At about the time that the importance of the K correction was becoming known, work was beginning in Berkeley on the authoritarian personality (Adorno, Frenkel-Brunswik, Levinson, & Sanford, 1950). In this work the item content was mostly different from that of the MMPI. Extreme groups were again used as a method of item selection, and the item format was even more vulnerable to response bias, since the pathognomic response was always in the same direction and since the degree-of-agreement format introduced a new opportunity for dispositional bias to enter the score. The failure of the Berkeley group to utilize more sophisticated methodology has doomed attitude research to years of methodological follow-up of minimal value for any purpose other than to show what the Berkeley people had

3. Some Limitations of Objective Personality Tests

reason to know at the outset, namely, that their item format produced excessive response bias. Again, however, this format went on being imitated by other psychologists long past the point at which its weaknesses were thoroughly documented.

I have a long-standing prejudice in favor of the item format I call "paired choice," that is, forced choice between a pair of alternatives more or less logically contradictory. The nature of my introduction to academic life had an influence in this matter. My first graduate year was spent as a teaching assistant at the University of Minnesota, with one of my chief duties being to contribute objective test items for the examinations in introductory psychology. Although I was a mediocre apprentice that first year at Minnesota, the following year at Berkeley I was a psychometric expert from Minnesota and was put in charge of the same task. Thus for several years, I was subjected to a pressing form of feedback in regard to test items, to wit, the complaints of irate students who felt that points were taken off their grades when they read the items differently from the way that determined the scoring key. True-false items were hopelessly vulnerable to such complaints. Too much depends on where you see the sentence stress. This is a vulnerability of the single stimulus item both in its MMPI form and its Berkeley F scale form. My main objection to the four-choice item that was, at least in my day, a favorite of Minnesota psychology professors is somewhat different, namely, that three different choices are scored the same (wrong), which discards information. The item as scored differs from the item as responded to. The best and least ambiguous items are those written in the two-choice format, in my opinion.

This item form is by no means original with me. Many persons have noted its merits in many contexts. William Owens (1947), one of my Minnesota classmates, did a fine study showing improvement in the validity of a personality test when it was changed from a single stimulus to a paired choice format. Kenneth Hammond (1948) did a beautiful study showing that forced choice between paired, equally inaccurate statements yielded a test that separated persons chosen from labor and management groups with 100 percent accuracy. Recent studies using this format include those of Rotter (1966) whose I–E test concerns the person's disposition to think in terms of internal or external control of reinforcement.

I used this format to study women's attitudes toward problems of family life beginning in the early 1950s (Loevinger & Sweet, 1961, pp. 110-123; Loevinger, 1962). It seemed to me that in tests like the MMPI and the Berkeley F scale there was a hidden hand that turned the answers. Use of the paired choice format, I hoped, would by-pass that response set. Yet when Dr. Blanche Sweet and I sat down to ponder the kinds of answers we were getting from the various groups that we had secured to test (women marines, student nurses, and others), the impression was strangely born in on us that something corresponding to that methodological artifact was still strongly present in our data. The proportion of women endorsing conventional thoughts, banalities, and moralistic cliches seemed quite disproportionate to the number of women who might behave in the corresponding fashion. For a moment we thought of giving up our whole enterprise. We concluded that paper-and-pencil techniques, no matter how careful one is to by-pass or to avoid methodological artifacts, simply do not reflect the way people act. On second thought, we decided to persevere, largely because we had included groups (notably Vassar women) who chose the opposite alternatives of the same items. We at least were picking up some stable individual differences in something; and, whatever it was, it appeared to be related to the hidden hand in test response. Despite the fact that our format excluded an acquiescent, or degree of agreement, response set as a source of variance, we seemed to be measuring whatever was the source of valid variance in response bias.

That there should be valid variance in response bias is a thought that has come as a sudden insight to many investigators who have taken it as an excuse for continuing with item forms heavily weighted with response set. But every voluntary action contains valid variance, in principle. The task of the psychometrician is to find the best measure, and as a rule that will be the one least tainted with methodological artifact. Most of the objective personality tests in use today are in direct line of descent from those that, in a more naive era, were modelled after ability tests or psychiatric interviews, or both. Such tests proved to be contaminated with methodological artifacts that certainly were not purposively planted there by the test constructors. Granted that there is some valid variance for some purpose in every test response, it would be most remarkable if those unintended artifacts should prove to be the best possible measures of anything.

The basic strategy used in constructing scoring keys for the Family Problems Scale was homogeneous keying, using the method of Loevinger, Gleser, and DuBois (1953). This is an alternative to criterion keying and, in particular, to the method of extreme groups used in both the MMPI and the Berkeley studies. It is equally empirical, however; so I decline to allow the method of criterion keying to preempt the title "empirical keying," as it customarily does. Using a heterogeneous group of 200 cases, five scoring keys were derived. On a cross-validation sample of 67 cases, four of the keys survived, the fifth turning up with a negative KR 20 coefficient.

3. Some Limitations of Objective Personality Tests

Although the method of homogeneous keying favors independent scoring keys, the results indicated that our strongest key, which we ultimately called Authoritarian Family Ideology, also operated as a central or general factor. Moreover, this factor resembles similarly strong and central variables in other studies using different methodologies and different types of subjects. The kinds of Family Problems Scale items that fell into this cluster confirmed many of the notions about the authoritarian personality that came out of the Berkeley study. If one made an a priori scoring key for punitiveness–permissiveness, it would be entirely dominated by this factor. At the same time, items logically relevant to punitiveness or permissiveness were in some cases unrelated to Authoritarian Family Ideology; hence we rejected punitiveness or permissiveness as a title. Approval of a hierarchical family structure is a strong element in the content. Antiintraception, acquiescence to moralistic cliches, intrusion into a child's inner life, and rigid control of the child's impulses appear as content in other items. Older psychoanalytic ideas (perhaps rather naively interpreted) did not form the basis for any of the clusters, although there were ample items to test the ideas. The items that concerned toilet training did not form a cluster or a statistical subcluster, nor did those concerning food training and eating. Rather, items concerning toilet training were as closely related to items concerning eating as they were to each other; they were included in the Authoritarian Family Ideology cluster (Loevinger & Sweet, 1961). Furthermore, the impression was strong that what we were measuring was indeed the source of whatever valid variance response bias contains. This train of thought led into new channels which I shall discuss shortly.

There is an interesting side issue here which is of immediate relevance to the MMPI as well as to other multiple-score tests. In the United States both our tests and our psychometric methodologies have usually been based on an orthogonal model of the universe of traits to be studied. We are usually looking for several more or less independent and more or less equally important traits. This point of view goes back to the earliest days of intelligence measurement. Hathaway, like Thurstone, was looking for multiple factors, but stubbed his toe on the K factor. We thought we would profit by his experience and eliminate the general personality factor by eliminating response bias. But Authoritarian Family Ideology operates as a general factor in the Family Problems Scale. The review by Campbell and Fiske (1959) of many kinds of psychological test data reveals that a similar finding is a general rule in psychology. Every test seems saturated with a methods factor that outweighs other kinds of valid variance.

To meet the problem of taking a test's general factor into account without letting it overpower all other kinds of variance, I have devised a graphic profile method (Figure 1). Along the x-axis, which goes from 1.0 on the left to 0.0 on the right, is represented the correlation of each subtest with the test's general factor. Each subtest is represented by an ordinate erected at the point of its correlation with the general factor. Thus, an ordinate erected at $r = 1.0$ represents the general factor. The chart is constructed so that one standard deviation is the same length on each ordinate. If we enter a subject's standard score on the general factor on the ordinate at the extreme left and connect that point with the point representing a standard score of zero at the point $r = 0$, the line will show the subject's predicted score on every subtest. If his actual score is also entered on the graph, it will be apparent at a glance whether he is above or below the mean (or any other given cutting score) on each subtest, and also whether he is above or below what would be predicted on the basis of his own score on the general factor. Thus a simple graphic device can partly handle the problem of the general factor, at the same time yielding a more meaningful type of profile for multiple score tests.

Dr. Kitty LaPerriere, Professor Abel Ossorio, and I met together a number of times to discuss the Family Problems Scale and its meaning and what further studies might profitably be done with it. I believe it was primarily Dr. LaPerriere who said on the basis of her own clinical experience,

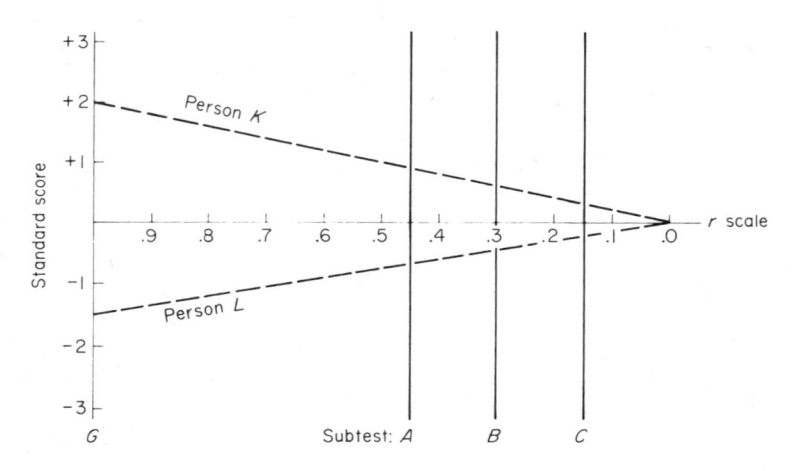

Figure 1. Test profile showing subtest scores predicted from general factor (G) of test. Example: $r_{AG} = .45; r_{BG} = .30; r_{CG} = .15$. Person K: $Z_G = 2.0$; predicted $Z_B = .60$. Person L: $Z_G = -1.5$; predicted $Z_A = -.675$.

3. Some Limitations of Objective Personality Tests 51

confirmed by that of Dr. Ossorio, that rigid authoritarian control is not a mark of the lowest ego levels, where a more chaotic picture prevails. From their work in public clinics they were familiar with what Oscar Lewis has since called "the culture of poverty," what we now would call simply a low stage of ego development. My current notion of ego development began to take form in these conversations. We formed the hypothesis that Authoritarian Family Ideology was, to a first approximation, a measure of ego level.

Dr. LaPerriere administered the Family Problems Scale to postpartum women in four maternity hospitals which were chosen to represent a wide social spectrum. The women were Catholic, Protestant, and Jewish, having first, second, or third babies, and they were of differing educational levels. It proved impossible to fill cells in the design calling for Jewish women of less than high school education. She found significant main effects in Authoritarian Family Ideology due to number of children and to educational level but none due to religion when education was controlled. There was a significant low association with age $(r = .29)$, with older women being less authoritarian than younger women. The correlation of Authoritarian Family Ideology with age, educational level, and experience in childrearing confirmed a developmental interpretation.

Following LaPerriere's work, our studies went in two divergent directions. We repeated the homogeneous keying and the ANOVA study, dropping religion as a variable and adding race; and we studied the relation of Authoritarian Family Ideology with other variables, in particular with a projective test of ego development. Both these lines of research led to findings that are pertinent to the general topic of what can be measured by paper-and-pencil personality tests.

Dr. Claire Ernhart (Ernhart & Loevinger, 1969) has replicated the homogeneous keying study with a new sample of women (over 900 cases) again very heterogeneous. All keyed items from the previous study were retained and new items were substituted for the discards in order to test hypotheses about the traits being measured. The one major change in her research design was the inclusion of black women (about 20 percent) in place of the previous all white samples. Using homogeneous keying again, she found the same general factor, Authoritarian Family Ideology, with minor changes in the exact items included but no major change in the overall substantive content. The other clusters she found, however, could not be collated with the small clusters of the previous study. In both studies we were able to spin hypotheses about the item content of each cluster and provide psychologically meaningful titles. These putative traits were at least as convincing as those to be found in all sorts of factor analyses and in other studies of family attitudes, such as those using the Parental Attitude Research Instrument. The fact remains that they were not replicable. We suspect that a fair test would show that most factors in other studies would not be replicable in new samples which differ demographically in ways which, according to reasonable assumptions, should not change the trait structure under study.

The emergence of different clusters of items as homogeneous keys in Ernhart's study (1969) meant that the pattern of relationships among items differed in her study as compared to the earlier one. A more detailed examination of her data showed that the inclusion of Negro women (20 percent of the sample) was the major source of differences. The changes in item groupings were, in at least some instances, quite intelligible in terms of the known differences in circumstances of Negro and white women in our cities.

Ernhart saw these results as leading to a much broader issue. To what extent are the homogeneity coefficients (KR 20) and the intercorrelations of a set of tests a function of the demographic composition of the sample? Her study contained a group of women tested postpartum after first, second or third births. Their educational level ranged from having finished only grade school to having finished college. There were white and black women. She divided the sample into cells on the basis of these variables. She then worked out an adaptation of ANOVA, permitting her to compute within-cell values of the KR 20 coefficients and of the intercorrelations of the scoring keys she had derived earlier from the broader sample. In effect, the statistical technique she worked out held constant statistically any stratifying variable or any combination of stratifying variables. She showed that large variations in the correlations could be produced by holding constant race, education, parity, or some combination of them. These were not merely variations in the size of the correlations but striking variations in pattern, that is, in the size of one correlation relative to others.

Ernhart's results throw into question the entire picture that has been accepted as defining the mission of psychometrics in relation to the study of individual differences. (No wonder neither *Psychological Bulletin* nor *Educational and Psychological Measurement* want to publish it, even though they have found no errors in it.) It has been assumed that there is some stable domain of traits awaiting discovery by some all-purpose methodology. Most people assume that that methodology will be some variation or refinement of factor analysis. It has often been asserted that rotation of axes will lift the factors discovered above the particularities of the tests and samples used, but

3. Some Limitations of Objective Personality Tests

this has never been proved either logically or empirically. Indeed, the weight of experience has indicated that it is very hard to match the factors of one study with the factors of a study with different tests or a different sample. If matching factors from one study with the next were so easy, why would the Procrustes method have been introduced?

Now, of course, Ernhart and I do not maintain that there can be no such thing as a robust trait, discoverable by different methods in different samples. On the contrary, we ourselves have found one such trait. Our measure of Authoritarian Family Ideology, which was robust by all other criteria, was also robust by the new criteria which came out of Ernhart's ANOVA techniques. It remains a strongly homogeneous cluster of items in all demographic groups. What we doubt is that there is any technique, factorial or otherwise, that will automatically lead to a family of such traits.

Let us turn now to the projective test approach. Once the notion of ego development and particularly of its dialectical course was strongly conveyed to me, I quickly perceived that many other people knew much more about it and had a more detailed picture of its dialectics than I had or could hope to evolve with my own unaided efforts. I began to study what others had said on the subject, beginning with the version of C. Sullivan, Grant, and Grant (1957) who called it interpersonal integration. I subsequently was influenced by Isaac's (1956) notion of interpersonal relatability, Peck's (Peck & Havighurst, 1960) stages of character development, and Kohlberg's (1964) stages of the moralization of judgment, as well as the classic work of Harry Stack Sullivan (1953), Piaget (1932), and others.

Miss Elizabeth Nettles became interested in correlating AFI with a sentence completion test scored for ego development. I discouraged this idea because making a scoring manual for the sentence completion test meant starting a whole new test construction project. I was overruled, and how right I was. That was eight or ten years ago, and our scoring manual for the sentence completion test was published in 1970 (Loevinger & Wessler, 1970; Loevinger, Wessler, & Redmore, 1970). Several able people have been devoting a major part of their time to its construction and evaluation since we first started on this task. At the outset we were fortunate to have the help of the late Virginia Ives Word, who had previously worked with Eric Gunderson, Douglas Grant, and Marguerite Grant (now Marguerite Warren) on their sentence completion measure. An intermediate version of the manual was largely the responsibility of Mrs. Nina de Charms.

The basic measurement strategy of the sentence completion scoring manual is as follows: The stages of ego development are seen as qualitatively different. They constitute a milestone sequence rather than a simple polar variable. Each bit of behavior to be rated (single response or total protocol) is matched against a rating scale that describes the successive stages or milestones of ego development in qualitatively different language. The stage names give a glimpse of the sequence: presocial, impulsive, self-protective (formerly called opportunistic), conformist, conscientious, autonomous, and integrated.

Compare this with the basic measurement strategy of the MMPI, the Berkeley F scale, and tests of ability. In those cases it is assumed that the amount of the trait is proportional to the number of different indicators marked correctly (or in the scored direction), with each item assumed to be a different indicator.

Take for granted for the moment that the sequence we call ego development is a psychologically meaningful one. There are many reasons for so thinking, and we have much data to support the usefulness of our version. Other research groups have similar data to support closely related versions. Now consider what happens when a psychologist approaches the area of research I call "ego development" with a behavioristic and quantitative bias. He will take namable and observable aspects of behavior, say, conformity, one at a time and treat each one as a polar variable. That is, he will assume that conformity is a trait that you have more of, the more signs of conformity you show. Similarly, other points on the ego development scale (the other milestones that make up the ego developmental sequence) will be treated as polar variables, and tests for them will be constructed on the cumulative model.

I maintain that nothing of any value for psychology can come of this enterprise. No amount of study of such variables, singly or together, by whatever version of the general linear hypothesis or by however high speed a computer, will ever yield a psychologically intelligible result, except by sheerest accident. Two such variables may have almost any correlation, including a very low one, even though both represent stages in the same sequence of ego development, just because they represent different stages. Such variables could be studied for years by the usual methods, including factor analysis, without ever yielding any inkling that they fit together to form a milestone sequence. Is that not, in fact, what has been done?

It is possible, moreover, to study variables that sound very much like the descriptions of stages of ego development without making any close connection with the topic. Something like this has happened in the study of the achievement motive. An interest in achievement partially supplants

3. Some Limitations of Objective Personality Tests

interest in appearance and in popularity or belonging as one moves from the conformist to the conscientious stage. As the achievement motive was originally defined, it meant achievement as measured by one's own inner standards. That is the form that interest in achievement takes at the conscientious level. There can also be a version of the achievement motive that is chiefly a matter of competition with one's fellows; that would characterize the self-protective, opportunistic level. Another version of the achievement motive is primarily a quest for recognition from one's fellows; that could appear at the conformist stage, though, of course, it need not completely disappear at later stages. My impression is that current methods of scoring the Thematic Appercepion Test for need for achievement do not distinguish these possibilities. At any rate, Dr. Carolyn Redmore found no relation between ego level as measured by our sentence completion test and need for achievement as measured by the Thematic Appercepion Test and scored by Motivation Research Center of Cambridge, Massachusetts.

The foregoing example illustrates the fatal flaw in all research projects that are predicated on vast data banks. The idea that untold riches in the form of data can be stored up and then dipped into at will is a misconception. Anything really new will involve rethinking of basic constructs and a consequent revision of the notion of what is considered to be relevant data. This is part of the thesis of Kuhn's (1962) essay on scientific revolutions.

Most investigators who work with the sentence completion test decide sooner or later that whatever they are measuring by it could be tested better, or at least almost as well, by a multiple choice form. Several such studies have begun systematically choosing typical answers representing different ego levels as the alternative responses. That this experiment always fails is shown by the fact that the relative frequencies of responses in the several levels change radically. High-ego level responses are unusual in the ordinary sentence completion format, but they are very popular when they are presented in the multiple choice format. To understand this result, one must understand something about the nature of the ego.

Alfred Adler used the term "style of life" which at various times he equated with self or ego, the unity of personality, individuality, the method of facing problems, opinion about oneself and the problems of life, and the whole attitude toward life. Let us say that the ego is the person's frame of reference. To get an adequate picture of a person's ego level you must give him a task that permits him to project and that permits the protocol to register, his frame of reference. A projective test does so. The multiple choice format, by contrast, presents the researcher's frame of reference. Thus, our use of a projective test instead of an objective one is not a temporary expedient to serve until psychometric technology advances further. The projective format is of the essence in measuring ego level.

Let me recapitulate my main points. If a categorical diagnostic decision is the aim of a new test, then quantitative measures are inappropriate. If quantitative traits are to be measured, then discrimination of extreme groups is too crude and inappropriate a method for item selection.

Although I remain loyal to factorial methods, including homogeneous keying and factor analysis, as evidence for one aspect of the construct validity of a test score, it is fallacious to assume that any factorial method automatically supplies test scores or trait concepts that are robust under demographic variation. Such robustness is essential to fulfill the implied program of construct validity. In order to test for robustness, systematic variation of the demographic composition of the sample is an essential element of future programs of test construction.

Such valid variance as the MMPI K factor contains is probably an aspect of ego development and better measured by some test specifically designed for that purpose. It is foolish to hope that unwanted and unplanned artifacts of measurement will provide optimal measures of anything.

The discussion has wandered a long way from the MMPI. But it was an interest in response bias, the hidden hand in objective personality tests like the MMPI and the Berkeley F scale, that led to my interest in ego development and to the conviction that such valid variance as response bias carries is, in fact, a manifestation of ego level. If you want to measure ego level, it would be best to do it directly by a test such as the sentence completion test. If you want to measure something else, like neurotic tendency (if that is a something), then a format free of response bias should be chosen.

If I were to draw a single conclusion from my own studies of personality measurement, it would be this: I consider it exceedingly unlikely that either by accident or by automation one will discover a measure of a major personality variable. There is no substitute for having a psychologist in charge who has at least a first-approximation conception of the trait he wishes to measure, always open to revision, of course, as data demand. Theory has always been the mark of a mature science. The time is overdue for psychology, in general, and personality measurement, in particular, to come of age.

REFERENCES

Adorno, T. W., Frenkel-Brunswik, E., Levinson, D. J. & Sanford, R. N. *The Authoritarian Personality.* New York: Harper, 1950.

Campbell, D. T., & Fiske, D. W. Convergent and discriminant validation by the multitrait-multimethod matrix. *Psychological Bulletin,* 1959, **56,** 81-105.

Ernhart, C. B., & Loevinger, J. Authoritarian family ideology: A measure, its correlates, and its robustness. *Multivariate Behavioral Research Monographs,* 1969, No. 69-1.

Hammond, K. R. Measuring attitudes by error-choice: An indirect method. *Journal of Abnormal and Social Psychology,* 1948, **43,** 38-48.

Isaacs, K. S. Relatability, a proposed construct and an approach to its validation. Unpublished doctoral dissertation, Univ. of Chicago, 1956.

Kohlberg, L. Development of moral character and moral ideology. In M. Hoffman & L. W. Hoffman (Eds.), *Review of child development research.* Vol. 1. New York: Russell Sage Foundation, 1964.

Kuhn, T. S. *The structure of scientific revolutions.* Chicago: Univ. of Chicago Press, 1962.

Loevinger, J. Objective tests as instruments of psychological theory. *Psychological Reports,* 1957, **3,** (9), 635-694.

Loevinger, J. Measuring personality patterns of women. *Genetic Psychology Monograph,* 1962, **65,** 53-136.

Loevinger, J., Gleser, G. C., & DuBois, P. H. Maximizing the discriminating power of a multiple-score test. *Psychometrika,* 1953, **18,** 309-317.

Loevinger, J., & Sweet, B. Construction of a test mothers' attitudes. In J. C. Glidewell (Ed.), *Parental attitudes and child behavior.* Springfield, Ill.: Thomas, 1961.

Loevinger, J., & Wessler, R. *Measuring ego development I. Construction and use of a sentence completion test.* San Francisco: Jossey-Bass, 1970.

Loevinger, J., Wessler, R., & Redmore, C. *Measuring ego development II. Scoring manual for women and girls.* San Francisco: Jossey-Bass, 1970.

Meehl, P. E. The dynamics of "structured" personality tests. *Journal of Clinical Psychology,* 1945, **1,** 296-303.

Owens, W. A. Item form and "false-positive" response on a neurotic inventory. *Journal of clinical psychology,* 1947, **3,** 264-269.

Peck, R. F., & Havighurst, R. J. *The psychology of character development.* New York: Wiley, 1960.

Piaget, J. *The moral judgment of the child.* (2nd ed.) Glencoe, Ill.: Free Press, 1948. (Originally published: New York: Harcourt, 1932.)

Rotter, J. B. Generalized expectancies for internal versus external control of reinforcement. *Psychological Monographs,* 1966, **80,** (1, Whole No. 609).

Rundquist, E. A., & Sletto, R. F. *Personality in the depression.* Minneapolis: University of Minnesota Press, 1936.

Sullivan, C., Grant, M. Q., & Grant, J. D. The development of interpersonal maturity: Applications to delinquency. *Psychiatry,* 1957, **20,** 373-385.

Sullivan, H. S. *The interpersonal theory of psychiatry.* New York: Norton, 1953.

4

PSYCHOMETRIC CONSIDERATIONS FOR A REVISION OF THE MMPI

Warren T. Norman

When I was a student at Minnesota in the years following World War II and the Boulder Conference, there was a story that circulated among the graduate students contending that the only way to get accepted into the clinical psychology program was to have either a Miller Analogies Test Score that was out of this world *OR* a Multiphasic profile that was. There were some who also believed that it was necessary to get through the entire Kent-Rosanoff list without giving a single high commonality response. Others doubted whether this latter was strictly required as long as a sufficiently extended series of mediational links could be *imagined* to have intervened in arriving at the responses.

Regardless of whether or not the story had some basis in fact, its mere existence is worthy of note. For among those who have designed and developed devices to assess noncognitive attributes, none have been more devoted to the need for providing requisite kinds of empirical data on which to base score interpretations than have the authors of the MMPI, their colleagues, and students. (Nor, if there is any truth to the story, have any been willing to go to such lengths to secure the kinds of cases needed to illustrate rare and bizarre response protocols!)

But despite the continuing effort to evolve a more efficient and useful instrument for clinical diagnosis, personality assessment, and psychometric research, the time has now come to ask more fundamental questions than can be answered by simple recourse to established methods and procedures. It may just be that what we have come to know as "objective" personality testing may be a blind alley or, at the least, a passageway so constricted that only the most limited conceptions may move along it.

Indeed, there is, in my opinion, little doubt that a number of fundamental changes in methods, data, and theory are required if we are to witness any substantial improvement in our efforts to assess personality and account for behavior—whether clinical or otherwise. The old items, methods, and interpretive concepts have had an extended day in court; and relative to their adversaries, they have not done too badly. But at this stage the question is not whether the MMPI, or empirical keying, or profile analysis can do better than the Rorschach, or judgmental key construction, or global interpretation of a case folder. It is, rather, how may we best incorporate what we have learned from the past thirty years, or more, of research with this and other techniques in order to generate the quantum jump in personality theory and methods of assessment and diagnosis which is, I believe, potentially attainable.

Thus, I come not to bury the Mult *nor* to praise it. The first would surely be premature, and the second unnecessary. Instead, I propose to consider some general issues and problems of theory construction, diagnosis, and measurement and relate them to some of the present characteristics and uses of the MMPI. If, in what follows, my comments sometimes seem critical of the Multiphasic or, by implication, critical of those who built, developed, or use it, that is both unintended and beside the point. My aim is to focus attention on some of those aspects of diagnosis, assessment, and theorizing in which there is some hope of improving contemporary practice, methodology, and conceptualization.

As a functionalist, I think the most fruitful way to begin an examination of this (or any) method is with its uses, aims, or objectives. In spite of the fact that the MMPI has sprung from a functionalist tradition, it has not always been entirely clear just what this device and all this effort has been *about*. Actually, it has been about many things—and therein lies part of the

4. Psychometric Considerations for a Revision of the MMPI

explanation of the confusion that exists and the source of continuing difficulties.

The MMPI was (and is) *not* intended to be solely a screening device for gross pathology, or a tool for differential psychiatric diagnosis, or a means to detect malingering and dissimulation, or an omnibus inventory of personality measures, or a means of operationalizing the constructs of some theoretical system, or any other of the myriad uses to which it has, at various times, been put. It was originally constructed and subsequently touted—sometimes by its authors and proponents and sometimes by others (often without "official" blessings, we must imagine)—for *all* of these purposes and many more.

As time has passed and the reputation of the MMPI and its availability has spread, uncounted numbers of students, practitioners, and researchers, in pursuit of useful tools for their own purposes, have turned to this device and applied it to an ever wider ranging set of problems. The variety of situational contexts in which these diverse aims were to be realized and the demographic variety of the respondent populations to whom the Mult was administered as well as for whom (or by means of whom) these differing objectives were to be met has led inevitably to disappointments and to the disenchantment that accrues at last to any *presumed* panacea.

It has often seemed to me that psychologists display an absolutely astonishing degree of naïveté concerning the tools and methods of their trade. Intelligent people who would never try to drive a nail with a screwdriver nor attempt to bore a hole in a sheet of metal with a pair of pliers frequently seem to act as though they believed that quite analogous kinds of behavior would be quite appropriate and effective with tools like the Multiphasic.

In a carpentry shop some tools have a wider range of potential use than others; but none is sufficient to accomplish all potential jobs equally well. John Tukey has made a related point with reference to statistical methods in what he terms the "law of the jackknife." Some tools and some methods, like the jackknife, do have a broad band of utility but usually at some cost in terms of precision for specific tasks. Others can be used to accomplish more limited jobs with a high degree of efficiency but are utterly useless for many other things that need to be done.

The general point I am trying to make is that *it is unreasonable,* given what we already know of the complexity of human behavior, the personological determinants of responses to inventory items, the effects of situational conditions on test performances, the ambiguities of verbal items both between and within various language communities, and the host of other things we have learned over the past several decades *to expect any single, fixed format, verbal stimulus and (quasi-) verbal response inventory to be a sufficient, or even a generally efficient, means for assessing human personality for all purposes.* The day is past when we can reasonably expect to get by with a jackknife, even a big and elaborate one, for all the things we have to do.

I do believe that verbal stimulus materials and resulting response protocols can yield large amounts of personality-relevant information about patients and other individuals. But, I also believe this yield will be realized only if we provide for much greater flexibility in the choice of which specific stimuli or questions are presented and when, only if a greater diversity of presentation formats for such stimuli and of instructional tasks or sets are used, and only if a far more specific (and hence complex) set of norms and calibrations of such behaviors by members of relevant language communities are developed. Even then, it is quite possible that we may have to turn to entirely different behavioral modalities and information sources to complete the picture(s) of personality organization, structure, and dynamics which we require.

But I want to return now to consider some more limited aspects of the problem and to be more specific about possible courses to follow in modifying our approach to *diagnosis, instrument design,* and *personality assessment*. By merely stating the matter in this fashion, I have made explicit what is perhaps the major source of our difficulties. For diagnosis, test development, and personality assessment are in no sense the same enterprise—or even necessarily mutually compatible ones.

The first, *diagnosis,* is a matter of identification, placement, or assignment of an individual (or element) to one of two or more distinguishable, if not always independent or disjoint, sets. *Test development* is essentially a psychophysical business in which one attempts to calibrate stimuli and determine their operating characteristics under relevant conditions. The last, *assessment,* is the most complicated of the three and is inherently a descriptive, conceptual activity, and one which typically entails characterization and evaluation of the individual in terms of his attributes. Although assessment could seemingly be carried out in terms of proximities or similarities of the individual to typal reference or diagnostic groups (a view of considerable relevance vis-a-vis the MMPI), such an approach is indirect and requires, in the last analysis, knowledge of the bases or attributes on which the reference groups themselves are distinguished from one another.

In effect, there are at least two fundamental or intrinsic facets to even the most rudimentary diagnostic, or assessment, or psychophysical study: the *individuals* and the *attributes*. In diagnostic identification or assignment, the attributes provide merely a means to the end and may be (indeed, often are) of little or no intrinsic interest. By way of contrast, psychophysical studies focus primarily on operating characteristics or properties of the attributes (or stimuli), and the individual plays the complementary, subordinate role. In assessment, however, both individuals *and* attributes are involved in an essential, focal manner.

For the diagnostician it is sufficient to determine who goes with whom. Assuming one knows effective treatments to apply to different members of different classes, all that is required is correct placement of individuals in the respective categories. To provide a complete attributive description or characterization of each individual could quite conceivably be both unnecessary and irrelevant.

In like manner, the task of scaling a set of attributes or otherwise determining their relations or probabilities of co-occurrence does not, as such, typically require the use, or even explicit knowledge of, the presence, absence, or degree of each attribute in each individual in order to determine such values or relationships. Indeed, some scaling theorists I have met seem to proceed with their work giving scarcely any thought whatever to whom their subjects are, where they come from, or anything else about them!

But the task of assessing personality and providing characterizations of the dispositions, traits, and behavior of individuals is intrinsically linked to both facets of the paradigm. To do the job effectively one needs reference points based on distributional characteristics of the set of individuals *and* operating properties of the stimuli, including relationships among them. Without the former, interpretations of uniqueness or commonalty are impossible. Without the latter, the intentionality and frame of reference is missing and the assessment becomes connotatively vacuous.

If I have been redundant in these last few paragraphs or have seemed to stress unduly the distinctions among these several viewpoints or orientations, it is because I think they are fundamental to any real appreciation of what has been going on in the field of late and of what the implications of these events might be for a possible revision of the MMPI. In the remainder of this chapter, I propose to examine in more detail the first two of these three major orientations to the MMPI—diagnosis and scale development—and, where possible, to suggest ways in which each set of objectives might be achieved more adequately or efficiently. Personality assessment, the most complex and difficult enterprise of the three, will receive only scant attention, although I will have a few comments concerning the development of adequate trait theories that have a bearing on the interpretation of assessment data.

Diagnosis

I have chosen to begin with the diagnostic problem (by which I mean to include selection, classification, and personnel decision making, generally) because I think I can be most specific in my analysis and recommendations in this area.

From a strictly diagnostic viewpoint, the Multiphasic is a mess! Its original clinical criteria are anachronistic; its basic clinical scales are inefficient, redundant, and largely irrelevant for their present purposes; its administrative format and the repertoire of responses elicited are, respectively, inflexible and impoverished; and its methods for combining scale scores and for profile interpretation are unconscionably cumbersome and obtuse.

Let us begin with the original criterion categories. Whether or not Kraepelinian nosology was an appropriate system on which to base a psychiatric diagnostic instrument in the early 1940s, its relevance for that purpose in the late 1960s has surely become tenuous, at best. In one respect, the MMPI already reflects this shift away from classical terminology by the substitution of numerical designations for the old scale names and by the shift in interpretative emphasis from the original, single scales to profile code types. But the scales themselves have remained, by and large, unaltered in this process. Whatever justification each scale derived initially from the nosological category it was designed to map is rapidly vanishing, if not already lost.

Far from decrying these changes in the criterional basis for clinical diagnosis, I am cheered by them. And I think diagnostitians, in general, and MMPI-ers, in particular, should be, too. At least *sometimes* changes result in improvements. What I am not so cheered by, however, is the continued use of the original scales as profile components and the unnecessary complexity, inefficiency, and obscurity this introduces into the specifications and interpretations of typal classes. Whatever one thinks of the desirability of the original construction of the basic clinical scales (granting the purposes for which they were then intended), it is abundantly clear that they are about as inappropriate and maladapted a set as one could imagine for their current uses in profile analysis and interpretation and typal class definition.

First, the individual scales in most cases are highly heterogeneous in content. Scores are, accordingly, difficult to characterize simply or to

4. Psychometric Considerations for a Revision of the MMPI

describe concisely and unambiguously. Although this lack of a clear *internal* basis for interpretation may have been tolerable when one could appeal to a well-established diagnostic type or syndrome as an alternative (at least for "high" scores), the gradual blurring and eventual abandonment of this external framework and the further complication introduced by the need to consider various configurations of two or more scales simultaneously made it virtually necessary to evolve an entirely new typal system to which to appeal for meaning.

And this, of course, was just what was done in the development of profile coding methods and in the construction of the Atlas. But if one were going to set out to build a new taxonomy of psychopathology on the basis of test behavior on the MMPI, what an extremely awkward and self-restricting way to go about it! Could the mere existence of all those old profiles laying around in files all over the country and the accumulated folklore regarding them have justified this perseverative use of the original scales for this purpose? Perhaps so. But the price we have paid in terms of impeded progress toward the development of a more adequate taxonomy of diagnostic classes has, in my judgment, been excessive.

But there are grounds other than just internal heterogeneity of content for objecting to these scales as *profile constituents*. They are also structurally and substantively redundant. Although, for reasons I will expand upon shortly, I do not think anyone really knows, as yet, what a reasonable estimate is for the upper limit of configural complexity of the MMPI, it is obvious we can never find out what this limit is by using the present scales as profile components. Their intercorrelations in both homogeneous and mixed general populations are much too high to justify retention of all the scales in the present profile on the grounds of the independent information they each contribute. What is worse, several of these intercorrelations are, in part, sheer artifacts created by joint keying of single responses on two or more of the component scales.

Finally, and perhaps most grievous of all, a great deal of potentially useful information contained within the item pool is not even available in the present profile. Not only are some items unused in any of the keys but the potential configuration properties of many others are masked by their embeddedness in the present, *statistically* heterogeneous, linear scales. When one combines a pair of negatively correlated items in a positively weighted linear function, as frequently occurs on these keys, their valid common variance components effectively cancel one another. When pairs of uncorrelated items are so combined, any potential configural information one might otherwise extract from their inclusion in separate profile components is also lost.

In brief, linear composites of items which are to be used as the component scales of a profile, the configural properties of which are of potential interest, must each be statistically homogeneous. It would also be desirable from the viewpoint of efficiency for the separate scales to be relatively uncorrelated with one another. And, of course, it would be nice if some interpretation of each component scale based on the content of its items could be given, although that would not be strictly necessary for purposes of diagnosis alone. There is no possible benefit or justification I can think of, however, for keying single responses on two or more of the component scales of such a profile set.

Thus far, what I have suggested is predicated on the assumption that diagnostic placements are to be made by means of a single-stage assessment procedure. That is, a set of type classes is assumed to exist into one (or perhaps, several) of which each individual is to be placed according to the features of the score profile derived from his responses to a single administration of the entire set of items. I would suggest that such a procedure requires too much irrelevant information from the respondent for many of the decisions one might want to make about him and too little information on which to base other conclusions. It is also too restricted in terms of the order and form in which the stimuli can be presented and the data elicited. And, finally, it makes assumptions about the structural organization or relationships among the typal classes that are certainly simplistic and quite apt to be entirely untenable.

Consider this latter point first. The model that underlies this approach is that each typal class is a discrete collection of individuals each characterized by a highly similar pattern of attributes which, in some generally unspecified way, is *merely different* from the configurations that characterize members of other classes. It is as though the diagnostic system were assumed to consist of classes only at the species level with no system for grouping these in turn to form genera, families, orders, and the like.

In psychiatric diagnosis, it may suffice initially to establish merely whether or not the respondent gives evidence of *any* form of gross pathology. That is, comparatively speaking, a simple task, and one would ordinarily not want (or need) to utilize a major differential diagnostic battery to accomplish this. Only if the initial testing revealed some evidence of gross pathology might one then reasonably proceed to narrow down the focus, say, to a determination of "psychosis" or "neurosis" or "character disorder" or "organicity."

4. Psychometric Considerations for a Revision of the MMPI

Given some resolution at this level, successively finer and more circumscribed distinctions (e.g., "conversion reaction" versus "anxiety reaction" versus whatever given "neurosis") might well be pursued, *but presumably within the frame of reference established by the prior findings from the more molar levels of inquiry.*

As any reasonably intelligent, adolescent, party-goer knows, all you get (or need) in order to identify any object in the world is twenty questions—even when they are only answered "Yes" or "No." He also knows that the first thing to determine is whether what is sought is "animal," "vegetable," or "mineral," *not* whether it is, say, "the upper left bicuspid in George Washington's cast-iron false teeth." He may eventually get around to asking questions which permit that sort of specific identification, but he does not *begin* that way unless he is either very foolish or very naïve. And even if he is unsophisticated initially, he usually learns the error of his ways long before he asks as many as 550 (or 566) such questions!

Even if one granted that the identifications sought in clinical diagnosis are neither so circumscribed nor so clearly defined as they typically are in the game of twenty questions, and even if the responses one gets to his inquiries cannot be trusted not to mislead, distort, or misrepresent the case (as they are honor bound not to do in this pastime), there are several relevant lessons to be learned (or relearned) from this analogy.

First, as Herbert Feigl used to say to us, "You need no razor blade to cut warm butter." And similarly, one does not need a protocol of a half thousand responses to detect grossly pathological mentation, affect, or perceptions.

Second, once you have established that you are looking for some kind of vegetable, you do not have to ask a lot of questions about locomotion, muscle tone, or crystaline structure. By the same token, if one is testing a 25-year-old male member of a motorcycle club who was referred by a law enforcement agency after being arrested and charged as an habitual offender for vagrancy and assault while drunk and disorderly, there are more pertinent things to focus on during the diagnostic inquiry than hallucinations, somatic complaints, or religious hangups. And one might not want to dwell at length on the poignancy and depth of his affectionate relationships with others either, for reasons of avoiding redundancy rather than any sheer probability of irrelevance. This argument has implications that bear on the design of diagnostic inventories, the choice of items to include, and how, as well as when, to ask them. I will consider these matters in more detail when we examine some problems of scale development a little later. But before we turn to that, I want to cite a brief example from the history of interest measurement that will, I hope, be instructive and illustrate the major point I have been trying to make in this section, that is, *the importance of establishing appropriate frames of reference in diagnostic testing.*

As I am sure you all know, E. K. Strong, in building the occupational keys for the Vocational Interest Blank, used as a reference group a heterogeneous sample composed of men drawn largely from diverse professional and managerial occupations—the so-called MIG group. Although considerable success was achieved in developing keys for specific occupations *at the professional and managerial level* using this reference group, attempts to build keys for skilled, semiskilled, and unskilled trade groups by the same means were largely unsuccessful. So recurrent were these failures, in fact, that a theory of occupational interest differentiation was invented to account for them. According to the theory, as one moved down the hierarchy of occupations from professional and managerial to unskilled, the interests of men at each successive level became less and less differentiated.

We now know this theory is false—or, what amounts to the same thing, that there are no empirical data which actually support it, and that there exists a mass of evidence to the contrary. Clark (1961), in fact, has shown that occupational groups at the nonprofessional level have interest patterns that are every bit as differentiated as those at the professional and managerial levels.

The explanation for the earlier findings lies, in large part, in the use of an inappropriate reference group to construct those scales. *Relative to professional and managerial interests,* those of men in various nonprofessional groups *are* quite similar and undifferentiated. But the reverse is also true! If one were to attempt to build an occupational interest scale for physicians and one for psychologists by selecting items on which groups from these occupations responded differently than a mixed group of tradesmen-in-general, he would also find a great deal of overlap in the two sets of items and an extremely high correlation between scores on the two measures. But, if he were a psychologist, I doubt if he would conclude from such findings, no matter how recurrent, that there exists an *inverse* hierarchy of occupational interest differentiation. There were, of course, additional reasons for the difficulties encountered in building occupational keys for nonprofessional groups using the SVIB, including the absence of certain relevant kinds of items on the Blank. But I've already promised to return to that sort of consideration later.

Perhaps a geographic, if somewhat homely, example can be used to make the point even clearer. If one wanted to get an accurate perspective of

4. Psychometric Considerations for a Revision of the MMPI

the relative locations and distances among buildings in downtown Minneapolis, he would do well to select a reference or viewpoint somewhere in the center of the city (perhaps atop the Foshay Tower) rather than one at some distance (say, along University Avenue or in St. Anthony Park). From such a distal viewpoint all the buildings would seem to be clumped together, and one would hardly be able to distinguish among them even with a good pair of field glasses or a telescope.

There are a number of experimental studies already available in the literature which lend support to this argument. The first, again drawn from the area of interest measurement, is the study by Philip Kriedt (1949) who, for the first time, successfully developed differential occupational keys for *subgroups* of psychologists on the SVIB. He accomplished this simply by replacing the usual professional men-in-general reference group with a sample of undifferentiated psychologists.

Actually, we need not have gone to another area of psychological measurement (much less to local geography) to illustrate my point. The work of Albert Rosen (1962) in developing second-stage, differential keys for the Multiphasic using a reference group of psychiatric patients instead of the usual "Minnesota normals" both exemplifies nicely what I am arguing for and provides a point of departure for further efforts along this line.

Both of these studies have demonstrated that one can achieve substantial increases in resolution or differentiation of diagnostic subgroups over that which has typically been attained by the very simple expedient of conducting one's search for discriminating items within an appropriate frame of reference. Once we have concluded that we are confronted with a patient who has either a neurosis or a character disorder, it hardly seems relevant to examine scores on variables whose main claim to fame is that they distinguish *normals* from one or the other of these two kinds of patients. But that is just the sort of thing we have been doing by limiting ourselves to the information yielded by the current clinical scales, virtually all of which were built to discriminate various diagnostic classes from a "distal" group of normals.

By now I hope that I have convinced you that diagnosis, if it is to be done efficiently and, in some cases, if it is to be done at all, is inherently a *multistage, sequential,* and *branching* sort of enterprise in which the discriminations that one must make at each stage depend upon what he has already learned, including both what he already knows to be relevant as well as what he knows to be impertinent.

There is one additional set of issues to which any contemporary discussion of diagnostic decision making must, at last, address itself; that is, the matter of *evaluating* diagnostic decisions and the attendant concepts of costs, payoff functions, and net utilities. There is, unfortunately, relatively little I can say that is either new or constructive about these issues.

When Cronbach and Gleser published the second edition of *Psychological Tests and Personnel Decisions* in 1965, they indicated in the Preface that they had not undertaken any substantial revision of the manuscript because, in part, their "thinking on this problem (had) not departed in any significant way from that of the original edition." If these authors had nothing new to add to their general formulation after eight years, it is only fair to say that the rest of the field had scarcely given the issues they had raised earlier a passing thought in the interim. Although the review of recent literature which these authors appended in their second edition cited some isolated applications of the various models and some efforts to cope with problems of values, costs, utilities, and methods of personnel accounting, it was obvious that a great deal of systematic and empirical work remained to be done.

The major objection, that one hears repeatedly, to a decision theoretic formulation of diagnosis is that there is no generally accepted solution to the cost and utility problems involved. Unless the outcomes of placement decisions can be evaluated and expressed jointly in a common metric or "coinage" with the costs of testing and treatment, the evaluation of net utilities accruing to different diagnostic regimens is not computable. And we must admit that the explicit determination of such costs and utilities *is* an extremely complex and difficult problem to contemplate, let alone solve, in real-life personnel decision contexts.

I must remind you, however, that diagnostic decisions *do* get made every day. Persons *are* assigned to various treatments and therapies on some basis or other. Mental health budgets *are* defended, hospitals and clinics *are* built, clinicians *are* trained and hired, and programs of testing, care, and treatment *are* operated. Implicitly, it would seem, these problems *do* get solved.

Within more circumscribed, clinical contexts, choices are made regarding which tests to adminster, whether to give a fixed battery routinely, or whether to give diagnostic tests at all. Patients (or clients) are assigned to therapists, are referred to other agencies or units, and are talked to and otherwise dealt with in a multitude of ways. They, in turn, get better or worse, happier or more miserable, less anxious or more so, or whatever.

Presumably which of these end states occur in each case makes some difference. There are values, however imprecisely specified or recognized,

4. Psychometric Considerations for a Revision of the MMPI

which attach to each of the potential outcomes. The basic question the decision theoretic formulation asks is whether or not we are behaving in such a way as to maximize the net utility that accrues to all this activity.

To answer that question *fully* and *precisely* requires an explicit specification of the values associated with each possible outcome and of the costs and losses attendant on operating the program from intake through final evaluation. And, as just mentioned, all costs, losses, gains, or payoffs must be commensurate, that is, expressed in terms of a common unit, or metric, in order to generate a solution.

It is not surprising, then, that we have witnessed no widespread application of formal decision theory to the problems of clinical diagnosis. Given the magnitude of the demands this formulation makes upon the user to provide inputs to the various models, it is at least understandable, if nonetheless regrettable, that so little attention is being paid to these notions. For whether or not the formal theory can be realized fully and precisely at present in any actual setting, its fundamental concepts are not irrelevant. The very fact that decisions do get made in such contexts implies a resolution of some sort to the very problems that many contend are fundamentally unsolvable!

The major problem seems to be in making these implicit bases for decision explicit. Perhaps what is needed as a first step toward the eventual acceptance of this framework is not a series of attempts to implement it "full blown," but rather an analysis of current practices in various settings to discover what decision rules are actually being used and what tradeoffs of costs and gains are implicit in the decisions actually being made.

Once the component elements of the general model as they are currently being used are better understood, it may become possible to see more clearly how to apply the general formulation and to evaluate the contributions of diagnostic procedures within it. Sooner or later, I believe, instruments such as the MMPI, or its successors, will have to meet such tests of their adequacy.

Whether it is premature to consider such matters in connection with a possible revision of the Multiphasic at present is not clear. I would at least hope that the matter would be considered seriously and pursued as far as imagination and ingenuity can take it. And a little more data would certainly not hurt either. Let us turn now to the second major set of considerations, those growing out of an interest in scale development and psychophysical research.

Psychophysics and Scale Development

The item pool for the Multiphasic was developed on the basis of an extensive examination of the relevant literature and of previously published questionnaires in the field. The content considerations that guided the development of the item pool played little or no part in the selection of which *response* categories to include in the various scales. I remember, at one time, thinking it ironic that the domain of relevant content covering "all the more important phases of personality (from the) viewpoint of the clinical or personnel worker" could be extensively defined by such an approach, while such rational considerations were presumed to be entirely irrelevant for developing scoring keys for particular "phases" of that domain. Of course, previous attempts to develop rational scales on the basis of presumed relevance for various traits had not been very successful. But then why trust such considerations to define the total domain?

Actually, of course, others have asked that question too, and some, such as Irwin Berg (1959 pp. 89–99), have argued that such a step was, indeed, unnecessary. Any content, Berg has contended, is sufficient just as long as one uses a contrasted-group method of key construction with whatever the items may be. (I have on occasion referred to this viewpoint as "empiricism gone mad as well as blind.")

Ultimately, I have come to view the matter not as ironic but rather as a commentary on the state of our knowledge at the time and as a reasonable and pragmatic (if not, indeed, an ingenious) adaptation to that condition. Who knew at the time what the characteristic responses of members of particular diagnostic groups would be to self-report items dealing with anything? But where better to look for distinguishing responses than among verbal descriptions of clinical symptomatology, beliefs, attitudes, and interests? And if one were inclusive rather than restrictive and extended the domain beyond narrowly clinical phenomena and symptom descriptions, then one might reasonably hope to uncover a sufficient number of indicators that would distinguish members of specific diagnostic populations from people in general, even if some, or perhaps many, of these indicators were not a priori obvious.

Well, it worked fairly well. But it had its faults as a general strategy. I have already discussed some of these and others deserve to be mentioned. First, it is now easy to see that the transformation of sympton descriptions and other traits, beliefs, and so forth, directly into self-report items represented an overly simplistic view of what is involved in self-description.

4. Psychometric Considerations for a Revision of the MMPI

The perception of an attribute of one's own, and the public acknowledgment or ascription of that attribute to oneself on direct inquiry are two different things. Even if one grants that the individual is a treasure trove of useful knowledge about his own behavior, feelings, attitudes, and the like, to assume one can elicit this information simply and exhaustively by direct inquiry under even the most benign conditions is not a very sophisticated position to take. Lacking any adequate theory, or any extensive empirical data, concerning the variety and effects of defense mechanisms, response sets, and other sources of distortion in self-reports, the only recourse was to empirical keying. But without such theoretical and empirical grounds on which to build, the direct translation of the elements of the domain into self-report items, while perhaps a plausible thing to do, was one which, in hindsight, must be viewed as overly optimistic and in need of a more enlightened approach the next time around.

What is needed most, of course, is the accumulation of knowledge concerning the determinants of responses to various kinds of items (or other stimuli) under a broad range of pertinent conditions. A mass of itemetric information for each stimulus we anticipate using in future diagnostic or assessment inventories simply must be generated ahead of time if we are to avoid the mistakes of the past. Among the kinds of information needed are general and specific desirability scale values, endorsement rates for diverse, demographic subpopulations, and their stabilities or sensitivities to change under a variety of implicit and explicit modifications in administrative conditions and imposed sets. We need to know the influence of the context in which the item appears in the inventory and to explore the effects of different kinds of response options including forced-choice and intensity rating formats. And we need to do all this on an initial, potential item pool that is vastly broader, more numerous, and more vaired in form and content than the present MMPI.

Some of these data are already in hand, of course, but only for a limited number of potentially useful items, such as those on the present forms of widely used tests. And, even in these cases, only rarely are the data available in the detail that is required to design and to carry out the construction and development of a new generation of assessment devices. The task that lies before us in this regard is staggering but of such fundamental importance that, unless it is undertaken, I see very little point in "revising" our present instruments or in expecting much improvement in our efforts to diagnose or assess personality with them. Until we acknowledge (as some of our sister sciences have long since learned to do) that we must take the time, effort, and resources to thoroughly calibrate our instruments and their components, there is little prospect of our being able to solve or clarify many of the pressing theoretical and applied problems we now face.

Out of all this empirical effort, one can hope that an adequate *theory* of the determinants of responses to self-descriptive items could gradually be constructed. To the extent that this occurs, the job will become less demanding of sheer effort, and the need to examine *all* conceivable types of items under *all* kinds of conditions for *all* specific classes of respondents will become less critical. But without an extensive substrate of such itemetric data to begin with, I fear we will continue to flounder around more or less ineffectually for an unnecessarily long period of time.

Now let us take a look at another class of measure variables on the MMPI and their prospects for the future. One of the hallmarks of the present Multiphasic is its "validity" scales and their role as a means to sanction and correct scores from other keys as well as to provide additional interpretative information regarding the respondent's personality, attitudes, and defenses. I believe any future versions of the MMPI, or similar instruments, will have to provide explicitly for a more diversified and effective set of such ancillary keys. I believe further that their uses in validating or providing a set of limiting conditions on the interpretations of the protocol and for assessing broadly stylistic aspects of the respondent's test behavior will continue to be cogent functions. But their prospective usefulness as suppressors or correction terms for the adjustment of other measures is doubtful.

There are many ways to defend, distort, and dissimulate; and the items of any lengthy, broadly based, personality inventory or questionnaire are likely to provide ample opportunities for the expression of a great many of them. Relative to only intentional sets to fake, the variety of direction keys and control procedures required may be very great.

An indication of the magnitude and diversity of such effects was brought vividly to my attention several years ago. I had built some self-report scales to measure a set of five molar traits originally assessed by peer-rating methods. Since the self-report scales were to be used for selection of applicants to a training program in the Air Force, some assurance was needed that the protocols had not been intentionally faked and/or that scores were not markedly influenced by whatever dissembling might have occurred and gone undetected.

We solved the problem by constructing a faking detection key that, on cross-validation, identified straight-take and faked answer sheets with false-positive and false-negative rates of less than 10 percent and by means of an item-selection technique for the content scales that yielded nearly congruent mean profiles for the two conditions and smaller variances under faking.

Somewhat later, we had occasion to administer this instrument to a group of Peace Corps trainees whom we asked to respond under both the straight-take condition and under a different faking set. In this second condition, the subjects were to fake so as to be selected as PC volunteers (rather than to gain admission to the Air Force Officer Candidate School). The straight-take mean profile on the content keys was only slightly different in this sample from that obtained from the original cross-validation sample. But there were marked disparities between the profiles from these two groups based on their respective faked performances. In addition, and of most relevance to the present discussion, the original (USAF-OCS) faking detection keys were much less effective in separating the straight-take and faked answer sheets for these latter subjects. I concluded the report (Norman, 1963) of these results with the following statement:

> One implication of these findings is (unfortunately) quite clear. Control over faking of the sort achieved by (these kinds of content and) detection scales, constructed for use in one setting with one class of respondents, may not generalize very widely. Just what the limits of generalizability attainable may be is as yet not fully known. But it does seem to be improbable that it will be possible to construct and standardize a single set of general purpose keys which can be used effectively in all settings for all classes of respondents. It may even prove to be necessary to build special purpose keys for each new context where they are desired. This is not a very happy prospect, but it is one we may have to learn to live with all the same [p. 240].

I don't believe that every different assessment context will require a totally unique set of devices tailor-made to the prevailing circumstances. But there is already ample evidence to indicate that a very much larger number of more specific detection, control, or "validity" keys will be needed on future "multiphasic" inventories or batteries, and that they will have to be specifically calibrated for diverse subgroups and conditions of administration in order to be effective.

This brings me to the matter of correction-keys or suppressor variables as a means for adjusting primary scales for individual differences in certain broad stylistic tendencies to respond to inventory items, but which are, themselves, not relevant to the criterion or to the specific trait status of the individuals. The K-scale of the MMPI, as you all know, was one of the first cases and is certainly the most famous example of this approach. The literature is equivocal regarding the effectiveness of K and opinion is split among users regarding when, or even if, K-corrections are useful.

The theory of the suppression of criterion-irrelevant, test variance is clear enough, and it is not a priori demonstrable that such an approach will, in general, fail to be effective. It all depends upon the nature of the criterion, the primary predictor, and potential suppresor variable. It is possible to demonstrate, however, that for a suppresor variable to be *very* effective, conditions must prevail which are, alas, not very common at present or very easily attained. In the first place, the reliabilities (proportions of nonrandom variance) of all three constituents should be high. Random error components do not correlate systematically with anything, and the success of a suppressor is contingent upon the magnitudes and the configuration of the intercorrelations among the criterion, the primary predictor, and the suppressor.

Second, the major portion of the reliable variance in the criterion should be well mapped or accounted for by the primary predictor. That is, the attenuation of validity should be due mainly to the presence of invalid (but reliable) variance in the *predictor* rather than to unaccounted for variance in the criterion. It is the test which is presumed, by suppression theory, to have the excess complexity not the criterion. Finally, the suppressor should be, as far as possible, a pure measure of those components in the predictor's variance which are unrelated to the criterion. (Other variants of this classic suppression case are, of course, possible, and some are even quite interesting from an abstract point of view. But we need not consider them here.)

If the aforementioned conditions prevail, then an optimal weighting of the predictor and suppressor can result in a substantial increase in the validity of the composite over that of the primary predictor alone, even though the suppressor has no valid variance whatever vis-a-vis the criterion. But these conditions just do not prevail in any very close approximation in most applied contexts.

First, the statistical complexity (i.e., the number of independent, reliable components of total variance) in the criterion measure is not likely to be less than that of the typical self-report or test predictor. Especially in clinical settings, where the criteria are frequently based on global judgments or membership in broad diagnostic classes, the criteria are apt to be the most complex set of variables with which we have to contend.

Second, the task of constructing a pure measure of the "excess" components of variance in the primary predictor is likely to be almost as difficult as building a primary predictor without those irrelevant components

4. Psychometric Considerations for a Revision of the MMPI

in the first place. Only when the components to be suppressed are some common method factors shared only by the two noncriterion variables does such a task seem potentially easier than the development of an uncontaminated basic predictor.

It is instructive to experiment with various combinations of correlations among the three types of variables and to examine what happens to the multiple correlation relative to the zero-order validity of the primary predictor as various degrees of suppression are assumed. For example, given the configuration shown in the following tabulation:

Variable	Criterion	Predictor
Predictor	.60	.40
Suppressor	.00	.40

which surely is about as good as one typically finds or can generate for contemporary personality scales against external criteria, the optimal linear function yields a multiple-R of only .65—a gain of but .05 over the zero-order correlation of the criterion with the primary predictor alone.

It would seem that as long as a primary predictor accounts for less than half of the criterion variance, one would be better advised to search for *other* primary predictors with which to account for independent portions of the criterion, or to raise the reliabilities of the criterion and predictor, or both, rather than attempt to suppress irrelevant variance in that particular predictor one has available.

Finally, it seems to me unlikely that any *single* scale that could be built on an inventory would prove to be an optimal suppressor for any substantial number of *different* criterion predictors—even if it were weighted differently for each one. Perhaps the K-scale or some other general stylistic measure of test-taking attitude is about as well as one can do with this approach. And that, it would seem has been none too satisfactory.

The question of *moderated* relationships, as distinct from suppression effects, does warrant further consideration. Moderators are variables whose effects on predictability are achieved by means *other* than their linear combinations with one or more basic predictors. Products between such variables and the primary predictors, higher order polynomial or transcendental functions of them and the other variables in a prediction system, or preliminary screening, or subclassification variables by means of which the population is segmented prior to the prediction, are all examples of moderated systems.

Actually, the use of *"?," "L," "F,"* or *"K"* to invalidate protocols (when they are used in that way) are examples of the method. It is assumed in these instances that the validities of the clinical scales hold only when one (or all) of these moderators fall within an acceptable range—otherwise, "bets are off," that is, the relationship between scale score and criterion is presumed to be different in the two cases.

The study I mentioned earlier in which we were attempting to develop self-report personality measures for use in selecting applicants for the Air Force Officer Candidate School provided a dramatic example of a moderated relationship of this latter type. The faked performances of our subjects provided no basis whatever for predicting their status on the peer-rating variables we were using as our criteria. Not only were the original scales (which were based on the straight-take data) entirely invalid when applied to the faked protocols, but, also, efforts to find items with which to build a different set of valid predictors for the faked performances met with utter failure. Thus, the detection scales, which were highly accurate at identifying response protocols of the two types, served as very effective moderators by dividing a total mixed set of protocols into two groups, in one of which validities were moderately good and in the other, nil.

Research and arguments by others, notably Saunders (1956) and Ghiselli (1960), deserve to be examined closely by those who wish to undertake major test development or prediction enterprises now or in the future. Actually, however, I believe the problem of moderated relationships can most profitably and effectively be dealt with as part of a general practice of *group-specific norming and calibration* of one's measure variables.

The problem, as I see it, is that too often we try to deal with relationships that are joint and heterogeneous functions of two or more sources of information. Thus, we combine both valid and faked answer sheets and estimate a single validity coefficient which describes neither set accurately. Or we mix males and females, lower and middle class respondents, adolescents and adults, defensive and exhibitionist patients, and so forth, often with no consideration of the possibility that we may be amalgamating between-group differences with intragroup, individual variation, and that the two may be related to what we want to predict in entirely different ways.

This principle has been well recognized by those who currently publish the better tests of cognitive abilities. Age specific norms have been a feature of the Wechsler for some time. The reason is that we know that the meaning and implications of given scores at different age levels are not the same, and that if we are going to validly interpret such information, we must know the class (i.e., age) of the person we are talking about.

4. Psychometric Considerations for a Revision of the MMPI

The point is not that between-group differences as such are generally irrelevant or unimportant. To the contrary, they are sometimes of the very essence. And, when they are, we need to know their magnitudes and the extent of their covariation with other variables as clearly as possible and unenshrouded by intragroup, interindividual differences and their attendant covariance structure which may be quite disparate. And conversely, when *individual* differences are of interest, it will rarely, if ever, be helpful to have substantial group variation confounded with them.

What I have been leading up to in these last few paragraphs is a theme which, in various guises, has arisen at several points in this chapter. It is that when one speaks about relationships between variables (or differences among persons, groups, or items), it is imperative that one make clear what *the context,* or *boundary conditions,* or *frame of reference* is within which such relationships (or differences) purportedly exist. It is *not* sufficient merely to give an intensive definition of the variables involved (even if one does so in nice, specific operational terms, although often that would be helpful, too). One must know also *for whom* and *under what conditions* the relationship holds.

When put bluntly, in this manner, the principle seems almost sophomoric. "Of course!" would seem to be the obvious and only reaction. And I would agree except that so much of what is written and said, even today and often by eminent and sophisticated people in our field, gives little evidence that any real and widespread appreciation of this point exists. Many of our most famous (or infamous) controversies have arisen, and some of our most cherished misconceptions have persisted, as a result of failing to recognize the importance or cogency of this matter.

I believe it was Walter Cook who first got me thinking about the issue of the context or boundary conditions of a relationship. I recall him saying one day during a lecture on the Binet to a class of us budding school teachers that we should remember that the youngest children in our classes were apt to have the highest mental ages. This puzzled me since I already *knew* that CA and MA were *positively* correlated. But his point was that within the classrooms of that day, with their policy of accelerated promotion for the highly able and retarded advancement for those who failed to achieve, CA and MA were *not* highly positively correlated. They might, in fact, be zero or even negatively related. Over the full school age range, of course, the relationship is highly positive. But the novice teacher who entered his or her first classroom expecting that fact to be pertinent *there* was in for a surprise.

It was some years later that I read Spearman's and Thurstone's accounts of their studies of intellectual abilities. Two things impressed me about the results of these studies. The first was the fact of positive manifold; cognitive abilities were positively correlated—all seemed in agreement about that. On the other hand, there was much disagreement, often vitriolic, concerning *how large* and *how uniform* these positive correlations were, and, in turn, what that implied about the structure of intellect.

We now know, of course, that the matter was more complicated than had been originally assumed involving issues of test design, analysis methods, aesthetic preferences and much more. But one aspect of these studies that has not received the attention it deserved is the matter of heterogeneity in the samples of subjects used in those early studies of Spearman's. The samples used by Thurstone and his students wery typically quite homogeneous with regard to age, socioeconomic status, educational background and other such demographic variables now known to be related to performance on tests of cognitive abilities. In contrast, the usual sample used in the British studies was rather highly heterogeneous in these respects. The result was that in the British studies between-group covariance components undoubtedly augmented the intragroup components (also positive) yielding higher positive correlations than would otherwise have been obtained. One major effect of this was to mask otherwise distinguishable subsets of abilities that would easily have been seen as separable if viewed within the context of the variation and covariation present *within* a more homogeneous group of subjects.

Now as long as one is interested in portraying the relationship among such variables in some given mixed population, there is nothing wrong with such a sampling design and analysis—it is, to the contrary, entirely appropriate. But, if one is interested in "vectors of the mind" (Thurstone) or relationships among "the abilities of man" (Spearman), then the appropriate frame of reference would seem to be not a diverse collection of minds or men but rather some one representative mind or man.

From this viewpoint, Thurstone's analyses were more appropriate than Spearman's for the investigation of mental structure since there was greater homogeneity in the samples of subjects used. That is, each respondent came closer to being a replication of other respondents in the sample than was true in the British studies.

But if such homogeneity is a virtue in analyses of structure, why not remove from consideration *all* main effect variation owing to individual differences rather than just a portion of it? Procedures for separating between-person main effects from other sources of variation in a battery of standardized test scores are both well known and easily accomplished. In situations in which the basic questions pertain to the structural relationships among a set of attributes, such "double-centering" of the data matrix would seem to be called for routinely if we are not to confuse main effects among persons on the entire battery with those intraindividual structural relationships primarily under study. Other examples of the use of such data analysis techniques and additional arguments for the intensive study of such "interaction" structures and relationships have been provided in recent years by Abelson (1960), Norman (1967) and Gollob (1968). Such approaches warrant more consideration than they have received by test developers, personality assessors, and trait theorists.

Personality Assessment and Conclusion

I have attempted to construe the tasks of diagnosis and scale development in terms of the two principal facets of a typical persons-by-items or persons-by-scales data matrix. It is tempting now to consider the remaining topic of personality assessment exclusively in terms of the remaining orthogonal source of variation in such a design, that is, the interaction components. What would be the meaning of such an approach and what would that imply for the task of assessing personality?

First, the dimensions of such an assessment system would be the factors or components of the interaction effects, that is, those that remain after the between-persons main effect, first centroid, or first principal component in the battery has been removed or, rather, after that component has been separately considered. The major reason for separating this main effect or first component from the others has already been mentioned; its size or magnitude is a direct function of the heterogeneity of the sample of subjects used.

In addition to this is a related matter. Most of the methods for rotating factors to a psychologically meaningful configuration are based on a "simple structure" rationale. Such methods find general factors (those with appreciable loadings on all or most variables) and sets of variables, most of which have complexities greater than unity, difficult to deal with adequately. But the between-person main effects constitute just such a "general" factor in most batteries, and personality measures are notorious for their high factorial complexities, if for nothing else.

In contrast to the domain of cognitive abilities, truly multiphasic or broad-band inventories in the personality area might not be expected to possess overwhelmingly large first factors. Some exceptions do exist, however. The MMPI itself, especially when given to "normal" subjects, displays a large first factor variously known as "alpha," "A," "ego strength," "social desirability," or "general pathology" depending on one's predilections. But, in general, with adequate domain sampling of traits and with application to relevant populations, a general personality factor seems less likely to appear or to be interpretable than is true in the ability and aptitude area. When such a factor is present, however, I would argue that clarity of interpretation and meaningfulness of the assessments are likely to be best served by dealing with such a component separately from the others implicit in the residual sources of variation.

Finally, I would make an appeal for an extension of this general argument to the analysis of the data from individual scales within such multiphasic batteries. Although we often fail to extract general factor information from multiscale batteries prior to analysis and interpretation, when we deal with separate itemized scales, such general factors are usually the only things we consider. A unit-weighted or differentially weighted composite of item scores; that is, the general factor among the items, is taken as the scale score and all residual variation is usually ignored or termed "unreliability," even when it may contain systematic, replicable information. Whereas individual item responses are not apt to be highly reliable (in any sense of that term), neither is it likely that they reflect only that one systematic source of variation that is common to all items in the set and in terms of which we label and interpret the single summation score we usually compute.

This chapter represents a combination of diagnostic and prognostic efforts. It is perhaps not surprising that I found the task of diagnosing what is wrong or deficient with the MMPI and other contemporary assessment devices and procedures easier than the task of prognosticating or prescribing what should be done to make things better the next time around. I am fairly certain, however, that if we are ever to come to a full measure of maturity in this field, our methods, procedures, and instruments are going to have to be far more sophisticated than even the most complex of those currently available. I am optimistic enough to believe we are moving in that direction even though the pace of that progress often seems to me unnecessarily and agonizingly slow.

REFERENCES

Abelson, R. P. Scales derived by consideration of variance components in multiway tables. In H. Gulliksen and S. Messick (Eds.), *Psychological Scaling.* New York: Wiley, 1960.

Berg, I. A. The unimportance of test item content. In B. M. Bass and I. A. Berg (Eds.), *Objective Approaches to Personality Assessment.* New York: Van Nostrand, 1959.

Clark, K. E. *The Vocational Interests of Nonprofessional Men.* Minneapolis: Univ. of Minnesota Press, 1961.

Cronbach, L. J., & Gleser, G. C. *Psychological Tests and Personnel Decisions (2nd ed.).* Urbana: Univ. of Illinois Press, 1965.

Ghiselli, E. E. Differentiation of tests in terms of the accuracy with which they predict for a given individual. *Educational and Psychological Measurement,* 1960, **20,** 675-684.

Gollob, H. F. Confounding of sources of variation in factor-analytic techniques. *Psychological Bulletin,* 1968, **70,** 330-344.

Kreidt, P. H. Vocational interests of psychologists. *Journal of Applied Psychology,* 1949, **33,** 482-488.

Norman, W. T. Personality measurement, faking, and detection: An assessment method for use in personnel selection. *Journal of Applied Psychology,* 1963, **47,** 225-241.

Norman, W. T. On estimating psychological relationships: Social desirability and self-report. *Psychological Bulletin,* 1967, **67,** 273-293.

Rosen, A. Development of MMPI scales based on a reference group of psychiatric patients. *Psychological Monographs,* 1962, **76,** (8, Whole No. 527).

Saunders, D. R. Moderator variables in prediction. *Educational and Psychological Measurement,* 1956, **16,** 209-222.

5
WHITHER THE MMPI?

W. Grant Dahlstrom

Most of the other contributions to this book have focused on the more general question of whether to use the MMPI or something quite different. A number of practical considerations make it seem quite unlikely in the near future that any feasible instrument for general personality assessment will differ greatly in general format from the MMPI. Ultimately, we will probably have at our disposal computer-based assessment procedures in which a subject at a stimulus-response console is led through a series of item samples each chosen on the basis of his prior pattern of responses and each series of questions pursued long enough either to dismiss the area as noncontributory or to pinpoint his momentary status. It is also likely that these systems will have computing capacities sufficient to develop direct links from item-configurations to descriptors without using intervening summary scale values or score profiles. It seems obvious, however, that these approaches are predicated on an immense increase in access to computers by means of consoles in schools, businesses, clinics, and hospitals. The present availability of such equipment is so limited and the growth rate so slow that any immediate test revisions almost certainly will be based on the portable test booklet with its answer sheet and on local scoring and interpretation options as we now know them. Radical departures will have to wait for yet another round of revisions.

Thus, from this practical standpoint, the question as stated in this chapter title involves how best to improve the MMPI without appreciable sacrifice of those many virtues which it possesses as a consequence of Hathaway's sage pragmatism and unbelievable serendipity. A long list of objections, complaints and criticisms of the MMPI was made during its first quarter century of development, many admittedly pointless, but some quite cogent and compelling (see Dahlstrom, 1969). How can these legitimate concerns be dealt with without extensive expenditure of time and energy while preserving the clinical and research value of the instrument? Thus, some consider the test too long, others find it too insistently probing of sensitive emotional areas in the subject's life, and still others feel it is too psychiatric or medical to be used in the widely different areas of application currently being used. The suggestions offered here are intended to be ways in which these and other related complaints may be substantially corrected or circumvented.

One way to begin this rehabilitation is to examine the content of the sets of correlates of recurring MMPI patterns as they are reported in various cookbooks, codebooks, and handbooks on this instrument (cf. Dahlstrom, Welsh, & Dahlstrom, 1972). Examination of these sources and the contents of many reports from computer-based interpretive systems suggests that there are two general kinds of assessment evaluations intermixed in these current applications of the MMPI: personality structure and current emotional status. That is, many of the descriptors pertain to the question: What kind of person is this? Whereas other items seem to deal more with the question: What, if anything, is wrong with him? In the first kind of appraisal, the configural correlates bear upon enduring attributes of the person: his character, his personality style, and his stability or lack of it. In contrast to these general characteristics, there are also many descriptors that refer to the person's mood and feelings, his contact with reality, or his present level of control.

Since the two kinds of descriptors become configural correlates of the MMPI, it is reasonable to presume that the empirical ties of test pattern and behavior pattern involve both broad summarizations and salient current symptomatology. Yet, there are reasons for dealing with these two kinds of appraisals separately. One obvious important consideration is that in their emotional status individuals do vary a great deal from one occasion to another or from one situation to another. Thus, scales which are to reflect such variations with fidelity must show appropriate shifts from one test

5. Whither the MMPI?

administration to another. If the existing MMPI scales are reflecting to any important degree some major personality stabilities, however, they may be expected to be correspondingly ill-suited to the evaluation of change in mood, feelings and control (cf. Schofield, 1950, 1953). For example, we know empirically that individuals with 27' codes are appropriately characterized as both prone to depressive moods and currently depressed and guilt-ridden. Yet, if the D scale covaries with shifts in manifest depression as suggested by the data from Endicott and Jortner (1966), then a low D scale value should be interpreted as relative freedom from serious depression at the time of testing. How then can the clinician use the D scale value as a predictor of significant degrees of depressive reaction at some later (or prior) time?

Another important consideration is that theorists like Foulds (1965) have proposed explicit ties between particular personality structures and the clinical manifestations which each will show when undergoing a particular emotional reaction, as well as the kinds of emotional reactions to which each are most susceptible. If these formulations are correct, then it would sharpen our assessment efforts considerably if we were to devise separate measures for the personological predispositions and the psychopathological states. In fact, if such measures were at hand, we could obviously do a better job of testing such theoretical assumptions and perfecting these formulations. As matters stand now, these distinctions are blurred and the accuracy of our appraisals is correspondingly limited.

A number of developments within the MMPI research literature and beyond indicate this kind of separation of personality appraisals to be both feasible and meaningful. Spielberger's (1966) efforts to develop separate measures for the trait of anxiety and for the momentary level of anxiety are a case in point (cf. Spielberger, Gorsuch, & Lushene, 1970). Additional encouragement comes from the success of Panton's (1970) studies of the special adaptational evaluations needed to supplement the basic MMPI scales in studying within-prison adjustment of North Carolina felons, and from Block's (1953, 1965) scales of personality style. Many lines of research, therefore, indicate that it should be possible to develop separate sets of measures that more accurately evaluate each of these basic assessment questions.

For the present, I would like to use a few examples to try to demonstrate the approach and illustrate some of the difficulties involved. Let us begin with a pair of specific cases to pinpoint some of the limitations in the present MMPI format. Then we will examine a few of the more promising leads for personological and symptomatic scale sets on these cases as well as on some experimental subjects. From these data, it will be possible to see some of the advantages offered from this approach as well as some of the methodological difficulties which their development and perfection will entail.

The first case was presented more completely in Dahlstrom and Welsh (1960) as one of the illustrative examples of serial MMPI interpretation (see Chapter 7, case III). At the age of 22, he was tested for the first time when entering the university. At that time he was described as follows:

> On entering the university, this man was twenty-two years old and a veteran of the Korean war. He was attending school on the GI bill without which he would probably have been unable to continue his education. He had married his high school girl friend while he was in the Air Force. At the time of the original counseling this couple was just establishing a home for the first time. The advisement procedures indicated he was intellectively capable (W–B, I: IQ 131), strongly motivated for college work, and interested in a political science major. The MMPI profile at that time suggested that he desired to impress the counselor favorably (the high K and moderate L scores) with his control, his personal adequacy, and his freedom from problems. It also indicated that he was energetic, sociable, and free of manifest anxiety and hampering inhibitions. He was able to create a favorable impression on others and seemed to hold himself in good regard. He was using denial and repression to some extent. All these implications of the initial profile were borne out in the counseling interviews at the time.
>
> Evidence of some instability was also noted in the test profile, and confirmed in the interviews. The relative prominence in the MMPI of scales 7 and 8 suggested inner tension and insecurity that was being handled by the denial mechanisms noted in the validity score configuration and in the neurotic triad. His social behavior was quite superficial; his manner was breezy and insincere. In many relationships he appeared cold and unresponsive. He was restless and seemed to be showing a flight into activity as a means of distracting himself from his feelings of potential inadequacy. He had a chronic need for social approval and acceptance. He appeared quite well integrated and controlled at this time, however.
>
> Two years later, the personality picture is markedly changed. (Profile 2 in Table 1 and the second profile in Figure 1.) The validity scale values indicate that he is no longer defensive and denying. The markedly elevated F score suggests a severe personality disruption, since on other grounds it is possible to rule out lack of cooperation or comprehension. The height of the profile, together with the peak scores on scales 2, 7, and 8, suggests severe distress, depression, and panic. He seems to be agitated, markedly anxious, and worried. His reactions are heavily toned with guilt, self-depreciation, and feelings of unworthiness. He may be expected to show some feelings of unreality, loss of efficiency, and indecision, as well as a tremendous feeling of hostility and rage (scale 4).

5. Whither the MMPI? 89

These interpretations were borne out in the subsequent interviews with the counselor. He had been making good progress on his college program up to the previous semester. At that time, his wife insisted that they move into an apartment in the home of her parents. Although she continued to work, his wife also became more and more intolerant of his college work and concerned about the length of time that remained before he could become self-supporting and productive. Apparently because of some jealousy of his being able to attend college while she had to be satisfied with a high school education, she repeatedly encouraged him to drop out of school and get a job. She also wanted to start having children soon. When they finally moved into his in-laws' home, his wife's pressures were augmented by those of his mother-in-law. He had increasingly greater difficulties studying at home, had more and more arguments and wrangling discussions with his wife and her family, and began to have doubts of his adequacy and of his vocational choice. In an effort to keep up with his studies, he stayed at the university for longer and longer hours, but the inevitable arguments when he did return home eventually bothered him to the extent that his grades began to suffer. He was continually restless and had difficulty concentrating. He then began to stay up all night, driving in his car for hours in a random, patternless course through the countryside. He occasionally stopped at roadside taverns. Then he began drinking, at first only moderately, but later in quantities that made him fear that he was becoming an alcoholic. He also had a few casual, adulterous affairs during these long rambles, although he did not feel that these sexual escapades were the main reason for his night-long trips. Rather, he felt he was constantly preoccupied with his marital and academic difficulties and with trying to resolve his problems, Finally he sought the help of the counseling center in regard to his problems with his marriage, his college work, and his ultimate professional goals. The second record was obtained at this time.

Although his depression was marked and the danger of some suicidal act was present, the previous MMPI profile and his current control seemed to indicate enough personality strength to warrant treatment on an outpatient basis. He was seen frequently, however, during the next several weeks.

Shortly after talking his situation over for the first time with the psychologist, he had taken the first step in resolving his marital difficulties. He moved out of the apartment and took a room near the university. This physical separation from his wife and her family reduced his tension and agitation noticeably according to the case notes. He was able to discuss the various aspects of his problems more coherently and constructively. He made several attempts to see his wife in the next several days to talk over his feelings and reactions and to arrive at some workable solution of their marriage. These talks invariably ended in further arguments and recriminations . . .. Each time, however, he would subsequently feel guilty and remorseful over his temper outbursts . . . and get in touch with his wife for further talks. Between times he stayed by himself and studied to catch up with his assignments. He reported having insomnia, however, and experiencing combat dreams when he was able to sleep. He did not at this time persist in his drinking, his sexual exploits, or (since he had let his wife have the car) his night-long rambles. Although he had a great deal of ambivalence and vacillation about his marriage, he was able to make up his course work and stay in school.

A month later (see profile 3 in Table 1) his acute disturbance had all but subsided. The validity scale configuration is similar to the premorbid pattern, although somewhat less protest and denial seem present. The depression is apparently resolved and the prominent features suggest extrapunitive hostility, oversensitivity, and avowal of control and personal adequacy. The subpeak on scale 6 indicates the possibility that he has resolved his previous guilt feelings by assigning blame and responsibility to someone else. Perhaps, the level of scale 4 is in part a strong effort to free himself from personal ties and close affectional feelings.

By this time, he had decided to maintain the separation and encouraged his wife to seek divorce settlement. He had continued to see his wife many times and reported, with great disturbance and anxiety, an episode in which he had suddenly got the feeling that a drink his wife had fixed for him during one of their conferences had been poisoned. Apparently he became very angry with her when this feeling came over him and had come close to assaulting her physically. Instead, he had rushed out of the house and had been afraid to see her or trust himself alone with her for nearly a week. However, this extreme hostility toward her had passed and . . . he was firm in his resolution to let the marriage dissolve. He had also started discussions in the interviews with the counselor about his vocational choice. He had finally decided to shift into a business sequence and give up any career in the area of political science. It was realized that many of this man's problems were not solved, but by this time he had worked through the most severe phases of his marital crisis and had achieved what was considered to be a more suitable choice of vocational goals [pp. 229–232].

Although the changes between the second and third testing are not as dramatic as the shifts from the first to the second, all three of these examinations imply that he was quite different on the three occasions. The clinical descriptions of his behavior and emotional status are in accord with these profile patterns and the differences appearing on these three examinations. A similar correspondence between clinical status and psychometric patterning can be noted in the second case.

This 29-year-old married woman was seen first as an inpatient in a psychiatric service of a university hospital. Briefly, she was a graduate nurse who had married a medical student and helped him set up a general medical practice in a small town. While the physician was struggling to get established, his wife worked closely with him in the office as receptionist, office nurse and laboratory technician. As he became more successful, he was gradually able to replace her in the office with other trained workers and they decided to start a family. She had four children in five years, showing some postpartum depression after each. The last episode was serious enough to lead her husband to have her hospitalized in the psychiatric service shortly after she brought her infant home. She was tense, restless, and

TABLE 1
MMPI T Scores and Codes of a Veteran under Study during an Acute Marital Crisis

Pro-file no.	Date of administration	L	F	K	1	2	3	4	5	6	7	8	9	0	Extended code	
1	8-16-52	53	50	72	62	58	62	64	61	62	69	69	70	40	9'7841365 − 2/0	K'−LF
2	3-21-54	40	80	55	59	99	67	90	65	79	95	96	65	64	2874*"6'3590 − 1	F''−K/L
3	5-04-54	40	53	66	49	53	60	69	55	65	60	65	53	37	'468 37 − 529/1:0	K−F/L

MMPI scales

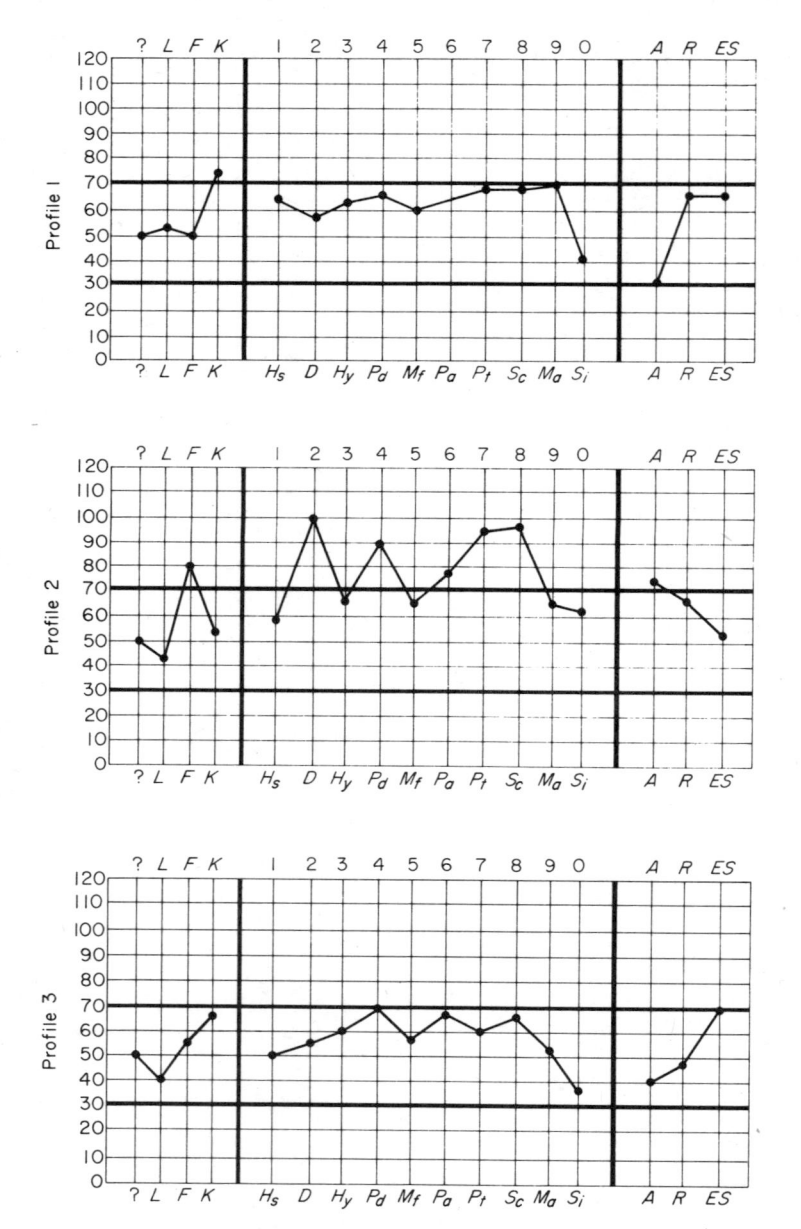

Figure 1. K-corrected profiles for three test administrations obtained on a veteran under study during an acute marital crisis.

5. Whither the MMPI? 93

agitated and had been taking phenobarbital to control her tensions and insomnia. Upon entering the hospital she rather quickly gave up her dependence upon phenobarbital, but developed a classic hypomanic clinical picture. She was examined for the first time with the MMPI and gave the results in profile 1 shown in Table 2 and Figure 2. Nurses noted at this time that she was talkative, overactive, and difficult to keep quiet. She sang aloud to records and read long passages from Shakespeare to others on the ward. She was constantly promoting new activities in the social room with the other patients, visited freely in other patients' rooms even after bedtime for the ward, and was openly flirtatious with the male patients and attendants. On one occasion she sallied forth from her room dressed in a bathing suit, with a necklace in her hair like a tiara, carrying a scarf, performed an energetic dance for the people assembled in the social room, and ended up on the floor kicking her feet in the air. She was contrite when told to return to her room and put her clothes back on. The salient elevation of scale 9 in her MMPI is quite consistent with this clinical picture. The smaller spike on scale 2, however, does not directly correspond to her clinical status at that time.

Her stay was only 14 days after which she was seen weekly in an outpatient psychotherapy series by a psychiatric resident. Progress was judged to be good and after six months her therapy was terminated. The resident was being rotated to another hospital for further training, and it was decided she should be discharged from treatment rather than being shifted to another therapist. One week after termination she entered the emergency room of the medical center after being found comatose with all reflexes absent as a result of having taken 1600 mg of Seconol in a suicidal attempt. She recovered after intensive care and was subsequently transferred to the psychiatric service again. The second MMPI record was obtained thirteen days after her suicidal attempt (see Table 2 and Figure 2). She was very depressed and withdrawn. She indicated that she was overwhelmed by responsibilities for caring for her children, meals, and household chores. She doubted she could fulfill the role of mother and wife adequately. The second test profile mirrors her change in emotional status with marked elevations now on scales 2, 4, 7, 1, 3, and 8 and a significant drop on scale 9.

The changes which this woman showed between the first and second testing have a general resemblance to the alterations in the MMPI profile noted for the young man presented in the first case between his freshman and junior years. Under therapy his MMPI changed back toward the level of his initial test scores and, since the young mother was now in psychiatric treatment, there would be an expectation, perhaps, that she too would subsequently show evidence of remission both clinically and psychometrically. Retesting six weeks later, however, did not confirm such an expectation (see Table 2 and Figure 2). Rather, the elevations on scales 2, 4, 6, 8, and 0 were as high or higher than they had been shortly after her suicidal attempt in February, although the values on scales 1, 3, 5, and 7 had come down to some extent. By this time she was judged to be less depressed

TABLE 2
MMPI T Scores and Codes of a Female Psychiatric Inpatient

Profile no.	Date of administration	L	F	K	1	2	3	4	5	6	7	8	9	0	Extended code
1	7-16-58	53	55	44	44	59	47	48	49	50	50	55	73	50	9'28670/5431 'FL/K
2	2-24-59	44	70	55	70	84	73	86	53	53	74	72	58	55	42''7381'−9056/ F'K/L
3	4-08-59	44	68	53	58	92	66	97	45	62	69	75	60	60	42*'8''73690−1/5 F−K/L

5. Whither the MMPI?

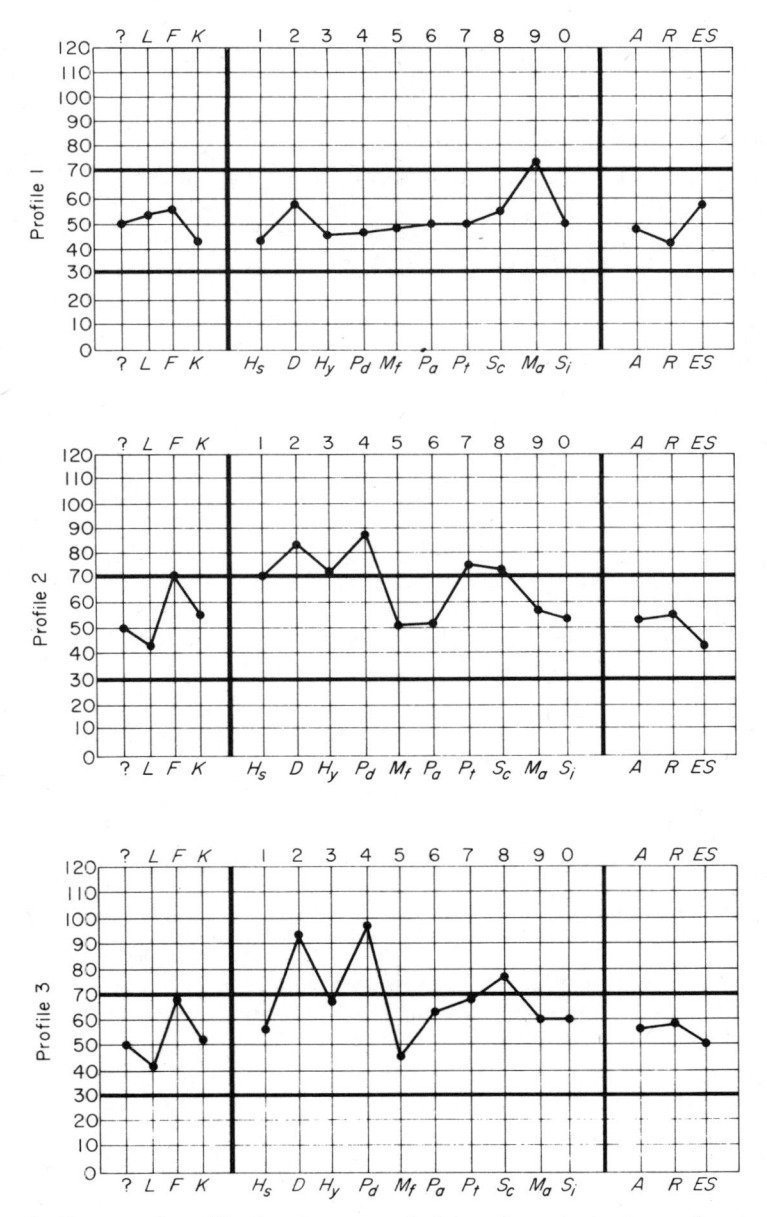

Figure 2. K-corrected profiles for three test administrations obtained on a female psychiatric inpatient.

clinically and had been granted permission to leave the ward. It was noted, however, that she felt very ambivalent about these new privileges and afraid of such freedom. When plans were being made to have her children come to visit her, she revealed that she had intense fears of giving way to an impulse to kill them. It was, in fact, this fear which had driven her to the suicidal attempt in February. Shortly after this psychological examination, she was transferred to another psychiatric institution for long-term care. Thus, in general, her MMPI pattern and score changes on the third occasion corresponded to her lack of clinical improvement and need for continuing hospitalization.

These two cases illustrate the problems raised earlier about the present MMPI profile. The sets of scores for each of these people on the three different occasions parallel to a considerable degree the alterations in their clinical status over time. Could the initial set of scores obtained on each, in addition to reflecting their emotional condition at that time, have given proper indication of the kinds of or extent of change that they would each show on the next examination? Similarly, on the second occasion, when each was in the midst of an acute and complicated depressive reaction, could the MMPI record provide more than a mirror of their emotional crises? Is there some way that the young man's remission could be anticipated or the young woman's deepening despondency be forecast from the personological features appearing in the MMPI record at that time? Are the effects of momentary emotional status so pervasive in the records obtained from acutely disturbed patients that it is meaningless to search for measures of more enduring characterological or personality features in their self-descriptions at those times? It seems well worth the effort to try to work out some means of accomplishing both kinds of assessment. It may, however, turn out to be an impossible task for the inventory approach.

One kind of analytic method that has been applied to inventory data in an effort to discover source traits or underlying personological uniformities by such investigators as Thurstone, Guilford, and Cattell is factor analysis of interitem correlations. Most of the factor analytic work with the MMPI (Dahlstrom, Welsh & Dahlstrom, Vol. II, in preparation) has been carried out at the level of scale interrelationships or on within-scale item sets, for example, Comrey & Souri (1960). Recently some interitem analysis findings have been reported (Barker, Fowler, & Peterson, in press; Lushene, 1967) based on larger groups of items, in Lushene's case on the whole intercorrelational matrix of MMPI items. However, only the work of Tryon, Stein, and Chu (Tryon, 1966; Tryon, 1967a, 1967b; Stein, 1968) has involved the

TABLE 3
List of Special Cluster Scales Developed for the MMPI[a]

	Scale name	No. of items	Correlations with basic scales
I	(Social introversion)	26	Si .92; Pt .77; D .71; F .54
B	(Body complaints)	33	Hs .97; Hy .77; Pt .71; D .68
S	(Suspicion)	25	Pa .16; Ma .58; Sc .52; K −.73
D	(Depression)	28	D .81; Pt .91; Sc .85; Si .76
R	(Resentment)	21	Pd .61; Pt .81; Sc .79; K −.79
A	(Autism)	23	Sc .82; Pt .79; F .58; Pd .51
T	(Tension)	36	Pt .93; Sc .85; D .76; Hs .73

[a]Tryon, Stein, & Chu (1969).

development of a new set of scales. Their research, based on special cluster-analytic methods, led to the isolation of the seven scales listed in Table 3. In addition to the titles and abbreviations given each of their cluster scales, Table 3 provides selected correlational values that Stein (1968) reported for each scale with basic MMPI clinical and validity scales. These values were calculated from data on a composite sample of 310 males made up of records from 70 VA outpatients diagnosed as schizophrenic, 150 additional cases diagnosed as neurotic, and 90 normal military officers. The values listed were selected either because the title of the cluster scale suggested some correspondence to an existing standard MMPI scale (entered first) or because they were the highest values obtained (positive or negative) for that scale with the basic scales.

Note also that these cluster scales are not statistically independent of one another. In fact, Stein indicates that the first three scales, *I, B,* and *S,* can be considered the main cluster variables, and the remaining four scales as being comprised primarily of these three sources of variance. The method of derivation of these scales could have been expected to yield basic source trait dimensions underlying the MMPI, but the kinds of relationships that these scales show with the basic MMPI scales suggest instead that they are more likely somewhat purified symptom scales. To explore this possibility, in a preliminary way, the two cases described above were scored on all seven of these *T-S-C* scales. Although the chapter by Stein (1968) provided a set of *T*-score norms for these scales, the values shown in Tables 4 and 5 are based on Minnesota norms. That is, these scales were scored at the University of North

Carolina on the Hathaway and Briggs' (1957) sample of Minnesota men and women so that they are comparable to the scales in the MMPI profile (Dahlstrom, Welsh, & Dahlstrom, Vol. II, in preparation). Values on these scales for these specific cases would have been rather consistently lower numerically on the California-based norms given by Stein.

Since these scale values are reported in terms of both central tendency and variance that are comparable to the regular scales in the profile, it is appropriate to collate both the set of initial values earned by these cases and the variations found when retesting on the *T-S-C* scales with the standard set of MMPI measures. Thus, initially the young university student falls below the adult means by .50 to 2.0 sigmas on all scales but *A* (autism) on which he is about at the adult male mean. These deviations are not in accord with the consistently elevated values on the basic MMPI scales that were reported for him in Table 1. His initial low score on scale *I*, however, does correspond to his low value on scale 0.

On the other hand, the initial values of the *T-S-C* scales in Table 5 appear to be more consistent with the levels of the basic scale values for the nurse shown in Table 2. Thus, the scale 2 and *D* scale values seem to correspond, as do the levels on scale 1 and the *B* scale, scale 0 and the *I* scale, as well as scale 8 and the *A* scale. However, there is little in the regular profile to match the elevations shown on the *R* and *T* scales. Conversely, the elevation on scale 9 that was so revealing of her clinical status is not represented in the *T-S-C* set. (Masculinity–femininity variance is also strangely absent in these clusters; perhaps a *symptom* scale set should not reflect this kind of attribute?)

Examination of the shifts in the *T-S-C* values on retesting each of these cases indicates that they do indeed show appreciable change and that the change is often quite in accord with the altered status of these two individuals. For the student in the midst of his marital crisis, the largest shift is on scale *D*, but there are changes of about two standard deviations or more on the *A, T, I,* and *R* scales, whereas only the *B* scale remains unchanged. Since he did become appreciably more depressed, withdrawn socially and emotionally, resentful and tense, these shifts seem quite justified, whereas his lack of somatizing during this crisis appears very consistent with both the level and the stability of the *B* scale values. For the nurse, too, there are two score shifts upward of this magnitude, on the *B* and *D* scales, which fit her altered clinical status after her suicidal attempt. Two other scales, however, show rather paradoxical drops on retesting: scale *T* is lower by more than a

5. Whither the MMPI?

sigma, whereas scale *S* also moves down nearly as much. Both her level of tension and her suspiciousness would seemingly have been *higher* after her suicidal gesture, not lower than in the midst of her hypomanic phase, but these are assumptions which may be proved erroneous after further experience with the *T-S-C* scales has accumulated a backlog of interpretive lore.

In contrast to the mode of development of the *T-S-C* scale set which seems to have generated a symptom-status complement, the way in which Haan (1965) devised her ego defense measures for the MMPI would appear to be a more promising method for obtaining basic personological attributes. The subjects in her investigation were adults who had been studied longitudinally in one or another of the Bay Area developmental studies (Jones, Macfarlane, & Eichorn, 1959). Ratings were made on these subjects based upon extensive interviews over their past and current social and personal status. Among these were ratings covering their typical utilization of effective coping techniques or reliance upon crippling ego defense mechanisms. These personality ratings constituted the criteria in Haan's efforts to develop scales for these attributes on both the MMPI and CPI. It is of some interest that the CPI proved to be a fruitful source of items for scales of the coping techniques but not for the defense mechanisms, whereas the obverse was true for the MMPI item pool. In addition to preliminary measures for the seven defense processes, Haan also developed a measure for a general defense attribute which she termed primitive defense, a factorial summary scale reflecting variance common to the scales in this set. These scales are listed in Table 6 together with data on the largest correlations that she found between her defense scales and the basic MMPI clinical and validity scales. These correlations were obtained on all her normal adult cases combined into a total sample. There is, of course, no direct correspondence between particular Haan scales and specific basic MMPI scales, although she offers various psychodynamic formulations for linkages between these two sets of measures. We can note in Table 6 that the magnitude of the correlations found with the basic scales does not match the levels of correlations between the *T-S-C* variables and these standard measures. This level of correlation may merely reflect the narrower ranges of variances in the Haan sample on the basic scales or may be a promising index of the desired independence from symptom-status variables needed in a set of characterological measures.

Normative data were obtained on the same Minnesota reference groups (Dahlstrom, Welsh, & Dahlstrom, Vol. II, in preparation) so that *T* scores could be determined for male and female subjects comparable to both the

TABLE 4
MMPI T Scores on Special Scales for a Veteran under Study during an Acute Marital Crisis

Profile no.	Date of administration	T-S-C scales								Haan scales							
		I	B	S	D	R	A	T	Prm	Rgr	Rpr	Prj	Dpl	Dnl	Dbt	Itl
1	8-16-52	38	46	30	41	38	52	44	62	55	55	50	47	53	47	65
2	3-21-54	60	46	40	90	55	72	70	38	45	45	55	57	40	67	50
3	5-04-54	42	42	32	48	42	50	40	38	43	45	50	47	48	40	65

TABLE 5
MMPI T Scores on Special Scales for a Female Psychiatric Inpatient

Profile no.	Date of administration	\multicolumn{7}{c}{T-S-C scales}							\multicolumn{8}{c}{Haan scales}							
		I	B	S	D	R	A	T	Prm	Rgr	Rpr	Prj	Dpl	Dnl	Dbt	Itl
1	7-16-58	48	44	50	54	65	50	57	45	53	55	70	53	30	57	65
2	2-24-59	52	64	40	74	58	53	43	50	58	60	50	63	53	57	55
3	4-08-59	58	58	48	78	50	48	55	55	58	65	45	60	33	60	50

basic scales and the *T-S-C* scales reported above. The two representative cases were scored on each of the Haan scales for the three testing occasions and the Minnesota-based *T* scores that they earned were also listed in Tables 4 and 5.

Until further interpretive material is available on this set of scales, it would seem reasonable to gauge the significance of score elevations and shifts on the same basis as that used for the MMPI basic scales (and as was applied to the *T-S-C* scales above). Thus, the young married student appears to be most clearly deviant on the primitive defense scale and the scale for intellectualization. General immaturity and a reliance on emotional insulation, then, would be suggested by this configuration which he presented upon admission to the university. The nurse, too, is apparently characterized by the Haan scale values as relying upon intellectualizing defenses to about the same extent but deviates in the opposite direction on the primitive defense measure and is, instead, typified by an even higher elevation on the projection scale, suggesting a disowning and externalizing mode of dealing with her impulses or conflicts. Thus, initially these subjects are characterized rather differently by salient deviations on these defense scales, although it is impossible to determine whether these deviations are statistically sufficiently prominent or atypical to signify predisposition to their subsequent manifest psychopathology. Similarly, it is not immediately clear whether these particular defenses are psychodynamically the processes one would expect in light of what is known about their concurrent adjustmental patterns.

The shifts which take place in the values on the Haan scales at the time of the second testing on each of these patients range from 0 to nearly 2.5

TABLE 6
List of Ego Defense Scales Developed for the MMPI[a]

	Scale name	No. of items	Correlations with basic scales						
Prm	(Primitive defense)	21	L	.56;	K	.28;	F	−.31;	Sc −.31
Rgr	(Regression)	41	Hs	.61;	Sc	.53;	Pd	.51;	Ma .44
Rpr	(Repression)	20	L	.51;	Mf	.21;	Pd	−.29;	Ma −.24
Prj	(Projection)	20	Pt	.29;	Hs	.25;	D	.25;	K −.32
Dpl	(Displacement)	29	Hs	.66;	Pt	.58;	D	.57;	Hy .56
Dnl	(Denial)	33	K	.50;	L	.44;	F	−.47;	Pt −.44
Dbt	(Doubt)	24	Pt	.71;	D	.57;	Sc	.55;	K −.48
Itl	(Intellectualization)	22	Mf	−.41;	D	−.38;	Pt	−.24;	F −.23

[a] Haan (1965).

5. Whither the MMPI? 103

sigmas, changes which are nearly as large as the range of alterations that appeared on the *T-S-C* set. The number of very large changes, however, is appreciably less so that the Haan set may, in fact, correspond more to the desired attributes of the characterological measures than the *T-S-C* set does. For the veteran in the marital crisis, there appears to be an important drop in primitive defense level, which remains at this new low level on the third testing, and decrements on the denial and intellectualization measures which return close to his previous levels on the follow-up examination. In place of his previous elevations on primitive defense and intellectualization, a new elevation on the doubt scale appears while he is in the midst of his difficulties, but this score drops to a new low after the acute crisis is resolved. Accordingly, the most reasonable interpretation of these alterations in the young man's MMPI performance would be that he changed the ego defense mechanisms on which he was relying on these different occasions.

Examination of the shifts appearing in the Haan scale values for the nurse indicate that she did not change as much as the student did during his crisis. Nevertheless, sufficient alterations occur to raise further doubts as to whether these preliminary measures of Haan's will be suited to the task of characterological description. In these changes found after her serious suicidal attempt, we can see a move toward greater psychological similarity to the young man. She, too, shows an appreciable drop in her score on intellectualization and a rise on the displacement score. Her projection score also drops coming closer to his general level. On the other hand, her primitive defense score rises on the second testing and continues to increase on the third occasion. (Is this possibly a clue to her continuing deterioration in self-management and personality integration?) In addition, her denial score rises abruptly and then returns to about the level it was when she was in her manic phase. Only her scores on the doubt scale stay essentially unchanged over these three administrations of the MMPI.

Single cases are, of course, only suggestive in providing a basis for judging the psychometric and psychodynamic implications of such scales. What is needed is a larger body of data to provide information on the status of some set of test subjects prior to, during, and after some reversible, but important, alteration in their symptomatic status over a sufficiently brief interval to reduce the possibility that gross alterations in basic personality have accompanied the symptomatic shifts. It would also be desirable to have some comparable set of subjects examined under similar circumstances who did not undergo the symptomatic shift but who had been through the sequence of re-examinations and other evaluations to assess simple retest effects. On the basis of a set of such data, these issues could be studied with more precision and the results judged with more confidence than isolated case studies can provide. Through the courtesy of Dr. Paul B. Fiddleman,[2] a set of MMPI records was made available that meet these requirements quite well in most respects except, perhaps, that of sample size. Examination of the shifts in these sets of scales over time in these groups can serve as an additional basis for judging the suitability of these particular scale sets for the present purposes and, in some ways also, the feasibility of this venture in MMPI revision in general.

As a part of his dissertation in 1961, Dr. Fiddleman examined sixteen volunteer medical and dental students who were to serve as subjects in a study of the effects of the oral administration of 100 gamma of LSD-25 on the psychological and psychophysiological status of young male adults. Part of the screening process involved administering the MMPI; this testing antedated the LSD session by two to three weeks.

The drug session lasted almost an entire day beginning early in the morning (without breakfast) with procedures to obtain a baseline of physiological recordings and self-descriptive checklist data. Then administration of the LSD-25 was followed by periodic interviewing, further physiological recording and checklist completions, along with continuous monitoring through a one-way vision screen. Two and a half hours after ingestion of the LSD, at what was judged a priori to be the height of the effect, the MMPI was readministered in the card form. Further studies and evaluations were carried out until later in the afternoon when a 50-mg dosage of Sparine was given six hours after the original LSD administration. Subjects were either sent home under the care of a spouse or friend, or, if no proper surveillance could be assured, they were admitted for an overnight stay in the hospital. Either the following day or within a three-day interval, the MMPI was administered for the third time along with an interview and other follow-up tests. Each subject was paid a fee for his participation in the study.

Fiddleman's original interest in the MMPI data was in the possibility that the nature and extent of the emotional alterations under this drug could be related to the previous personality characteristics of these experimental subjects. Somewhat surprisingly one-half of his research subjects did not show much, if any, alteration under LSD, whereas the other half underwent a quite dramatic behavioral and experiential change. Some of his analyses in the

---

[2] The author wishes to gratefully acknowledge Dr. Fiddleman for supplying the data for these analyses.

5. Whither the MMPI?

dissertation involved contrasting these two subgroups formed on the basis of this amount of change. That is, eight of his subjects were characterized as LSD reactors, whereas the other eight were called nonreactors. It is this difference that will be explored further in the present discussion; other concerns germane to his dissertation, such as the relation of paranoid reactions to anger-out versus anger-in dispositions, will not be examined further here.

The initial profiles in Table 7 and in Figures 3 and 4 show the breakdown of the standard MMPI scale data on these two groups of subjects in Fiddleman's study. The two groups of subjects give means well within normal limits on all of the basic scales, and both subgroups are quite comparable on initial testing. Simple *t*-tests run between these groups show no statistically stable differences on any of the validity or clinical

It may be of some interest, however, that the difference on scale 4 between these otherwise very similar subjects is in the direction expected if the data on relative LSD "immunity" in the literature are taken into consideration. Earlier, Belleville (1956) reported rather small alterations in his reformed opiate addicts, who had rather prominent elevations on scale 4, when given this same dosage of LSD-25. More recently, Ungerleider, Fisher, Fuller, and Caldwell (1968) have reported the relationship of scale 4 elevations and the absence of "bad trips" with repeated LSD usage. Alcoholics with prominent scale 4 elevations, as reported by Kurland, Unger, Shaffer, and Savage (1967), actually appear to gain therapeutic benefit from a strong dosage of LSD rather than experiencing an acute emotional disorganization. This possible special role of scale 4 in anticipating the reaction to a substance like LSD-25 bears further investigation.

When examined under the influence of LSD, however, the reactor group in Fiddleman's study showed a dramatic rise on scale 8 *(Sc)*, which was statistically stable at the .01 level when contrasted with the nonreactor group's mean, and smaller shifts on scale 1 *(Hs)* and scale 7 *(Pt)* which were significant at the .05 level. (These mean values are designated by superscripts in Table 7). For the reactor group, the changes on the MMPI are quite in accord with the findings on a group of University of Illinois medical students studied under similar dosages of LSD-25 as reported by Lebovitz, Visotsky, and Ostfeld (1960). The effects of this psychodelic agent on the Illinois subjects and on Fiddleman's susceptible subgroup are quite similar to patterns of MMPI response of acute schizophrenic patients (cf. Peterson, 1954).

The third examination, obtained on the average two days after the LSD session, indicated that the alterations under the drug were short-lived; their

TABLE 7
MMPI T Scores for Reactors versus Nonreactors in a Study of Effects of LSD[a]

Test administration		L	F	K	1	2	3	4	5	6	7	8	9	0
							Reactors ($N = 8$)							
Initial	Mean	42.6	51.0	56.9	49.5	47.3	55.3	54.3	62.6	50.8	53.4	50.9	58.9	44.3
	S.D.	0.9	2.2	2.3	2.2	1.3	2.8	1.4	3.1	2.3	2.2	2.3	2.8	1.7
LSD	Mean	42.9	60.0	53.1	63.9[b]	56.3	60.0	52.6	60.4	57.5	63.4[b]	76.5[c]	68.1	49.5
	S.D.	1.2	3.7	4.6	4.0	5.8	3.7	2.8	3.8	2.8	3.5	5.0	2.8	2.8
Post	Mean	42.8	52.9	59.3	48.0	50.9	51.3	55.6	61.0	52.6	52.3	51.3	60.0	43.6
	S.D.	1.3	2.7	2.0	1.3	1.6	2.6	3.0	2.8	2.6	1.4	2.3	2.3	1.3
							Nonreactors ($N = 8$)							
Initial	Mean	42.3	52.1	57.4	50.8	53.1	55.3	61.4	58.9	50.6	54.1	54.1	62.8	46.0
	S.D.	1.1	1.7	2.6	3.0	2.3	2.8	2.6	3.7	2.4	2.6	2.8	5.4	2.0
LSD	Mean	42.0	53.1	56.4	50.8[b]	53.0	55.9	56.9	64.1	50.6	53.0[b]	57.1[c]	62.0	45.8
	S.D.	1.5	1.8	2.5	2.7	2.6	3.0	2.4	1.7	1.8	2.1	1.7	2.5	2.1
Post	Mean	43.5	51.0	58.3	49.3	47.3	54.8	60.8	65.4	52.6	52.8	53.5	60.3	45.6
	S.D.	1.5	0.9	2.7	2.8	2.9	2.6	1.6	2.1	2.8	2.8	2.3	4.8	2.1

[a] Fiddleman (1961).
[b] .05 level.
[c] .01 level.

5. Whither the MMPI? 107

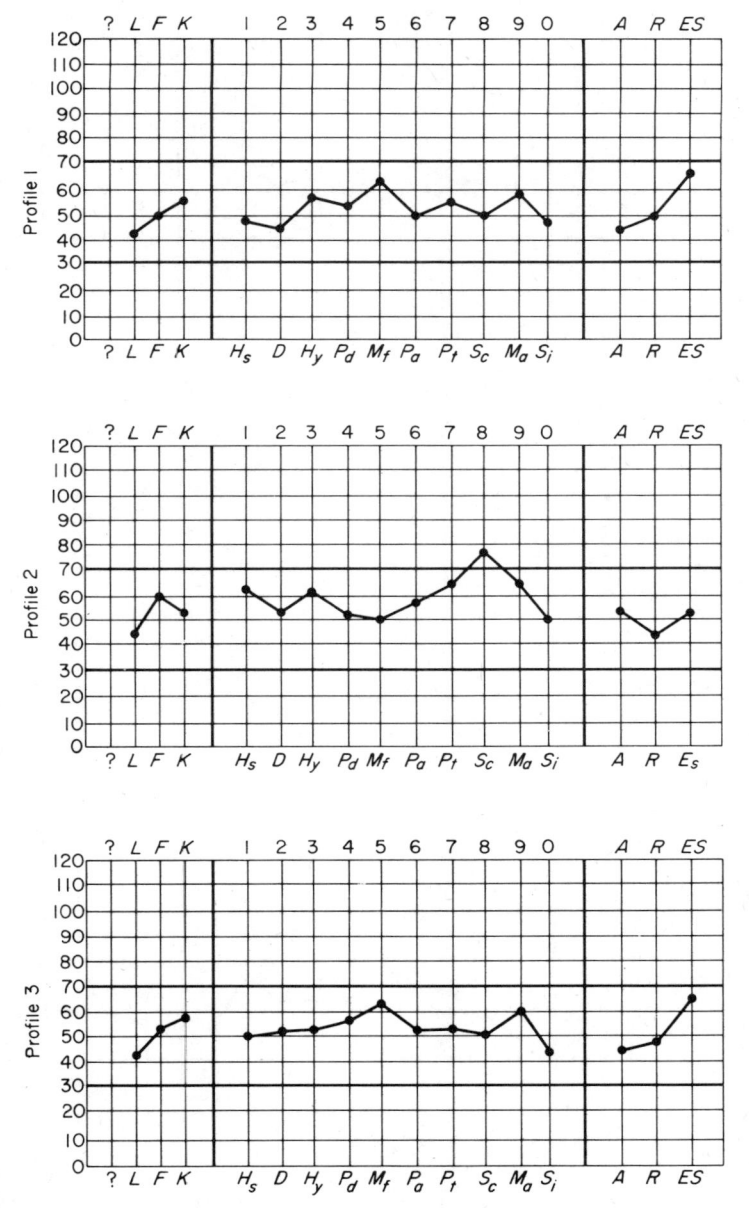

Figure 3. K-corrected profiles for three test administrations obtained on LSD reactors pre-, during-, and post-LSD experience.

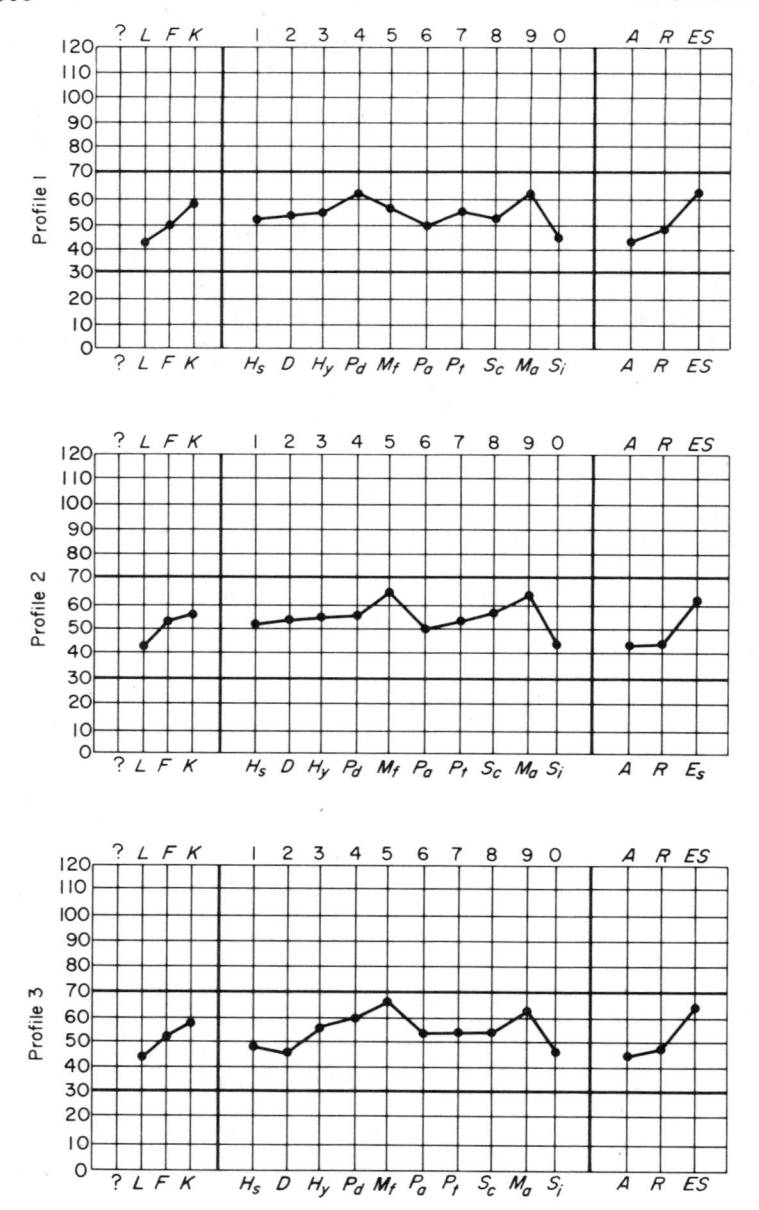

Figure 4. *K*- corrected profiles for three test administrations obtained on LSD nonreactors pre-, during-, and post-LSD experience.

5. Whither the MMPI?

postdrug means were quite comparable to the results obtained a few weeks before. The two groups again did not differ from each other to a statistically stable degree on any of the basic measures of the MMPI.

The basic questions to bear in mind, then, when these MMPI protocols are scored on the special *T-S-C* and Haan scales are: Do the symptom-status measures formed by the set of *T-S-C* scales show these two groups to be similar in initial clinical status? Are the differences in response to LSD mirrored in their scores on these scales too? Do such alterations disappear on follow-up testing as well? Are there any initial differences on the Haan scale values which might serve to herald their differential response to the psychodelic agent? And, lastly, are the Haan values sufficiently stable through the changes known to take place in the reactor group to provide characterological evaluations in the midst of an acute emotional disturbance? Admittedly, the data from the Fiddleman study may not be sufficient to give definitive answers to these questions; but they may serve as exemplars of the kinds of information that will be needed to evaluate this approach and generate this kind of format for the MMPI in the near future.

Table 8 summarizes the means and sigmas, as well as the *t*-test results, on both sets of scales scored on these two groups of men on each testing occasion, reported in terms of the *T*-score norms generated on the Minnesota male normative sample. On the *T-S-C* scales both groups of subjects initially scored lower than they did on the basic MMPI scale norms. The differences between them were quite small; the largest difference, on the *D* scale, is in accord with the difference on scale 2 reported in Table 7. The difference in Table 7 noted on scale 4, however, does not seem to be represented in any of the *T-S-C* variables. It may be represented in the Haan scale means, however, in terms of the difference on the *Rgr* scale. Examination of the *T-S-C* mean values of these groups under LSD intoxication suggests that these scales only partially reflect the altered clinical status of the reactor group. That is, the statistically stable shift on the *B* scale corresponds to the change reported in Table 7 on scale 1, but there is little indication among the other scales of the kinds of change which were detected by the basic clinical scales 7 and 8. Scales *T* and *A* should have shifted more if they were to mirror adequately what is manifested in the basic MMPI profile under the influence of this psychodelic agent. The final set of means on the *T-S-C* scales show the appropriate return to predrug levels which would be desired in this kind of symptom-scale set.

Turning to the Haan scales, we can see in Table 8 that no difference between these two groups on these variables is initially statistically stable as

TABLE 8
MMPI T Scores on Special Scales for Reactors versus Nonreactors in a Study of Effects of LSD[a]

Test adminis-tration		I	B	S	D	R	A	T	Prm	Rgr	Rpr	Prj	Dpl	Dnl	Dbt	Itl
				T-S-C scales								Haan scales				
								Reactors ($N = 8$)								
Initial	Mean	47.8	46.3	40.3	37.3	51.0	47.9	43.3	40.0	38.5	58.8	46.9	45.5	43.1	44.6	66.3
	S. D.	3.0	0.8	2.1	5.6	3.0	1.9	2.2	3.3	2.0	3.5	2.1	2.3	4.0	3.0	7.1
LSD	Mean	50.0	59.1[b]	43.0	48.0	52.0	56.1	51.8	42.0	47.5	54.4	50.0	59.5	47.3	53.0[b]	64.4
	S. D.	3.2	2.7	3.6	3.3	2.9	3.0	3.6	2.1	2.2	3.5	3.4	2.0	3.9	2.8	3.2
Post	Mean	48.3	43.3	39.5	43.6	49.6	47.0	43.0	41.0	38.5	56.3	49.4	43.8	46.8	44.3	68.8
	S. D.	2.7	1.3	3.3	2.0	2.4	1.2	2.3	2.7	2.2	3.4	3.1	2.2	3.7	1.9	4.3
								Nonreactors ($N = 8$)								
Initial	Mean	48.8	49.1	41.3	42.8	50.8	46.3	46.3	40.0	46.8	55.6	48.8	45.6	45.8	45.0	66.9
	S. D.	2.6	2.6	4.4	2.0	3.7	2.7	3.0	4.7	3.5	3.7	2.3	4.5	3.1	3.0	4.4
LSD	Mean	46.1	48.9[b]	38.5	43.1	48.3	50.4	46.8	40.0	42.4	52.5	51.9	51.6	48.4	44.6[b]	65.6
	S. D.	2.8	2.0	2.3	1.5	3.1	3.1	2.6	3.0	3.1	4.0	1.9	3.1	2.2	1.6	2.0
Post	Mean	50.8	46.0	41.5	40.0	49.1	45.3	44.5	35.0	45.1	57.5	51.3	50.3	47.3	45.9	69.4
	S. D.	3.1	2.1	4.2	1.7	3.2	2.6	2.7	3.4	3.7	3.7	3.0	3.1	1.5	2.6	3.3

[a] Fiddleman (1961).
[b] .05 level.

evaluated by simple *t*-test. The difference noted on the *Rgr* scale in this discussion is suggestive, but is no more supportive of this formulation than the trend noted on scale 4 in Table 7. Both groups are most elevated on the *Itl* scale, reminiscent of the pattern of the college student discussed earlier. On retesting under LSD, five of the eight means on these Haan scales remain essentially the same, even in the reactor group, but three scales, *Rgr, Dpl,* and *Dbt,* rise appreciably under this alteration in emotional status. The rise in the *Dbt* value is stable statistically at the .05 level and corresponds to some of the variations noted in the basic MMPI scale set. On some Haan variables, then, it would have been somewhat misleading to draw inferences about preexisting defense modes of these subjects if data in the acute phase were the only basis for such depictions. It is important to note, however, that the postdrug mean values are in excellent agreement with the predrug values on both subgroups.

Using the application of the two sets of scales (the *T-S-C* and Haan) to the data from Fiddleman's dissertation subjects as a model, it would appear that the proposed revisions of the MMPI along the lines of separate symptomatic and characterological components might be feasible but certainly not easy. There are, of course, several other sets of scales at hand which recommend themselves for consideration for one or the other of these purposes. Comrey's (1971) scales resulting from his factor analytic studies cut across the clinical scale domain in quite different dimensions. Wiggins (1966) has offered a set of content measures in place of the standard clinical variables in the MMPI profile. The factor scale sets of Welsh (1956) and of Eichman (1962) also seem to concentrate crucial variance in the clinical profile into a small number of nonoverlapping scales. They also seem to covary with important changes in the emotional status of clients or patients. Many of the new scales offered by Finney (1965) would also appear to be good candidates for the role of indicators of momentary clinical status. On the other hand, some of the other scales in the Finney set would seem to be potential measures for the characterological set. There is no special reason either for all of the scales in either subset to have been generated by the same author or the same method. For example, one kind of characterological measure may come from the research of Pepper (1964) on test-retest stability on the MMPI itself.

We must admit, however, that the present MMPI item pool (or any questionnaire item pool, for that matter) may not yield the requisite measures for our purposes. Perhaps, some new items will have to be generated. Or items may have to be rewritten, revamped, or added. Schofield (1966) summarized the kinds of personological referents which he felt were underrepresented in the MMPI and in several other instruments as well. Block (1965) suggested the kinds of omissions that he felt were particularly crippling in using the MMPI item pool for some of his stylistic evaluations. Most important, however, for the two general kinds of discriminations proposed here, the temporal referents of some of the MMPI items may have to be made more explicit. For example, consider MMPI item number 33: "I have had very peculiar and strange experiences." When answered "True," this item is scored on scales 4 and 8 (psychopathic deviate and schizophrenia). In its role in scale 8, when this item is answered (truthfully) in the negative direction, then, we can presume that it is helping rule out both a proclivity to schizophrenic reactions and any current state of schizophrenic disturbance. When answered in the scorable direction it may either be reflecting current difficulties or mirroring the fact that an individual has had in the past some episode of this sort from which he may now have recovered. Although there is no assurance that this kind of confusion could be minimized by rewording such an item, the addition of some temporal referent could, perhaps, reduce the interpretive uncertainty generated by such items in the component scales. Some test subjects deal with this problem themselves by adding qualifiers of their own (sotto voce), such as, "not for years" or "except for that time in the hospital," and go on to deny recent experiences of this sort. Others, however, get trapped into permanently characterizing themselves as this sort of person on the basis of reporting some long-since resolved emotional difficulties.

It will not be easy either to determine a priori the specific nature of the component scales in these sets. The typifying set, we trust, would cover such features of personality as: tendencies to blame oneself, tendency to blame others, inability to handle guilt and blame, femininity, repression, openness to threat, and character defects in loyalty, responsibility, and self-denial. It is questionable whether global measures of maturity, ego strength, or propensities for neurosis and psychosis would provide the requisite precision required in this typifying set. More promising, perhaps, would be the various separate control styles as reflected in some of Block's scales (1965). Some measure of social participation or preference for various kinds of interactions with others would also be valuable.

The syndromic set would be likely to include: depression, manifest anxiety, anger or hostility, and excitement or euphoria. A serious effort should be made to generate a measure of current sexual deprivation. In addition, measures of content disorders and current somatic preoccupations would be desirable. Here, too, the list should probably be short. The

5. Whither the MMPI? 113

configurations mount rapidly within each set and between patterns from each set.

The best strategy would seem to be to choose two such sets of criterion separations initially, try them out, and reset subsequent goals on the basis of the initial successes and failures. Hathaway, in the second chapter of this book, expresses great pessimism about the worth of any of the judgments available in contemporary clinical work-ups as a basis for the kind of empirical scale construction or refinement that he and McKinley pursued before World War II. Perhaps any revision of the MMPI will have to proceed in large part on the basis of a composite of present-day MMPI discriminations and refined clinical judgment. The old MMPI will provide the bootstraps for the new.

The final result of such developments could be three profile plots for a subject on a revised MMPI: validational scales, typifying scales, and syndromic scales. Assuming that this general approach pays off in scale development and in the generation of interpretively powerful configurations, it would then seem to be desirable to consider altering the present format one other way: by partitioning the test booklet into sections. I could envision Section 1 as made up of three kinds of material: the validational items, the typifying items, and some basis for determining the result to be expected from administering the remainder of the test. With luck, this first section would be discriminating in the scores and patterns it reveals of personological types, would be of reasonable length for screening, and would be sufficiently innocuous in referential content to be used without threat in most assessment contexts. The third kind of material suggested for inclusion in Section 1 is perhaps the most debatable. Can stop-items of considerable neutrality be devised that will still be effective in the crucial screening task? Should subtle items be tried in a configural scoring format? How can these indices be evaluated with sufficient speed and reliability to make the determination of whether to stop testing at Section 1 or to administer the full examination?

Section 2, of course, would contain the items for the syndromic assessment and the content would surely have to be more intrusive and potentially abrasive. The total test could turn out to be as long as the present test and, in this form, would be used most frequently in settings in which complete assessment evaluations are nearly routine. The labor of a rewriting, reconstruction, and restandardization of both the component scales and the score configurations is sobering, but the result could be a retention of the existing virtues of this clinical instrument and an even greater potential range of application.

REFERENCES

Barker, H. R., Fowler, R. D., & Peterson, L. P. Factor analytic structure of the short form MMPI in a VA hospital population. *Journal of Clinical Psychology*, 1971, **27**, 228-233.

Belleville, R. E. MMPI score changes induced by lysergic acid diethylamide (LSD-25). *Journal of Clinical Psychology*, 1956, **12**, 279-282.

Block, J. The development of an MMPI-based scale to measure ego control. Mimeographed materials. Berkeley: Institute of Personality Assessment and Research, Univ. of California, 1953.

Block, J. *The challenge of response sets: Unconfounding meaning, acquiescence, and social desirability in the MMPI.* New York: Appleton-Century-Crofts, 1965.

Comrey, A. L. *Comrey personality scales.* San Diego: Educational and Industrial Testing Service, 1971.

Comrey, A. L., & Souri, A. Further investigation of some factors found in MMPI items. *Educational and Psychological Measurement*, 1960, **20**, 777-786.

Dahlstrom, W. G. Recurrent issues in the development of the MMPI. In J. N. Butcher (Ed.), *MMPI: Research developments and clinical applications.* New York: McGraw-Hill, 1969.

Dahlstrom, W. G., & Welsh, G. S. *An MMPI handbook: A guide to use in clinical practice and research.* Minneapolis: Univ. of Minnesota Press, 1960.

Dahlstrom, W. G., Welsh, G. S., & Dahlstrom, L. E. *An MMPI handbook.* Vol. I. *Clinical interpretation.* Minneapolis: Univ. of Minnesota Press, 1972.

Dahlstrom, W. G., Welsh, G. S., & Dahlstrom, L. E. *An MMPI handbook.* Vol. II. *Research developments and applications.* Minneapolis: Univ. of Minnesota Press (in preparation).

Eichman, W. J. Factored scales for the MMPI: A clinical and statistical manual. *Journal of Clinical Psychology*, 1962, **18**, 363-395.

Endicott, N. A., & Jortner, S. Objective measures of depression. *Archives of General Psychiatry*, 1966, **15**, 249-255.

Fiddleman, P. B. The prediction of behavior under lysergic acid diethylamide (LSD). Doctoral dissertation, Univ. of North Carolina, 1961. (*Dissertation Abstracts*, 1962, **22**, 2873-2874.)

Finney, J. C. Development of a new set of MMPI scales. *Psychological Reports*, 1965, **17**, 707-713.

Foulds, G. A. *Personality and personal illness.* London: Tavistock, 1965.

Haan, N. Coping and defense mechanisms related to personality inventories. *Journal of Consulting Psychology*, 1965, **29**, 373-378.

Hathaway, S. R., & Briggs, P. F. Some normative data on new MMPI scales. *Journal of Clinical Psychology*, 1957, **13**, 364-368.

Jones, H. E., Macfarlane, J. W., & Eichorn, D. A progress report on growth studies at the Univ. of California. *Vita Humana*, 1959, **3**, 17-31.

Kurland, A. A., Unger, S., Shaffer, J. W., & Savage, C. Psychedelic therapy utilizing LSD in the treatment of the alcoholic patient: A preliminary report. *American Journal of Psychiatry*, 1967, **123**, 1202-1209.

Lebovits, B. Z., Visotsky, H. M., & Ostfeld, A. M. LSD and JB-318: A comparison of two hallucinogens. *Archives of General Psychiatry*, 1960, 390-407.

Lushene, R. E. Factor structure of the MMPI item pool. Master's thesis, Florida State Univ. 1967.

Panton, J. H. *Manual for the prison classification inventory for the MMPI.* Raleigh, N.C.: North Carolina Department of Corrections, 1970.

Pepper, L. J. The MMPI: Initial test predictors of retest changes. Doctoral dissertation, Univ. of North Carolina, 1964. (*Dissertation Abstracts,* 1965, **26,** 1780-1781.)

Peterson, D. R. The diagnosis of subclinical schizoprenia. *Journal of Consulting Psychology,* 1954, **18,** 198-200. (Also in G. S. Welsh, & W. G. Dahlstrom *Basic readings on the MMPI in psychology and medicine.* Minneapolis: Univ. of Minnesota Press, 1956.)

Schofield, W. Changes in responses to the MMPI following certain therapies. *Psychological Monographs,* 1950, **64,** (5), 1-32.

Schofield, W. A further study of the effects of therapies on MMPI responses. *Journal of Abnormal and Social Psychology,* 1953, **48,** 67-77.

Schofield, W. Clinical and counseling psychology: Some perspectives. *American Psychologist,* 1966, **21,** 122-131.

Spielberger, C. D. (Ed.) *Anxiety and behavior.* New York: Academic Press, 1966.

Spielberger, C. D., Gorsuch, R., & Lushene, R. E. *State-trait anxiety inventory.* Palo Alto, Calif.: Consulting Psychologists Press, 1970.

Stein, K. B. The TSC scales: The outcome of a cluster analysis of the 550 MMPI items. In P. McReynolds (Ed.), *Advances in psychological assessment.* Vol. I. Palo Alto, Calif.: Science and Behavior Books, 1968.

Tryon, R. C. Unrestricted cluster and factor analysis, with application to the MMPI and Holzinger-Harman problems. *Multivariate Behavioral Research,* 1966, **1,** 229-244.

Tryon, R. C. Person-clusters on intellectual abilities and on MMPI attributes. *Multivariate Behavioral Research,* 1967a, **2,** 5-34.

Tryon, R. C. Predicting individual differences by cluster analysis: Holzinger abilities and MMPI attributes. *Multivariate Behavioral Research,* 1967b, **2,** 325-348.

Ungerleider, J. T., Fisher, D. D., Fuller, M., & Caldwell, A. The "bad trip"—the etiology of the adverse LSD reaction. *American Journal of Psychiatry,* 1968, **124,** 1483-1490.

Welsh, G. S. Factor dimensions A and R. In G. S. Welsh and W. G. Dahlstrom (Eds.), *Basic readings on the MMPI in psychology and medicine.* Minneapolis: Univ. of Minnesota Press, 1956.

Wiggins, J. S. Substantive dimensions of self-report in the MMPI item pool. *Psychological Monographs,* 1966, **80,** (22), 1-42.

6

THE PRACTICAL PROBLEMS OF REVISING AN ESTABLISHED PSYCHOLOGICAL TEST

David P. Campbell

For the past ten years I have been associated with the Strong Vocational Interest Blank (SVIB), and I have been partially responsible for the 1966 revision of the men's form and totally responsible for the 1969 revision of the women's form. I am drawing on this decade of experience to offer some comments on test revision to those who aspire to update the MMPI.

One paragraph of history might provide some helpful perspective. The SVIB was first published in 1927. Eleven years later, in 1938, Strong revised it slightly and installed the scoring system and profile that then became widely used. In 1949, another eleven years later, Strong retired from Stanford University and began to think seriously about revising the inventory once more. He spent several years pondering what to do, and held several informal conferences with from five to twenty-five participants, to grapple with the problems. In the middle 1950s some decisions about procedures were made; and in the late 1950s work actually began at the University of Minnesota under the direction of Kenneth Clark, then chairman of the psychology department, and Ralph Berdie, Strong's son-in-law and the director of the Student Counseling Bureau.

I became involved in about 1959 as a graduate student doing their data processing. Over the next few years, my involvement increased until, in 1963 or 1964, the responsibility for the revisions became mainly mine. I emphasize that it was about twenty years ago that Strong first started thinking about these revisions and ten years ago that the work actually started. Those have to be sobering figures to anyone thinking about beginning to revise the MMPI.

There are three main obstacles facing those who would revise the MMPI. The first is technical ignorance; there is not enough solid data available to make wise decisions about how the test should be changed. The second is user acceptance: If the test is revised drastically, most practitioners will continue to use the old form. The third will be making the practical arrangements to carry out the work which mainly means securing the necessary funds and giving someone enough authority to make the decisions.

Technical Ignorance

The first problem here will be to decide just why the MMPI should be revised, since that will determine most of the revision strategy.

There are four possible reasons:

1. The items are out-of-date or otherwise unacceptable
2. The scales are out-of-date. The items in a specific scale are no longer descriptive of that characteristic—schizophrenia isn't what it used to be
3. The attributes or traits that are measured by the scales are no longer useful in psychological assessment and should be replaced with others
4. The entire system of empirical keying, using criterion groups, is no longer useful and should be replaced

If either of the first two is the major motivation for the revision, then the MMPI could be revised within its present form. The unacceptable items could be eliminated and at least 75 percent of the current pool retained. The scales could be revised by collecting new criterion groups much like the origi-

6. The Practical Problems of Revising an Established Psychological Test 119

nals—schizophrenics, depressives, psychopaths and so on—and deriving new scoring weights for these groups on the retained items.

The end result would be booklets and profiles very similar to the current ones. In fact, if done carefully, there would be almost no disruption to the system. A user, for example, would be able to look at the new profile—with familiar scales and T-scores—and know what the scores meant without consulting a new manual. Some new items and scales could be added, still within the earlier framework.

If the MMPI were revised because of the other two reasons, because the concepts reflected by the scales are no longer useful or because the whole system of empirical keying is no longer worthwhile, then the revision would, in effect, be a new personality inventory and would quickly drive away MMPI followers. For, if one is disillusioned with the current MMPI, he has many other current options, such as Gough's California Personality Inventory, Edward's Personality Inventory, Jackson's Personal Research Form, Thorndike's Temperament Schedule, or Berdie and Layton's Minnesota Counseling Inventory, the expurgated MMPI.

The decision as to which revision strategy to follow cannot be made wisely now because there are insufficient technical data available to answer clearly and firmly the questions about what techniques personality testing should adopt. No one can say, on the basis of solid data, which item format should be used, what types of scales should be used, what kinds of criterion groups, if any, should be used, what form of profile should be provided, what interpretive aids should be developed, or to what use the entire system should be put. The answers to these questions require a variety of information, including data analogous to that found in engineering handbooks. To date, personality researchers have not been willing or have not had the facilities to accumulate and organize this basic information for this purpose.

This general area of testing technology is the only aspect of test revision for which the typical psychometrician is trained. In the other areas, we are even more abysmally ignorant of how to proceed.

I will make one other parenthetical comment about technical ignorance. Because we do not have the necessary data to make objective decisions, fads tend to dominate the field; the MMPI reviser will be under tremendous pressure to incorporate whatever is faddish at the moment. For example, response set, acquiescence and social desirability, are currently popular, and the reviser will have to pay attention to those concepts even though the data in support of them are will-o'-the-wispy, at best, and, at worst, probably simply superstitious. Except possibly for factor analysis, no other psychometric issue has channeled so much high-powered wisdom into such trivial matters. Yet, any MMPI revision which does not deal specifically with response set must expect continual scathing from that small but vocal coterie of psychologists who believe that people don't read the items before responding.

There is another important area of ignorance which, to distinguish it from the first one, I will call practical ignorance. Here even, or, perhaps, especially, the skilled psychometricians are lost. I doubt that the following list of questions can be answered by anyone, yet a reviser would have to have this information to proceed sensibly.

1. How many MMPIs are given each year?
2. How many different versions of the booklets are there?
3. How many foreign translations are there, and how much volume do they generate?
4. How many times is the average MMPI booklet used?
5. How are the MMPIs scored? What percent are hand-scored, what percent machine-scored, and what percent computer-scored? What are the costs of each method?
6. What are the unusual ways in which the MMPI is used, and how would the revision affect each of them (e.g., in Braille)?

Information of this nature is extremely important if the revision is to be done with a minimum of disruption, yet it is very difficult to acquire. For example, probably no one knows how many MMPIs are taken each year; as a crude guess, I would say between one and two million. If these basic usage figures are not available, how can one make informed decisions about how many booklets to have printed, about how fast the change-over can be accomplished, and about a dozen other practical—but important—matters?

User Acceptance

The second main obstacle to be overcome if the MMPI is to be revised is user acceptance. This problem can be viewed graphically: Visualize a line, representing the amount of revision done, running from 0 to 100. The 0 represents "no change" and the 100 represents "complete and total revision." A checkmark representing the amount of MMPI revision could fall anywhere along that line, depending on how much change is made. If only trivial modifications are made, for example, replacing 10 or 15 percent of the items,

6. The Practical Problems of Revising an Established Psychological Test

then the checkmark could fall around 5 on the scale. This will not happen; for anyone who expends any energy on the revision will want to make at least a detectable change, perhaps going to a minimum of 35 to 40 on the scale. If significant changes are not made, why spend time and money on the revision?

On some other point on the scale, as yet undetermined, we can place another mark to represent the maximum amount of change that the average user will tolerate. If the MMPI is changed more than that, the user will refuse to switch from the old form. This second checkmark will, I believe, fall below that of the reviser's checkmark; that is, the average user won't tolerate as much change as the reviser will make, and he (the user) will ignore the revision and continue to use the old form.

The MMPI reviser must be very aware of this problem of user acceptance, and he should adopt two strategies to overcome it: First, he should make the changes as adroitly and quietly as possible to create a minimum of disruption; second, he should utilize whatever forces are working for the revision.

On the first of these points, the reviser will quickly learn that there is virtually nothing about a widely used test that can be changed without adversely affecting someone. Curiously, the responsibility of the test author and publisher to maintain consistency in the system has been little recognized. There is absolutely nothing on that point in the *Standards for Educational and Psychological Tests and Manuals* (American Psychological Association, 1966). Because so little emphasis has been placed on the need for consistency, I would like to give you several examples of how even trivial changes can create problems. Such examples seldom appear in the professional literature, yet they are very real concerns for anyone working on a test revision.

The first example is the number of items on the test. When a test is changed, the new form should have a different number of items so that it can quickly be distinguished from the older form, especially when answer sheets are involved. In the initial planning of the men's revision of the SVIB, we added 5 items (for a total of 405) to make the new form unique. After those plans became public, I received an anguished letter from a user stating that if the new test had 405 items, it could no longer be scored on the IBM-805 scoring machine because that answer sheet takes a maximum of 400 items. That did not seem to be a major problem since most people do not use the IBM 805 anymore and, anyway, answer sheets are flexible so that a few more items can always be added. The problem loomed larger when I found that 80,000 IBM answer sheets had been sold the preceding year, so clearly someone was using them, and the problem became hopelessly complicated after I spent an afternoon trying to cram five more items onto the answer sheet and finally concluded that it was impossible. (I found out much later that the reason that the original SVIB had 400 items was because that was the maximum number that could be fitted onto that answer sheet.) Since we were at a point where we could still make changes, we dropped one item, rather than adding five.

The second example consists of profile transparencies. One way to improve test interpretation is to construct transparencies to lay over profiles which demonstrate how various groups score. Also, there have been some attempts to develop scoring stencils for use with the profiles. These essentially are configural scoring schemes, and they depend on a standard profile format. Any change in the profile, even simple scale rearrangement, makes these transparencies obsolete. What would you say to an agitated colleague who has just found out that a new "Biologist" scale is going to be inserted in the profile (thereby moving each scale down one position) when he says, "I just had $1000 worth of transparencies prepared for our counselors—are you telling me they are now useless?"

The third example consists of new scales. Hardly anyone would argue with the virtue of updating occupational scales, and that has been done whenever new data have become available. For example, in 1966 the old Aviator scale was dropped in favor of a new Air Force Officer scale. Although the two scales correlated about .85, the new scale has a slightly different flavor than the old one and is a clear improvement. Yet, in a series of imaginative studies, Joseph Kunce, has developed an Accident Proneness Index for the SVIB, and has shown that this was related to accident frequency and also to the tendency to select risky occupations (Kunce, 1967; Kunce & Worley, 1966). He derived his index by subtracting the SVIB Banker scale score (presumably a measure of caution) from the SVIB Aviator scale (presumably a measure of risk taking) and this index does indeed, from his data, have moderate validity. Now, because the Aviator scale no longer appears on the profile, Kunce's index has been destroyed by the revision, and a promising line of research has been interrupted.

The fourth example is the Interest Maturity scale. This is my best anecdote about the impossibility of change without problems. In the 1930s, Strong developed the Interest Maturity scale by comparing the interests of young and old men; he wanted to find some way of determining whether a person's interests were mature enough to be stable or still adolescent enough so that further change would be expected. The scale was studied thoroughly by several investigators, and the overwhelming conclusion was that it didn't work—it had no validity. Thus in 1966, it was removed from the profile in what seemed to be the most defensible change ever made.

Sometime later, I was contacted by the personnel director of a large firm who wanted to know what happened to the Interest Maturity scale. I told him, and he said, "Well, you really shot us down. We hired a consulting firm to do a large selection study of the hiring of technical salesmen. The end product was a regression formula that we used in our hiring decisions, and one of the entries in the formula was the score from the Interest Maturity scale. Without that figure we cannot use that formula, and that study cost us $20,000."

These are four examples of what I would view as trivial changes; yet they caused considerable grief for some people. Consider what impact really big changes have had.

As I indicated earlier, the two strategies the MMPI reviser should adopt are the minimization of disruptive changes whenever he can and the utilization of whatever factors are operating to facilitate change. With regard to these strategies, we had several advantages in the SVIB revision that the MMPI reviser will not have.

First, some of the items in the Strong booklet were so clearly out-of-date that some change had to be made; we were asking students to report if they liked or disliked magazines that had gone out of print before they were born. Because of items like these there was enormous pressure for revision, and that has been an excellent argument for change that everyone will accept. In actual fact, the problem was not that severe; only a few items were affected.

But this pressure does not exist with regard to the MMPI because the items are still fairly modern. Only one item is dated and it is not extreme, especially in light of the peculiar diversity of the MMPI item pool. That one item is "Horses that don't pull should be beaten or kicked." Even though that statement is anachronistic, most people probably understand what it means, and some of us will continue to endorse it. Whatever other problems the MMPI item pool has, it is not contentually out of date and, from the reviser's standpoint, that is a loss of leverage.

The second factor facilitating change on the SVIB is that because the profile is essentially a listing of occupations, the addition of another occupational scale is welcome. Because such new scales are similar in nature to those already on the profile, the user immediately knows how to interpret them. On the MMPI profile, in contrast, new scales require much more study, and a user confronted with six or eight new ones has to go to the Manual to know just what he has. There is no simple way to add new scales, routinely.

Another advantage with the SVIB is that the system is more under central control because of the complicated scoring. Almost all Strongs are scored by a few commercial agencies; and when the revision was ready, we asked them to discontinue the old form and adopt the new one. Although a few psychologists continue to use the old form, the changeover after one year was between 75 and 90 percent which, considering the usual inertia, was remarkable and mainly due to the centralized control.

This is not true of the MMPI; most of these are scored in-house and the changeover will be more difficult to accomplish. Any user well equipped with booklets and answer sheets and an IBM 805 scoring machine can go on forever using the old system. There is no direct way to change his methods. Since it will cost money to replace the old booklets and convert the scoring weights, many institutions will stay with the old system for economic reasons. The reviser and publisher will have to think up some clever approaches to overcome this inertia.

The Administrative Arrangements

The third major obstacle for the MMPI reviser concerns the necessary practical arrangements. These can be subdivided into three main areas: first, the establishment of some administrative structure so that the work will get done. Essentially this means deciding who is going to be responsible and then giving him enough authority to carry out that responsibility; second, the provision of the necessary funds to support the activity; and third, the assignment of credit for doing the work to include both authorship listing and royalties.

These three points are intimately intertwined and to talk of one without bringing in the others is difficult. But let me try to discuss them separately here. First, the administrative structure. There are many individuals and institutions with vested interests in the MMPI. Some of them have direct, legal interests. These include the original authors or their estates, the publisher (The Psychological Corporation), the University of Minnesota which holds the copyright, and those who have prepared foreign translations. Others with less tangible legal rights but with real, practical concerns are *researchers* who have collected huge mounds of data on the current form and who want some guarantee of consistency between forms, the *scoring services* who have made widespread use of the MMPI possible and who have some

6. The Practical Problems of Revising an Established Psychological Test

considerable investment in the new computer interpreted profile, *users* who have expended money on booklets and answer sheets, and finally, the *practitioner* who has accumulated over twenty years of experience with a profile that he has come to regard, in many ways, as sacred.

All of these interests must be considered in the revision. The standard way to represent diverse viewpoints is to establish a committee, and this is, perhaps, the strongest point buttressing my pessimism regarding the possibility of successfully revising the MMPI. For—I will say it bluntly with absolute certainty of being correct—a committee cannot do it. A committee can provide different points of view, it can expand the scope of concerns that are to be considered before starting, and it can act as a brake on someone who is ridiculous or reckless. But a committee cannot do anything positive, it cannot take chances, it cannot handle a huge diet of what can only be described as menial, grueling work, nor can it stay constituted long enough, say five years, to complete any large portion of the work.

Somehow, one person (or, at the most, two or three) must be given enough authority to see things through; enough authority here means that he must have enough freedom to fail. He needs this freedom for two reasons: first, the revision will surely require some changes from the old way, and the reviser must be free to make the necessary changes in the face of powerful forces to maintain the status quo; and, second, there is no better safety check on the reviser's actions than the knowledge that if he makes some very bad decision, it will all be over. If he knows he can do virtually anything he wants and that he, and he alone, will have to answer for the results, then he will work nights, weekends, and vacations trying to determine what the impact will be before making any disruptive changes.

The point might become more vivid if we look at actual examples. Choose a likely person to be given the revision responsibility and ask yourself if you would allow that person to make the following decisions:

1. Should the MMPI be revised?
2. How long should the new test be?
3. What should the new title be?
4. What should the item format be?
5. Should the new scale weights be made public or kept secret? (Because of the widespread problem of piracy of answer sheets and test booklets, I think it is only a matter of time before all item weights are kept secret.)
6. What color should the new test be?

Even the more trivial decisions collectively add up to considerable impact, and one would have to have generous faith in the reviser before giving him this responsibility.

The question of the color of test was included in the list because I would like to cite one more incident of how seemingly trivial decisions can backfire on a test reviser. When we were ready to choose a new color for the men's SVIB revision, the decision was made in the following manner: the printer came in with samples of colored stock and, since time was short, we decided to choose a color from those he had on hand. After the colors used in previous booklets were eliminated, there remained gray, brown, pink, and blue. The blue stood out as lively and attractive, so the new men's booklet was printed on blue paper.

About two years later, we went through the identical procedure with the women's revised booklet. After again eliminating the colors which had been used, gray, brown, and pink remained. We all chuckled and chose pink. It was overly cute, I admit, but we were under time pressure again, and we needed the forms. Besides, there was some mild rationale to it and it seemed unimportant.

In the months, since, almost everyone who has heard about these colors has grinned and taken them with good humor. One of the few exceptions caused me to lose some valuable data.

When revising the women's form, I tried to collect a criterion sample of high-level women managers because those who counsel older women returning to the occupational world have lamented the lack of any tool to help women decide if they would enjoy managerial positions. I discovered that high-level women managers are very hard to find. However, I finally found an organization that had over 800 women holding very responsible managerial positions. I approached their executive secretary, and though she was dubious about testing, in general, I thought I had succeeded in winning her cooperation. After all, it was very much to their benefit to have a Manager's scale on the women's profile to attract more women into their activities. Everything was going reasonably well until I made the mistake of showing her the new booklets. She looked at the men's booklet—blue—then at the women's—pink—and literally exploded. She dressed me down in no uncertain terms about the nefarious nature of male and female stereotypes and what damage we were doing to little girls by only giving them dolls and what dastardly rogues we were in promoting the blue-pink split, and the result was that she would not allow me to collect the information from their membership.

6. The Practical Problems of Revising an Established Psychological Test 127

Finally, to add a scale for managerial women, I tested WAC and WAVE officers, and scales for them appear on the new profile—the presence of which will probably result in the accusation that I am a militarist.

The cost of the revision will be determined, of course, by what is done. For the discussion here, let me assume that the revision will include modifying the item pool, collecting new criterion data, building new empirical scales, adding some kind of factor or cluster scales, and modifying the scoring and computer-interpreted output. To begin this would require something like $50,000 annually for five years. Assuming that the MMPI total annual sales are around $75,000, then to begin the revision would require a commitment roughly equal to three years total sales. It would require a very persuasive psychologist to get that amount from a test publisher. Consequently, other sources of funds would have to be tapped. Government agencies such as NIH or NIMH or the Office of Education are possibilities; however, a grant proposal submitted to these agencies requesting funds to be used to revise the MMPI would not be approved. The MMPI is a commercially viable property and to use Federal funds to revise it is considered by some to be corrupt.

Another possible source of funds is the commercial scoring services. However, because most MMPIs are scored in-house, these services are not as important in the MMPI system as they are for the SVIB, and they may be more reluctant to provide funds. Still they can help in valuable ways by providing services. Test Score provided a great deal of help to E. K. Strong and his associates over the years by donating free scoring for research purposes; National Computer Systems has made their staff and computer available to our Center for perhaps $20,000 worth of scoring and data analysis.

Yet another source of funds for the Strong revision was the various occupational organizations. Some were willing to help finance the work on their occupation; for example, the Society of Petroleum Engineers helped a great deal in surveying their membership, as did the National Association of Funeral Directors. Because of the different populations served, such help may not be available to the MMPI reviser; no national society of manic depressives is likely to come forward with a mailing list. However, hospitals or clinics may be very helpful.

The other side of the economic coin is the problem of how to reward those who do the work. Because we in the academic world wish to project a blasé image of disdain for money and glory—we are only interested in the search for truth—we cannot be straightforward about issues of authorship and royalties. We are overly polite in the initial negotiations; then afterward we sit alone in our offices seething because we have done the work and someone else is reaping the benefits.

Not the smallest problem is the differential perception that each person has of his own contribution. I am convinced that if you chose any multiple-authored work in psychology and asked the authors independently what percentage of the total they were responsible for, the sum would be a minimum of 200 percent. Each person, on the average, believes he contributed twice as much as his colleagues think he did.

And the quest for glory is clearly involved here, for having one's name connected with a widely used test is a powerful way to gain professional visibility. Names like Wechsler, Strong, Kuder, Miller, Hathaway, and Rorschach are familiar to virtually all psychologists, and I do not mean to detract from their considerable accomplishments when I point out that the accident of test authorship assured them of a brighter place in history than that of their equally competent colleagues who happened to make other contributions. Probably few can name the man who directed the Psychological Clinic at Penn State for almost twenty years and then moved up to become a vice-president for student affairs for another ten years, yet the name Bernreuter is a familiar one to most psychologists in another context.

(Bernreuter recently told a funny story on himself about his fame. At a recent APA convention, he was alone in an elevator going down to a hotel lobby. The elevator stopped at an intermediate floor, and a graduate student, still high from the evening cocktail hour, reeled in. He steadied himself against the wall, and leaned over to squint at the stately white-haired university vice-president's name tag and stammered over a tongue that almost would not obey him, "Bernreuter, for Christ's sake, I thought you'd been dead for twenty years!")

The point is that association with a test is a valuable commodity; if it does not seem important to you now, spend ten years working on a test and see whether you develop some possessiveness.

Incidentally, one of the frustrations that the MMPI reviser is going to have to live with is being second generation; no matter how excellent his output, no matter how imaginative and how worthy his work is of being recognized on its own merit, he will be known as the man who followed Hathaway.

There are several ways to handle the authorship problem. The following four examples range from the most to the least recognition of the reviser's efforts:

The first example is the Allport-Vernon Study of Values. After revision, it became the Allport-Vernon-Lindzey Study of Values.

The second example is the Strong revision. The test name was unchanged; but the names of the four revisers, Strong, Kenneth Clark, Ralph Berdie, and myself went onto the test booklet as authors, and my name went on the Manual as reviser.

The third example is Clark's Minnesota Vocational Interest Inventory. I came in at the end of his research on that and helped him prepare the test for publication which included writing much of the Manual. For that, my name appears as junior author on the Manual.

The fourth example is the Miller Analogies Test. The test is continually revised by simply making up another form. I think the publisher simply contracts for someone to produce and norm another hundred analogies, and whoever does it is probably paid a flat "one time" rate. As far as I know, no other name but Miller has ever been identified with either the test or the Manual.

The designation of authorship will certainly be related to the assignment of royalties. The amount of money involved is just the wrong amount to facilitate negotiations among the participants. It is not enough to merit legalistic and friendship-destroying quibbling, yet it is too much to treat blithely. Before the work is started, the final splits should be negotiated formally and legally. Yet, because no one knows just how much work will be done nor exactly who will do it, such negotiations are difficult. All concerned wish to remain friendly, to maintain their academic facade of not really caring about money, and to treat the other fellow fairly. Yet no one wants to be taken advantage of.

After all of this, I still do not have any recommendations to make about royalty negotiations. On the Strong, we just blundered along until everyone felt at least comfortable enough not to speak out. In retrospect, this casual approach was probably as good as any.

If this picky discussion about authorship and royalties leaves a slightly queasy feeling in your stomach, and if you feel that I am a distasteful sort of fellow with a large slice of professional pettiness—good, I have succeeded in capturing the right tone. Because academicians refuse to treat these issues openly and because we act as if we are above it all, we are especially vulnerable to the vicious disagreements that arise when people will not level with each other about important topics.

Those of us working on the SVIB revision survived with our friendships intact and on close professional terms partially because each participant was willing to give—the Strong family, for example, relinquished two-thirds of their royalties, one-third to go into a research fund and one-third to be split among the other members of the revision team—partially because we had a publisher who was willing to leave us alone, even while providing some of the funds, and partially because we got some breaks. For example, when it was time in the progression of events to decide who was going to have the final authority, that decision was made by fate. Strong became ill and passed away, Clark left Minnesota to become a dean elsewhere, and Berdie was immersed in the administrative work necessary to run the huge Counseling Bureau at Minnesota. The power fell, by default, into my hands and because I made enough more correct than incorrect decisions, I was allowed to keep it. Had the quartet remained in existence, scattered over 2000 miles, making the decisions jointly, with everyone trying to explain his thoughts to everyone else, I seriously doubt that the project would ever have been finished.

Although many vested interests were present and occasionally conflicted, the SVIB revisers succeeded in this venture and survived with our personal and professional relationships intact, indeed, strengthened. I wish the MMPI revisers, if such there be, equal luck.

REFERENCES

Kunce, J. T. Vocational interests and accident proneness. *Journal of Applied Psychology,* 1967, **51**(3), 223-225.

Kunce, J. T., & Worley, B. Interest patterns, accidents and disability. *Journal of Clinical Psychology,* 1966, **22** (1), 105-107.

7
REACTIONS, REFLECTIONS, PROJECTIONS

When Professor Butcher invited me to comment on the papers in this volume it was roughly a week after the appearance of Professor Douglas N. Jackson's definitive paper, "The Dynamics of Structured Personality Tests: 1971." Somewhat shaken by this powerful attack upon my rather bodacious 1945 manifesto (Meehl, 1945a), I accepted without much enthusiasm. However, I agreed to make a small contribution to the present important volume and I laid down as conditions that (1) I would not be expected to function as sort of a "reviewer" of the book's chapters, a function I consider a work of supererogation, especially given the calibre of the contributors; and (2) that I should feel free to "do my thing," in the sense of using my reading of the manuscripts mainly as a springboard for some free associations of my own. If my explicit references to the main contributors appear minimal, this should not be misconstrued, since I have read each chapter twice and portions of each chapter three times before embarking upon this personal combination of reactions, reflections, and projections into the future.

A preliminary question must be put: "Is the psychometric description of personality worth doing?" One reason why this is an important question is that there is a respectable body of opinion in American psychology that would answer it negatively, for reasons discussed by Professor Butcher. Even for those of us who are old-fashioned enough to persist in this endeavor, the justification for spending scientific and professional time building and validating tests and the patient's or taxpayer's money administrating and interpreting them—not to say the dreadful waste of time typically involved in communicating them by inefficient means, for example, case conference—has to be settled, however preliminarily and arbitrarily, in order to provide a framework in which one can ask how good a test must be to justify the efforts spent on building and applying it. As I pointed out a dozen years ago (Meehl, 1959a), it is not sufficient to show that a psychological test, when purporting to "measure personality," has nonzero validity. In that paper I set out four rough levels of construct validity, emphasizing that the only level clearly defensible clinically was a kind of incremental validity for pragmatically significant inferences—hardly begun to be properly studied. It will not do, I think, for clinicians to argue that describing the human personality is "just something intrinsically worth doing" by analogy with such descriptive scientific enterprises as comparative anatomy, or taxonomy, or historical geology. Having been trained at Minnesota during the intellectual dominance of the late, great Professor Donald G. Paterson, I acquired an intrinsic interest in the subject matter of individual differences under the aegis of two teachers (Paterson and Hathaway) who had very little respect for psychological theory. Professor Paterson rationalized his interest in such questions as physique and intellect, and the inheritance of general intelligence in terms of his pragmatic frame of reference. I do not, of course, see anything objectionable about the scholarly position: "Describing the human personality is simply part of the subject matter of psychology." But that would not suffice to justify spending time on the building and validating of structured personality inventories such as SVIB, CPI, 16 PF, EPPS, MMPI, or PRF, unless it were shown that the validity of these devices exceeded that of less costly "criteria" employed in the validation process. Unless one can make a respectable case that a structured personality inventory can assess the personalities of people (1) better or (2) quicker-easier-cheaper than competing methods of assessment, should we bother with it? But this comparative criterion doesn't leave us as discouraged as one might think, for a reason that Dr. Hathaway mentions: It is far from clear that other assessment methods, including some that it is currently fashionable to become enthusiastic about, do any better—if as well. And I cannot resist the temptation to second Dr. Hathaway's all too brief reference to the preinventory research by personnel and educational psychologists—not to mention the research (going back into the last century)

7. Reactions, Reflections, Projections

on the general untrustworthiness of human testimony and the sources of error in human judgment—which a whole generation of young clinical psychologists have probably never heard of. The rise of clinical psychology has had the bad effect of our sometimes ignoring a vast body of data that led our intellectual ancestors of the 1920's to a healthy skepticism about what they called "anecdotal" or "impressionistic" evidence. Doubtless they overdid it a bit, with some maliciousness toward laymen's doctrine and an inferiority complex toward the advanced sciences (cf. Meehl 1971), but their empirical findings cannot be airily dismissed. Anecdotal evidence is just not good evidence, and that's as true today as it was in 1925. Some clinicians seem to believe that a big brain-changing mutation has occurred subsequent to the classic studies of Hollingworth, Starch, Münsterberg, Valentine, Thorndike, Rice, and Whipple showing the poor ability of humans to observe, judge, record, retain, report, and generalize accurately. If a clinician answers the direct challenge "What makes you think the Midwestern Tennis-Ball-in-a-Bushel-Basket Projective Technique has appreciable validity? I don't believe it!" by saying, "I have noticed it works peachy in my clinic," something important was missing from his undergraduate education in psychological science. One's "clinical experience" can often be a fairly legitimate justification for doing something; that justification occurs in the pragmatic context requiring us to "do something, don't just stand there." And clinical experience is a rich source of theoretical hypotheses. I will go further and maintain that sometimes clinical experience may countervail purported "scientific research" because to a critical mind much of such research, while quantitatively pretentious, is worthless. Despite these admissions, my main thesis remains that when one's clinical experience is challenged, either by another clinician or by unexceptionable quantitative counter-evidence, merely to reiterate "My clinical experience shows . . ." is a pretty feeble reply. Changes in psychologists' attitudes toward validation over the last quarter century are sociologically so important as to deserve an extensive discussion in themselves, but I shall not provide one here.

Returning to the question "Why bother with personality testing at all?" I here record an article of scientific faith and will go on from that. I find it almost inconceivable that precisely the same "treatment" is optimal for all personalities and problems. It does not discourage me that specific indications relating treatment to psychometric findings are largely lacking, although some would say it should. Psychologists often talk about the primitive state of the science and art of treatment and assessment in a way that suggests they do not really mean it. But when I say that clinical psychology is in a stage roughly like medicine in the days of Paracelsus, I mean it. There is unfortunately more than a verbal connection between the "empirical" emphasis in personality testing (I, of course, include here my half-right, half-wrong 1945 article) and the less honorific use of the word "empiric" as that term is used in medical scholarship. I believe—and my "faith" in this future development is, unaccountably, as strong today as it was when I was in graduate school—that the psychological clinic team of the future will make almost as powerful use of social and psychological diagnosis in treatment selection as the internist now does in medicine. I am aware that such a prophecy will strike some, perhaps most, of my readers as preposterous. To put some flesh on the bones: My clinical experience leads me to conjecture (note the word) that there are several distinct kinds of depression, at least five (two "psychotic") and possibly as many as seven. (I am pleased to note that since formulating these notions almost wholly on impressionistic grounds, some quantitative support has begun to appear in the psychiatric literature distinguishing varieties of depression, for example, the genetically distinct "unipolars" and manic-depressives.) I find it easy to fit into this speculative scheme of things the sometimes discouraging results of antidepressant medication, and the fact that electroshock therapy—the closest thing we have to a "specific" in the whole field of psychiatry, although many clinical psychologists fanatically refuse to admit this fact—does not always "work" and sometimes (actually very rarely) seems to make the patient worse. If there are five to seven kinds of depression which are not being identified, we are lumping together many patients characterized by different quantitative parameters. Sometimes, even different specific, qualitative etiologies underlie their mental suffering and aberrated behavior. I am confident that in the next twenty years the development of psychotropic drugs will exceed anything we have yet seen or most practitioners have even imagined. But the ingenuity of the biochemist and psychopharmacologist will be running too far ahead of clinical psychology and psychiatry unless the notion of specific CNS parameters is taken seriously and investigators accept it as a working hypothesis that the differential diagnostic and drug selection problem is going to be an extremely complicated one, clinically and statistically. It is just not going to be possible in the future to assign drugs to patients on the basis of a few slick paper brochures mailed out by the drug houses or one's casual impressions about which sorts of cases need which drug. I pick the brain chemistry area as the most obvious one, the one in which I have the greatest confidence for my optimistic psychometric projections of future practice. But I have only a slightly lesser degree of conviction about the choice of nonchemical treat-

7. Reactions, Reflections, Projections

ment regimes as a function of patient personality makeup. We already have some quantitative evidence for the importance of interaction between therapist and therapeutic theory-cum-technique and patient personality. I believe from my experience that future investigators will look upon these interactive studies as the merest primitive beginnings. Any practitioner who has had occasion to get feedback on his referrals in a certain community over a period of years (I always extract a "promise" from patients, when I refer them, to let me know by telephone, letter, or preferably by dropping in at my office, "How it went" with Dr. Jones) will have developed pretty strong convictions about certain kinds of patients that don't get along well with Therapist X and others who do very well with him. I need hardly say that as a scientist I realize that these anecdotal impressions must be researched, and I am fully aware that some skeptics who doubt that psychological intervention ever has any effect would not expect these clinical impressions to be supported by systematic quantitative research. I believe, for instance, that classical psychoanalysis or a strongly psychoanalytic kind of uncovering therapy is beneficial to a few people. However, I also believe that watered-down psychoanalytic therapy in which the mental processes of the therapist are fundamentally modelled after those of the psychoanalyst, but in which interview density and other features are markedly removed from the psychoanalytic context, is a relatively ineffective form of treatment and for many of our patients is counterproductive. Like every psychotherapist I have my notions about what kinds of patients are appropriate for psychoanalytic therapy, rational therapy, desensitization, behavior modification, and the like. I admit that I cannot prove these contentions scientifically at present, but I believe that in the future the evidence to that effect will be persuasive.

My utopian fantasy does not "dispense with the clinician," and there is, so far as I know, no locus in my writings that says, or implies, this. I do, however, propose to plug the clinician in at stages in the decision-making process where his talents will be used more effectively and his numerous defects, especially as a data-processor and information-storer, will be capable of introducing less noise into the system. One stage of data collection and data processing at which the skilled clinician will be indispensable for at least the foreseeable future (and perhaps longer) is the level of the diagnostic interview. Such "simple" things as noticing a patient's rigidly smiling facial expression, or sociopathoid "animal grace," or the "quasi-sleepy" voice texture of some schizotypes, cannot be discriminated by a computer or a clinically unskilled clerk or interviewer. Furthermore, the elicitation of certain kinds of diagnostic behavior requires the skilled interviewer to know when to interrupt, what to say and how to say it; I see no good reason to think that this skill will be dispensable in favor of an automated interviewing procedure in the foreseeable future any more than we have found it convenient in clinical neurology to stop training neurological residents in the proper use of the percussion hammer in eliciting the patellar reflex. I shall not be astonished if automation at the clinical "firing line" proceeds more rapidly than I here suppose, but I just want to make clear for the record, since my views on this matter are widely misunderstood, that this raw data eliciting and transducing function is one of those at which I conceive the human perceptual-cognitive system to be highly sensitive and superior to hardware. Since this is something that only skilled clinicians know how to do, it is desirable to have them spend more of their time doing it and less applying subjective equations with nonoptimal beta weights.

The psychological assessment of the future I fantasize will involve a combination of a semistructured mental status interview and a semistructured life history interview together with improved structured and projective tests, plus selected psychophysiological and "soft neurological" measures that lie somewhere among psychometrics, experimental psychology, and clinical neurology. The analysis and interpretation of this mass of material would be largely computerized, although we would, of course, include certain impressionistic, "global" and theory-mediated inferential judgments by clinicians among the variables—assuming that they survive critical scrutiny as to whether they contribute more information than noise, a question still open on present evidence. I do not anticipate that the computer's output in that utopian stage will be confined to any one of the kinds of "clinical decision" presently advocated as more worthy of our attention than others—any more than diagnosis in internal medicine aims to eventuate with the single decision "remove appendix" or "try Indocin," although we should not blink at the fact that for a patient with an acute abdomen or an osteoarthritic flare-up these two specific decisions as to first-step treatment choice are far and away the most important things that can be said. Point: A thorough description of a patient's medical condition will properly emphasize those aspects of the current clinical status that have highest priority for immediate therapeutic intervention, the limiting case being a finding that somebody is moribund (e.g., due to an airway closure or massive hemorrhage or cardiac arrest). But nobody thinks that when these high-priority statements have been made, the thorough physician has said all that it is appropriate for him to say in his assessment of a patient's physical condition. I reject the notion that clinical psychology will have to make up its mind whether to aim at diagnostic and

7. Reactions, Reflections, Projections

prognostic statements that are phenotypic versus genotypic, specific versus general, possessed of high bandwidth versus high fidelity (Cronbach & Gleser, 1957; Cronbach, 1960), content versus form, acquired versus innate dispositions, dispositions of low order versus high order (Meehl, 1972a), "Galilean" versus "Aristotelian," dimensional versus taxonomic, short-term versus long-term dispositions, phenomenal versus behavioral. For my part, each of these distinctions—while pointing to something important and in some cases critical—is a convenient handle for designating kinds of data, methodological techniques, and metatheoretical categories, but is not honorific or pejorative. It is stupid to pronounce (as many clinicians do) that "we shouldn't put patients in pigeon holes" because there are no disease entities in functional psychiatry, as if the recondite and technical questions involved in the meaning and uses of typological or taxonomic analysis could be settled by a few cocktail party cliches (Meehl, 1972a). It is hard enough to make clinical psychology intellectually respectable and socially relevant without having first to clean out the Augean stables of a pretentious dilettantism passing for sophistication.

But even in the present non-Utopian stage of our knowledge, some of us find the deliverances of a test like MMPI worth gleaning—especially since, as Dr. Hathaway points out in his paper and has always emphasized to his students, a device that takes a negligible amount of time for the skilled clinician to administer or interpret is often worth using even when the inferences it permits are of only moderate validity. I confess to the clinician's usual reliance upon "clinical experience," whether my own, or transmitted to me as part of Multiphasic lore from other practitioners. One who thinks rationally about the difference between the pragmatic context—where all of our professional behavior, including "not doing anything," is a form of action (Meehl, 1973b)—will recognize that the shifting of methodological standards in moving from laboratory or theory seminar to clinic need not always represent an irrationality or an incoherency on the part of the clinician who is scientifically trained and oriented. It is a difficult line to draw, and I do not know precisely where to draw it. But what is clear, whether one belongs mainly at the "simple minded" or the "muddle headed" end of the famous Russell-Whitehead continuum, is that the following three statements are quite compatible:

 I. Inasmuch as experienced practitioners sometimes disagree about the validity of diagnostic device X, it is highly desirable that this conflict of clinical impressions should be researched, employing investigative procedures as objective and scientific as is achievable given the subject matter. As Aristotle puts it, "It is the mark of an educated man to look for precision in each class of things just so far as the nature of the subject admits."

II. If experienced practitioners disagree as in (I), and a dispute is in progress between a pro-X practitioner and an anti-X practitioner, once that collision of "clinical experiences" has become manifest and is not plausibly attributable either to the fact that one of the two regularly contaminates his inferences or that the other one really doesn't know anything about the instrument having never bothered to learn skills with it, then it is not a rational contribution to the discussion for either of them to say, "My clinical experience refutes yours:"

III. Pending adequate quantitative research that will err neither on the side of simple-mindedness (by using an inadequate criterion) or on the side of muddle-headedness (by inadequate attention to contamination and the like), and being in a clinical situation where daily decision-making is demanded of me as a professional person, I intend to rely on diagnostic instrument X as part of my information base.

Applying this reasoning to the MMPI, I exemplify with three instances from my current clinical practice. They are garden-variety examples; there is, with the exception of the suicide case, nothing particularly exciting or unusual about them. They are not "selected instances" to grind my pro-MMPI axe, but are chosen because they happen to be current patients of mine of three different sorts, with whom I believe MMPI is clinically useful.

First Example: I have recently begun seeing a 31 year old lawyer, referred to me by a psychologist colleague for a marital problem, where the manifest precipitating factor in his wife's leaving him was the patient's tendency not to come home for dinner but to spend the evening drinking beer with the boys. He has never been in any trouble occupationally or legally because of alcohol, and he almost never drinks hard liquor. The patient's purpose in consulting a psychologist was "to find out whether I really need to go into some kind of long-term deep psychotherapy, or simply to face up to the fact that I am behaving stupidly and get hold of myself." Without going into the details of the case, my main diagnostic problem at this point—as of the present writing the patient has, interestingly enough, managed to avoid taking the MMPI group form which I sent home with him after our first session three weeks ago—is to assess the "sociopathoid" element of his temperament, as compared with the kind of thing that we would commonly label "acting out neurotic." Several features of the man's history and attitudes (e.g., "I become bored very easily with almost anything—once I find

7. Reactions, Reflections, Projections

out that I can surmount the challenge") would be consistent with sociopathic features.

Unlike some practitioners, I do not use the terms "psychopathic" or "sociopathic" with primary reference to an objective life history fact of school difficulty or legally adjudicated delinquency and, hence, for me, terms like "psychopathic deviate" are not a "mere wastebasket category" for patients that I don't happen to like or whose life style, social class, etc., differs greatly from my own. What we "Multiphasikers" were likely to call, prior to the advent of Hathaway's code (Hathaway, 1947), the "psychopathic deviate syndrome" and, more often today, by explicit reference to the code, the "49 syndrome," has primarily a personality-pattern meaning, and, second (but by no means unimportantly, for me as clinician) a theory-sketch of the basic temperamental parameters or the psychodynamics. I conceive the "true P_d" as basically (= constitutionally, perhaps genetically) having a deficient anxiety parameter resulting in a quantitatively weakened capacity to acquire aversive controls and, therefore, both adequate superego constraints and anxiety-derivative affiliative hungers (Schachter, 1959; Lykken, 1957; Hare, 1965a,b, 1966; and see footnote 10 in Meehl, 1970a), together with certain genetic "modifier" or "potentiator" factors such as primary narcissism, high energy level, and Sheldon's mesomorphy. The 49 configuration of the MMPI is one of the more valid patterns, whether we rely on the lore of clinical experience or the published research data. It is particularly nice that certain rather indirect phenotypic criteria, where one would theoretically expect the concurrent or predictive validities to be low or moderate, at best, because of their remoteness in the causal chain from the postulated genotypic entity "sociopathoid syndrome," tend to hold up (see, e.g., Cronbach & Meehl, 1955).

So I have a rather complex network of phenotypic and genotypic connections in my head concerning the 49 syndrome, of widely varying degrees and, with systematic validation absent, varying amounts of subjective conviction on my part. The patient's financial situation at the moment is such that he prefers not to enter into any long-term psychological exploration if it can be avoided. For my part, I do not especially enjoy working with persons in whom the sociopathoid element is predominant; nor do I consider myself skilled at it. To my way of thinking as a psychotherapist, it makes a considerable difference whether this man's habitual (and only moderately) excessive beer-drinking is behavior maintained by anxiety-avoidance reinforcement, the preference for "going out with the boys" involving deep seated ambivalence toward his wife, unconscious homoerotic determiners of a preference for male company, and his marked underachievement in his profession, given the fact that he was first in his class as a freshman in law school and in his senior year, having become bored and neither attending class regularly nor studying hard, "dropped to second place" (!), reflects a neurotic work inhibition, fear of success such as achieving commensurate with father (a highly successful and hard-driving attorney), and the like. And the point is that, unlike some clear-cut cases where a well-trained clinician can say of the hard-core sociopathoid personality syndrome, "You have seen one, you have seen them all," this man presents a mixed bag. Thus, for instance, a certain motor restlessness in the interview shown by fooling with his clothing and drumming on the arm of his chair is the kind of thing we see in some sociopaths but also in many persons with a fair amount of free floating anxiety. Nor does his own verbal report as to what the beer does for him illuminate much for us because, without necessarily buying all of Cleckley's "semantic dementia" (Cleckley, 1964), experienced clinicians are familiar with the fact that when sociopathoid types use words like "ashamed," "embarrassed," "anxiety," or "depressed," they do not operate from the same baseline of feeling intensity as normal or neurotic patients do. Point: I want to see the MMPI profile on this individual because neither the history, nor the mental status, nor the four hours of exploration to date tell me some of the things I want to know. And, as usual with clinicians who are fond of a particular diagnostic instrument, I am relying in addition to the research literature, the local lore, and my own clinical experience, on the (much-abused but nevertheless, sometimes unavoidable) "unpublished research" of my own, a twenty-year-old study of file data in which I showed that among the criterion cases diagnosed "psychopathic personality, asocial amoral type" on which MMPI scale P_d was derived, the pure 49 profiles differed significantly—and by an amount large enough to be of clinical importance—from "mixed" profiles with neurotic and psychotic features competing or predominating over the 49 configuration in respect to how clinically psychopathic they were as opposed to psychotic or neurotic ("acting out" being the apparent administrative reason for the psychopathic diagnosis being applied to these more complicated patients). So a "bootstraps" effect had occurred that was capable of manifesting itself even when profile analysis was applied to the original criterion patients, all of whom had the same diagnosis and all of whom had entered into the item analysis on which the derivation of the P_d scale took place.

Second Example: A college freshman referred to me from another campus comes in with presenting complaints of loss of interest in his studies

7. Reactions, Reflections, Projections

(in which he is still doing very well, getting top A's in the courses) and difficulty in concentrating. He also reports hard-to-verbalize feelings that "things do not appear quite real." We have here an extremely bright, overly-protected, hyperintellectual young man without anything clearcut that could be considered psychotic, but with an ominous ring that suggests an early schizophrenia. Anamnesis reveals three relatives on the father's side with rather clear schizoid makeup, two of whom were hospitalized in state mental hospitals; the one who was never hospitalized is a food faddist maiden aunt recluse described by the patient as "not in a hospital, but a real nut who ought to be." The patient, despite a certain interpersonal coolness and flatness, can certainly not be described as showing marked social withdrawal or inappropriate affect. Furthermore, an assessment of his way of relating to me is rendered difficult by his extreme verbal cleverness, sprightly sense of humor, and a youth-subculture that affects verbal cynicism and "objectivity." How I handle this, what I say to the father, what my long-term goals are, and, by no means least important, whether I ask my psychiatrist colleague across the hall to see the patient (with trial of one of the phenothiazines in mind) depends in part on my degree of conviction that he is a schizotype in an early stage of decompensation. The MMPI profile is the classic "gull-wing" type we find in many early and pseudoneurotic schizophrenias, and my diagnostic switches are set accordingly.

Third example: In over a quarter-century as a psychotherapist I had until this year not experienced the clinician's trauma of a patient making a "genuine" suicide attempt. But, as it does to most therapists, it finally has befallen me. The patient had originally come to see me following my successful treatment of his son, for whom the relationship to the father was an important part of the picture. Psychotherapy was a mixture of psychoanalytically oriented handling and, in somewhat larger dosage, rational psychotherapy. A great deal of progress was made, as judged by me, the patient, and his family, from whom I happened to have more than the usual informant inputs. However, a malevolent confluence of happenstances (the character of which is not relevant here but which involves events in the patient's reality-situation, partly vocational and partly family) combined with my taking a month's vacation. I was quite conscious of the extent to which this somewhat lonely widower's having a kind of "artificial fee-based friend" (Schofield, 1964) was important, at least as important as my rational therapeutic maneuvers and considerably more important than my sparse psychodynamic interpretations. When I returned from my vacation the patient was obviously depressed, and used that word to describe himself. On the basis of our previous contacts, and the fact that the patient had managed to get through my protective secretary and my wife to make an appointment somewhat earlier than I had said I would be available, I construed part of the depressive verbalizations as reactions to the interruption of therapy and as a cry for help and "testing" operation. In retrospect, I now believe that this was a mistake, although no doubt there was some element of truth to it. While I was aware that this patient had many years previously been hospitalized with a depression whose quality and depth was unquestionably of psychotic character, and had in fact been treated with EST by his psychiatrist on that occasion, I employed a denial mechanism qua clinician and refused to face the fact that he was now much more severely disturbed than he had ever been in my professional contact with him during the course of a two-year period. The extent of my denial can be indicated by the fact that I did not, when the patient spontaneously reported unremitting headache and severe pain in the neck, both of which can be found in some of the statistical studies of depression severity, and both of which are (in my opinion) while not by any means pathognomonic signs, strong indicators of a psychotically depressed rather than a neurotic or reactive depressed condition, follow through adequately to assess such cardinal signs as amount of insomnia, amount of weight loss, and the like. He did talk about the idea of suicide in an interview, as he also had done (during the same week) with his internist. It passed through my mind to give an MMPI that very afternoon and have a look at the profile, but partly out of consideration for the patient's discomfort and partly due to my own denial mechanisms I did not act on this impulse. Two days later, the patient made what was unquestionably a "genuine" suicide attempt, foiled by an unforeseeable inadvertence. Now the question is not whether straight actuarial MMPI prediction of suicide risk, given the discouraging properties of Bayes' formula (Rosen, 1954; Meehl & Rosen, 1955; Lester, 1970) is a powerful suicide predictor over the general population or even over the general clinical population. The Bayes-denominator subgroup here relevant is admittedly a somewhat fuzzy subpopulation, but we are not in a position of knowing absolutely nothing about its defining properties. It is, roughly speaking, the subpopulation of psychiatric patients currently in psychotherapy for whom the therapist has a baseline of mild and certainly nonpsychotic depression, who begin to show signs of psychotic depression. Application of the MMPI to this assessment problem is mediated by strands in the network that come from different sources, that is, not all presented in a single study. As Lester points out in his excellent review, the MMPI does somewhat better at suicide potential assessment than most psychological tests, but

7. Reactions, Reflections, Projections

still (especially in the light of the Bayes' Theorem consideration mentioned above) leaves much to be desired. In wishing I had administered the MMPI to this patient on that critical afternoon I would have been putting together various kinds of information from different sources, examples of which would be: The excellent clinical assessment scale for depth of depression developed by Beck (1967) correlates .75 with MMPI D-score. Although Dr. Beck himself appears not much interested in the neurotic/psychotic depressed division (at least his book does not emphasize this differential), that doesn't prevent me as another clinician from making use of his MMPI validation data along with my own belief that while depth of depression cannot be identified with the nosological entity "endogenous (usually psychotic) depression," (because affective pain is a dimension that shows overlap between taxonomic entities) nevertheless depth of depression is unquestionably one of the indicators for psychotic over neurotic reactive depression. Thus, for instance, loss of the "humor reflex" is a differential sign, because you can usually make a neurotic or reactive depressed patient, or a patient who has depression associated with some other major diagnostic condition such as schizophrenia, laugh (or at least smile) by telling a sufficiently good joke or recalling some humorous family anecdote, whereas a psychotic depressed patient cannot, in almost 100 percent of the cases in my experience (and psychiatrists with whom I have checked this) be made to laugh. Along with this evidence I put the evidence that psychotic depression is in considerable part a genetically determined disorder which, of course, leaves quite open the psychodynamics of this precipitation in a particular individual at a given time. There is, furthermore, some respectable genetic data to suggest that there exists a nosological entity, "unipolar psychotic depression," which is genetically different from the "down phase" of manic-depressive psychosis—no doubt one of the main reasons why clinical experience and published statistics in the older literature reflect an asymmetry in the incidence of depressed versus manic phases. There is, of course, no reason, unless one is addicted to a vulgar kind of psychodynamicism, for supposing that a person with a neurotic or reactive depression is, by virtue of that being the diagnosis, somehow immunized from the occurrence of a psychotic depression, including one precipitated by an unfortunate confluence of events. I am convinced, in retrospect, that that is what happened to my patient. Of course we know far too little about the interpsychotic affective level of persons prone to psychotic depressive upset, although I myself have a distinct impression that they are frequently, when not bipolar types, given to a kind of "free-floating 'blue,' worrisome pessimistic tone." Now, quite apart from development of suicide prediction scales or the wonders of Bayes' formula in a psychometric context, something can be said here that is mediated by the nosology: Numerous statistical studies in the literature indicate that the suicide risk for patients with a psychotic depression is not merely significantly higher than it is for other kinds of patients (let alone the general population), it is very markedly higher, and high enough so that once we know we are working within a psychiatric population Bayes' formula no longer prevents the nosological information from being predictively useful. The exact frequency of suicide or of what appear to be "sincere, genuine, for-real" suicide attempts varies in different studies; but we know, for instance, that even so-called "recovered" psychotic depressions manage to suicide with an incidence as high as 5 or 6 percent within three years after discharge from a mental hospital. Prior to the introduction of the electroshock therapy, nonhospitalized patients diagnosed involutional melancholia or manic depressed had a successful suicide incidence as high as 1/6 or 1/5 of all patients with that diagnosis! Now this is a figure that is obviously of more than merely academic interest. Had I insisted that my patient take the MMPI before leaving my office that afternoon, and had I then contemplated what would probably have been a 27 curve with $D \geqslant 90$ (I have seen D-scores as high as 120 in psychotically depressed patients) I think I can say with considerable confidence that I would have been psychometrically estopped from my denial mechanisms and practically forced to see this patient as having undergone a "change of quantity into quality" that would have led me to hospitalize him. Admittedly, this is talking about what the test could have done rather than what it did do, but I believe that is a correct account of the situation.

Given my belief that computerized actuarial interpretation is (except perhaps for the most gifted and experienced MMPI-user—and I am not convinced of that) preferable to "clinical eye-balling" of the profile, the best evidence of the test's validity should be found in studies relying on the various "cookbooks" now available. Strangely enough, validation of actuarial descriptions has lagged unduly long behind their construction (for an excellent summary of this situation see Manning, 1971). One thing is clear, that this approach requires huge samples in order to achieve coverage of the profile domain. The application of Marks and Seeman's otherwise excellent atlas in other clinical settings has been shown to leave a disappointingly large proportion of cases "not found," even when considerable relaxation of their multiple criteria for curve "types" is permitted in an effort to increase coverage. It is not even possible on presently published evidence to state a typical figure for cross-validative Q-correlations, distance measures, or hit-

7. Reactions, Reflections, Projections

rates (for either single trait-attributions or taxonomic sortings) attained by these cookbooks. It goes without saying that research of this kind is of the highest priority, especially since ethical issues concerning automated interpretation have arisen.

A difficult problem here is that of the "gross miss," that is, the patient whose profile satisfies the cookbook "rules" for subsumption under one of the listed types, but who is psychologically not the same type at all. The typological approach puts a patient "in" or "out" of a listed profile-class, and the computer is stuck with whatever Q-sort or paragraph of verbal description goes with that class. That the average "validity" of this type's descriptions is good (i.e., fits most patients with that profile) does not allay the practitioner's anxiety about the case before him, and, despite my proactuarial position, I share this feeling as a clinician. One possible approach would be to research the "bad typological misses," attempting to identify a subset of critical traits or symptoms having three properties:

1. The trait or symptom can be assessed from interview and history with high accuracy by most clinicians.
2. The trait or symptom is "pivotal" in the cookbook description, that is,
a. It has a very high or low actuarial placement.
b. It has a small dispersion among the criterion cases with that profile type.
c. Its actuarial placement is discriminative among profile types.
3. As a probable result of properties (1) and (2), but to be researched empirically, marked discrepancies between the clinician's assessment of the item and the cookbook's placement of it are strongly predictive of a low Q-correlation for the total array.

The reasoning (which needs statistical treatment but is plausible enough to warrant expending research effort on the straightforward empirical question) runs: The confidence we have in single item-placements hinges on a postulated profile typology being correctly applied to this single individual. If he doesn't "belong to the type" —if the MMPI has "got him all wrong" —then our confidence is unwarranted. The cookbook says strongly that he should have a lot of traits A, B, and C, and very little of trait D. This trait-pattern is highly characteristic of patients validly typed by the cookbook. But the expected (A, B, C, $\bar{D}$) pattern doesn't fit him clinically at all, and we know that these particular traits are accurately judgable from non-MMPI information. Therefore it is probably safer not to subsume him, and, hence, we will not attribute the cookbook's other trait-positions to him either. I need hardly add that this kind of clinical "stop"-item, should it prove effective, can itself be included in the actuarial recipe.

Despite my conviction that tests like SVIB, MMPI, and CPI, possess, even now, sufficient construct, concurrent, and predictive validity to justify their use (I repeat, relying heavily upon Hathaway's point about the economics—which I think would not justify anything like the near-routine use of low validity but costly projective devices such as Rorschach and TAT), I share with the MMPI's creator a certain skepticism about the situation, and I do think it important for us to ask the question why structured personality tests have not, after all these years of effort by hard working and able psychologists, achieved anything like the validity of intelligence tests, achievement tests, interest tests, tests of special ability, and so forth. Every paper in this volume represents a valuable contribution to that vexed issue. I am unsure that I have anything worthwhile to add, but at Dr. Butcher's insistence, I shall try. Before examining the question "Why are personality tests no better than they are?" I want to reiterate loudly and clearly that I consider it—perhaps scandalously, unaccountably, and in Asch-solitude—still an open question just how "valid" the present instruments could be if optimally used. (For "could be ... optimally" one may, of course, read "are," in the sense of construct validity.) Anyone familiar with my writings on actuarial prediction will be prepared for me to say that they are not, for the most part, used optimally (Meehl 1954a,b, 1956a,b, 1957, 1959b, 1960, 1965, 1967, 1970; Meehl & Dahlstrom, 1960). For that matter, we do not know for sure that the EEG is used optimally (should physicians "eyeball it" or let the computer do a thorough analysis of the Fourier components?). Similarly, some have argued that radiologic interpretation is suboptimal (Kleinmuntz, 1968, 1969; Newell, Chamberlain, & Rigler, 1954; Hoffman, Slovic, & Rorer, 1968; Hoffman, 1968). I am convinced that we are not currently extracting all the blood out of the MMPI psychometric turnip, and I shall make some constructive suggestions (some of which I am carrying out with my colleagues Glueck and Schofield) for estimating the upper limits of blood-from-turnip extractions. Why do I believe this is important? Because in order to decide what to do next (e.g., Should we build a new MMPI or not?) we need to know how well we could do with the present MMPI profile if we were doing the best we could, which we aren't. If the "best job" do-able with MMPI is very bad indeed, the empirical lesson could plausibly be read as, "Structured personality testing (of this general kind) is a blind alley; let's do something else." If the best job is very good indeed—say, "pushes the criterion"—revision from scratch would probably not be worth the trouble merely to eke out another 5

7. Reactions, Reflections, Projections

percent of construct valid variance. So it is worth while excluding these two extreme answers, if we can.

I might distill the essence of what I fear may be so when I am in a "down" phase of my psychometric cyclothymia, in agreement with some of what Dr. Hathaway says in his contribution to this volume, by a quotation from Albert Einstein. During one of the "discouraged" phases among theoretical physicists (I cannot trace the source of this story, so I do not know whether it was concerned with quantum mechanics or relativity), a newspaper science writer asked Einstein, "Professor Einstein, just what is wrong with physics these days?" to which Einstein replied, "It is too hard for the physicists." I have often thought that psychology is much too hard for us psychologists. And it would be intellectually dishonest to continue the present discussion without saying explicitly that I remain open—as I think befits any rational psychologist who doesn't have blinders on his eyes and wax in his ears—on the question, "What are the upper, permanent, intrinsic limitations on the construct validity of personality tests—limits which cannot even theoretically, 'in principle,' be passed because they are limits set by the complexity of the state of nature rather than by considerations of time, money, or the cleverness of psychologists?" Psychologists intoxicated by physics (and frequently not knowing much physics) are sometimes inclined to assume that our science and art is in its largely primitive and low-validity condition just because we came late on the scientific scene. It is, of course, no accident that we came late on the scientific scene; but, leaving that aside, I do not see any persuasive reason for thinking that the science of psychology and its associated art and technique must somehow inevitably converge toward the conceptual beauty, theoretical rigor, and pragmatic power that was attained by classical mechanics. Meteorology is a branch of physics. It does not involve any kind of entities or processes that transcend "physics" as a subject matter. But meteorology is not an exact science, and will never become one. This is not the place to exfoliate my views on the inherent limitations of personology as a science and technic, but I feel obliged to make it clear before proceeding that I think Einstein's remark about physics applies *a fortiori* to the psychometrics of personality.

Einstein's dictum has, to my mind, an encouraging aspect which I would like to stress and which is, perhaps, the main "message" I hope my readers will take from these reflections. The encouraging aspect is that we psychologists who work in applied psychometrics (test construction or validation) and personality assessment generally have tended to think—and we have almost always acted even if we did not officially think—on the presupposition that personality measurement is relatively "easy." And I have a very strong suspicion, amounting to a subjective moral certainty, that this seductive but erroneous notion has been, and continues to be, a large part of our trouble. I predict that psychometric personologists fifty years hence will find our behavior somewhat puzzling, because they will see us as having proceeded with methods and resources that, by their lights in A.D. 2022, will appear pitifully inadequate. More to the point in speaking to our present generation, the 2022 psychometrician will say that we operated with methods that were already discernible on the basis of the present knowledge as being inadequate to our task. Future psychometricians will find our behavior hard to understand, because they will see us as having not done, or even tried to do, "as well as we knew how." A large part of test development and validation proceeds as if things were so that nobody really believes are so. To take one of my favorite methodological examples (Meehl, 1959a,c) the choice that a personologist constructing or "validating" a measuring device commonly faces with limited resources is the unpleasant choice between (1) knowing a lot, in the joint sense of qualitative richness and quantitative mass, about a rather small number of intensively studied individuals (patients, clients, or subjects), and (2) knowing rather little, in the sense of skimpy information of low qualitative richness (as well as low reliability-validity) about a large number of subjects. Now it seems to me blindingly obvious that both of these alternatives must be, for most test construction purposes, viewed as thoroughly unsatisfactory. If I want to make or validate a multivariate testing device for, say, psychiatric outpatient assessment, I need to know a lot about each individual in the sample, and I need to know the reliability of this knowledge, for example, interclinician consensus, since the patient who is judged by Clinician A as being extremely dominant and by Clinician B as extremely submissive, is, whatever he is, probably not in the middle of the population, as Allport pointed out a third of a century ago in his great book on personality (Allport, 1937). Second, whether one has an idiographic or nomothetic methodological bias, one wants to have a large number of individuals studied because of the intrinsically stochastic character of any structured test item. There is little justification, in my opinion, for embarking upon a project in test construction where you can foresee that you will only have a few dozen patients carefully studied by competent clinicians, or where, *per contra*, you are going to have many subjects in your sample but the only "criterion" properties available on them will be superficial ratings by casual acquaintances, sorority sisters, or whatever. (I do not, of course, dispute that some bootstrapping can take place on these unsatisfactory bases; and some of the MMPI scales were perforce not in much better shape than

7. Reactions, Reflections, Projections

this with respect to their initial criteria; but that was in 1937.) Psychology research costs much less than physics or chemistry (or most branches of genetics or medicine). We can make an honest case to fund-granting agencies for a research grant to include as a very sizeable part of its budget provisions money for paying skilled clinical judges at a rate sufficiently in excess of what they make as practitioners per time unit to get adequate cooperation, including tape recordings of interviews that will permit one or more experts to make assessments on the same set of dimensions for purposes of interjudge "reliability" determinations. In our current research on the relationship between MMPI and MHPA variables, we have data which, I suspect, are qualitatively and quantitatively unique—some 800 patients or clients described by their psychotherapists or counselors on the basis of a minimum of 10 hours of interviewing (and ranging up to much more than that), on two very carefully constructed pools of phenotypic and genotypic items, and of course uncontaminated by the patient's MMPI profile (cf. Meehl, Lykken, Schofield, & Tellegen, 1971). But 800 cases is not adequate for the kind of actuarial cookbook construction that seems necessary and feasible. My point is that the time has passed when one can build and validate even a personality scale, let alone a multivariate instrument, on the basis of a few casual judgments concerning a bunch of laboratory volunteers. Even in the clinical setting, as I pointed out in an earlier publication (Meehl, 1959a), there is really little point (except at the crudest initial exploratory phase of inquiring whether a certain instrument or method has enough going for it to be worth investing research time on at all) in "validating" personality tests against the ordinarily available clinical judgments of psychiatrists or psychologists. Why not? Because what we usually want to know is whether the test contributes incremental information or does a more accurate job than the clinical workup routinely available as "criterion." Obviously, you can't answer that question unless you have a kind of workup that goes beyond "what is routinely done." This necessity arises from the fact that in psychology we do not have anything corresponding to the quasi-definitive validation of inferences provided by the pathologist's report—there is no comparable criterion, in most instances, for setting up a "psychological clinicopathological conference." (Meehl, 1973b; Castleman & Dudly, 1960; Castleman & Richardson, 1968).

One reason for the difficulties of psychometric personology, a reason that I did not appreciate adequately in my "dustbowl empiricist" paper of 1945, is the sad state of psychological theory. The superiority of mechanical, actuarial prediction and interpretation arises from several factors, one of which is theoretical inadequacy. The clinician who attempts to mediate predictions or other kinds of inferences, whether from test or history or interview raw data, by utilizing a psychodynamic causal model will, no matter how clever he is, almost never be able to meet the conditions which any undergraduate student of chemistry or physics knows are necessary in order to forecast the subsequent state of a physical system (or to infer to as yet unobserved aspects of its concurrent state) on the basis of scientific theory. In order to mediate predictions (using the word epistemically rather than with a time reference as to the state of nature) by theoretical constructs, one must satisfy two epistemic conditions:

1. One must have a powerful (high-verisimilitude) theory, that is, he must "know" how the system works.

2. One must have reasonably accurate knowledge of the initial and boundary conditions of the system, that is, he must have an accurate measurement technology.

Now it is perfectly obvious that the clinical psychologist, for the most part, does not satisfy either of these two conditions for powerful theory-mediated prediction, whereas it is necessary in making predictions on this basis that one should satisfy both. That this is an obvious limitation, admitted by all competent scholars, gives me continued faith in the general line of empirical-actuarial predictive and interpretative methods—despite my recognition that such a monolithically "criterion-statistical" view on item-analysis as that of my 1945 paper is too strong.

However, skepticism as to the predictive power of current psychological theory relying on current assessment technology does not, unless we conflate issues that are separable, imply that our test development strategy should be completely atheoretical. Those are two different questions, and the answer to one in the present state of knowledge does not give us the answer to the other. I now think that at all stages in personality test development, from initial phase of item pool construction to a late-stage optimized clinical interpretative procedure for the fully developed and "validated" instrument, theory—and by this I mean all sorts of theory, including trait theory, developmental theory, learning theory, psychodynamics, and behavior genetics—should play an important role. In this view I seem to diverge from my mentor Hathaway, whose skepticism about personality theory as a basis (or even as a potentially valuable auxiliary) for personological psychometrics remains, if I read his paper rightly, as strong as it was when he embarked on the construction of the MMPI a third of a century ago. It remains to be seen who is right.

If we were going to make a new MMPI, how might we proceed? All I dare offer is a few suggestions in which I have varying amounts of confidence and which I could defend on varying amounts of presently available evidence.

7. Reactions, Reflections, Projections

I shall bypass completely the important (and, in my view, still unsettled) issues concerning item format, on which the other contributions to this volume show some consensus and some disagreement. The evidence, especially with respect to the much-debated malignant influence of response set, leaves us in doubt. For simplicity of exposition, but I hope not prejudicial to the issues discussed, I am going to consider the case in which the present true/false item format is employed, meanwhile admitting that Professor Loevinger's objections to it may well turn out to carry the day.

One of the first questions that arises in adopting a psychometric strategy involves the dependence of a rational-empirical method upon theory, where I am now inclined to line up with Loevinger against Hathaway. I believe that psychology can no longer afford to adopt psychometric procedures whose methodology proceeds with almost zero reference to what bets it is reasonable to lay upon substantive personological horses. The "theory" may be a relatively impoverished one, and may be only weakly corroborated (Popper, 1959, 1962; Bunge, 1964; Lakatos & Musgrave 1970; Lykken, 1968; Meehl, 1967, 1970), but I think we have to make do with it anyway. An example of a substantive thesis which, while psychologically skimpy, nevertheless does make an ontological wager about the way things are and intends psychometrically to "carve Nature at its joints," is the postulation of a taxonomic rather than a dimensional ("Aristotelian" versus "Galileian") situation for the underlying causal structure. Like Dr. Loevinger, I have been struck by the paradox that Lazarsfeld's latent structure analysis was applied to soldiers' attitudes (presumably a Galileian construct), whereas the MMPI scales, a set of quantitative indicators, were built with psychiatric nosology (presumably taxonomic constructs) as the motivating idea. However, admitting this to be paradoxical *prima facie*, I am not persuaded that the latter case is as incoherent as Dr. Loevinger believes it to be. I do not see anything inherently absurd about employing quantitative fallible indicators for the probabilistic identification of a taxonomic entity, as examples from the genetics of loose syndromes—or, for that matter, the numerous dimensional indicators employed in internal medicine—attest (cf. Meehl, 1972a). If there were any structured test items that behaved as quasi-pathognomonic dichotomous signs—and such signs are extremely rare, even in medicine—it would not be optimal to combine them in a linear scale and simply "add up the points." But unfortunately, there do not seem to be any such quasi-pathognomonic structured test items. However, the test constructor ought to think through whether, when he constructs a "depression" key, he has in view primarily the assessment of degree (depth of depressed mood) cutting across nosological categories, or whether he wants instead to build an instrument that will classify individuals as belonging, say, to the taxon "endogenous psychotic depression, unipolar type," where the aim is one of minimizing classification errors in a two-category population with specified base-rates. In arguing that the investigator should have in mind his preferred substantive views as to the existence of a certain taxonomic entity when proceeding with his psychometric job, I do not deny that the behavior of the test items may itself contribute to the corroboration or falsification of that substantive position.

In this connection it is important to be as clear as we can about the causal meaning of a taxonomic claim which will include a clarification of what I may call the "strong" or "weak" meanings of words like "disease entity," "taxon," or "type." I hope that others are clearer about these distinctions than I am, but I see little evidence of it (see Meehl, 1972a). At the extremes, it is not difficult to make the distinction between something that is really taxonomic and something that is merely an arbitrary cut for some administrative (e.g., legal, educational admission, or employment) purpose. Cutting an intelligence test distribution arbitrarily at a certain IQ for the purpose of adjudicating mental deficiency (along with appropriate non-psychometric social adjustment criteria) is a pretty obvious example of an arbitrary cut that does not purport to reflect any kind of taxonomic situation in the state of nature. Within the mentally defective group, it is generally agreed that there are some individuals scoring below a certain IQ who represent merely the low end of the polygenic distribution of inherited intellectual capacities interacting with varying amounts of environmental deprivation, whereas there are other individuals, especially in the lower mentally deficient bracket (and not, as in the former case, appreciably correlated with social class) who represent Mendelizing genetic syndromes or nongenetic developmental anomalies. The clearest case of a taxonomic situation is that in which the specific etiology is a germ or gene, such as Huntington's Chorea or pulmonary tuberculosis. Let me note in passing that the existence of a dichotomous specific etiological agent, such as a mutation at a certain genetic locus or infection with a certain species of microorganism, does not preclude either (1) important causal contributions by nontaxonomic (dimensional) variables (e.g., polygenic potentiators yielding high family-strain correlations in age of onset of Huntington's disease) nor (2) the necessity to utilize fallible quantitative phenotypic indicators in identifying those persons in whom the specific etiology is present. It is a mistake to assume that if there is a specific etiology that is genuinely dichotomous, we must anticipate nonoverlapping symptomatic indicators. We cannot even be

7. Reactions, Reflections, Projections 153

confident that we will get a clear-cut bimodality. The most methodologically obscure situation, which may unfortunately predominate in personality psychometrics, is one in which identification of types or syndromes is nonarbitrary but not etiologically dichotomous. That is, an appropriate statistical search procedure (there are over 50 such floating around at present, and I heard a score of new ones presented at the 1971 meeting of the Classification Society) would discern "objective" clumps or clusters of individuals in the phenotypic hyperspace; but despite this phenotypic clustering, no qualitative causal factor, comparable to a germ or a gene (see, e.g., Murphy, 1964; Meehl, 1972c), underlies the clustering. Example: Consider the distinction between bridge players and nonbridge players. Restricting ourselves to a single dimension, suppose we construct a simple achievement test measuring verbal knowledge of bridge concepts (rules and "principles," in the sense of tactics and strategies of bidding and playing). A 50-item bridge achievement test would not have to be "taxonomically rigged" in order for it to generate a rather clear bimodality in raw score distribution when administered to a random sample of Americans. Roughly, it is an empirical fact that Americans divide themselves into "bridge players" and "nonbridge players," that is, the bimodality is a real social phenomenon rather than a psychometric artifact or an administrative convenience. Yet no one supposes that a person's belonging to the class of bridge players or nonbridge players reflects presence/absence of a qualitative, dichotomous, etiological agent in the life history, comparable to receiving the Huntington's chorea mutated gene from a parent, or having been invaded by *Mycobacterium tuberculosis*. The category "bridge players" is an environmental mould type (analogous to Cattell's concept of an "environmental mould trait"), and this etiological type is intrinsically fuzzy at the edges, in a way that the genotype for Huntington's chorea is not. The fuzziness involved here is not merely the phenotypic indicator fuzziness, which we can also find in early cases of Huntington's chorea or "subclinical" tuberculosis; it is also a fuzziness at the etiological (latent or historical causal) source. One statistical consequence of this inherent fuzziness in the type as it exists—quite aside from the "fallibility" of our quantitative measure—is that it would be impossible in principle to improve our measure so as to increase the bimodality to the point of nonoverlapping phenotypic distributions. We can conceive of doing this for Huntington's chorea, and, as a matter of fact, the full-blown case would show zero overlap in a quantified multivariate index of choreic movements, dementia, paranoid irritability, etc., with the population of healthy adults. But we could not achieve this (except, perhaps, by some psychometric skulduggery that would wash out on cross-validation) in the case of our bridge achievement score. Because while it is true that the majority of persons found in a random sample of Americans would have come out of environmental moulds (social or family life) which either got them to learning bridge systematically and playing it fairly frequently or in which they never bothered to learn it at all and would receive a (guessing-corrected) score near zero on the scale; nevertheless, intermediate cases representing all degrees of "bridge knowledge" exist, and an unrigged psychometric assessment device would identify persons at all positions on the achievement test dimension. Thus, for example, there would be a few examinees from a nurturing environment where nobody played bridge but who had overheard their grandparents playing whist (the ancestor game, which evolved into auction bridge, which developed into contract bridge). Such persons would obtain achievement test scores slightly higher than chance because they would dimly recall hearing terms like "bid," "trump," and "trick." The problem persists if we try to reduce distribution overlap between the two fuzzy "types," by putting in more items at an intermediate difficulty level and greatly lengthening the test. With a small sample it might appear superficially that we thereby succeeded in generating two nonoverlapping distributions of bridge-knowledge. But with increasing sample size this psychometric achievement of an apparent dichotomy on the continuous indicators would be revealed as illusory, because a minority of Americans could always be found somewhere in the middle, so that every score would be represented by a few persons in any large sample. Example: There would be men who once, having been snowed in with three hunting companions, were dragooned into making a fourth for bridge for a couple of days but who never played the game again. Such individuals would obtain middle region scores in the "valley" between our two distributions. However long we made the test, we could always find persons who would attain any prespecified score at k items out of m. This noncontroversial example shows why the existence of a bimodality on one variable (generalizing: a clearly evident "clump" or "cluster" in a multivariate indicator-space) is not a sufficient condition for inferring a dichotomous etiology (for an interesting discussion of which point see Murphy, 1964). It would be interesting to examine the theoretical bases on which, in the absence of a dichotomous etiology like a germ or a gene, a typological situation nevertheless arises. A general treatment of this question, so far as I know, does not exist. Relevant are Langmuir's concept of "divergent causality" (Langmuir, 1943; London, 1946; Meehl, 1970b, p. 395, and citations thereat; Hoering, 1969) and the theory of stochastic processes (Kemeny,

Snell, & Thompson, 1957) that assures us that two very different "end-states" (e.g., Pulitzer Prize for poetry versus backward state hospital burnt-out schizophrenia) need not reflect a big, systematic factor but the chance outcome of a random walk (cf. Meehl, 1972c; Gottesman & Shields, 1972).

After provisionally adopting a taxonomic or nontaxonomic causal model, the preliminary item pool should be constructed in reliance upon all of the facts and theories bearing upon the test. Even one who advocates a relatively atheoretical "blind empirical criterion keying" (Loevinger is, of course, correct in refusing to confine the honorific term "empirical" to external criterion keying) need not deprive himself of whatever theoretical insight is available at the item-construction stage. I would incline, however, to combine theoretical considerations bearing on item content with a variety of item-finding procedures such as therapy protocols, adjective checklists, and sentence completion responses elicited from large numbers of patients. I now believe (as I did not formerly) that an item ought to make theoretical sense, and without too much *ad hoc* "explaining" of its content and properties. But going in the other direction, I would still argue that if an item has really stable psychometric (internal and external) properties of such-and-such kinds, it is the business of a decent theory to "explain" its possession of those properties in the light of its verbal content. If the theory can't handle such item-facts, it is inadequate to that extent. Presumably, the more such theoretically puzzling items turn up (I repeat, with stable psychometric properties), the more inadequate the theory. Hence, the less trustworthy the theory is for our psychometric purposes, both test construction and construct validation. The theory-oriented psychometrist must pay the usual price in this business, which includes an "item-explaining" task. If he won't accept nontheory-based instruments (because, he alleges, theories are needed to justify using instruments), he should, by the same token, worry about theoretically inexplicable instrumental properties (because good theories are supposed to explain the facts). Point: The argument cuts both ways!

An example, which I am willing to forecast will succeed, of reliance on knowledge from previous "blind empirical criterion keying" plus theory, plus clinical experience—the convergence of the three yielding, one hopes, a higher prior probability of successful item-choice than would be the case were we relying upon only one, or only two, of these bases—would be insertion into the item pool of numerous items whose carefully chosen content is intended to reflect the schizotypal patient's "soft neurology" as subjectively reportable. It is interesting to note that MMPI Scale 8 [= S_c] derived by blind empirical criterion keying (diagnosed schizophrenics, 1937-40 vintage, as against Minnesota standardization normals) turned up a small set of items whose content reflected the patient's awareness of what a neurologist might call "soft neurological signs," to wit:

> I have never been paralyzed or had any unusual weakness of any of my muscles (F).
> I have numbness in one or more regions of my skin (T).
> I have little or no trouble with my muscles twitching or jumping (F).
> I have no difficulty in keeping my balance in walking (F).
> I do not often notice my ears ringing or buzzing (F).
> Once a week or oftener I feel suddenly hot all over, without apparent cause (T).
> My hands have not become clumsy or awkward (F).
> My speech is the same as always (not faster or slower, or slurring; no hoarseness) (F).
> Sometimes my voice leaves me or changes even though I have no cold (T).

I recall that in the late 1940's, after delivering a colloquium lecture at another university (vigorously pressing the atheoretical criterion keying position I then held) I received some criticism on the grounds that those "somatic" items had no business being scored for schizophrenia. At that time, I had no theoretical answer. It is interesting to note that these items do not all appear on the somatizing ("neurotic") scales H_s and H_y, and that, correspondingly, the numerous somatic complaints involving other organ systems (e.g., GI tract) do not tend to show up on Scale 8. In the 1940's, I was either unaware, or had failed to make the connection, that the great nosological systematizer Kraepelin (in his lectures on clinical psychiatry) was given to demonstrating quasi-neurological phenomena found, not with high frequency to be sure, but often enough to be worth noting in a presentation to medical students of schizophrenic symptomatology. Bleuler noted the same thing in his classic *Dementia Praecox: The Group of the Schizophrenias* (1911); and Paul Schilder, who had the rare qualifications of being both a first-class neurologist and a psychoanalyst, said that many psychiatrists, having decided that the patient was schizophrenic and, hence, a "functional" case, did not pay sufficient attention to the occurrence of soft neurology in their schizophrenic patients. I can recall as a graduate student hearing the late Dr. J. C. McKinley (co-author of the MMPI) warn the junior medical students—who had just observed McKinley elicit a rather pronounced dysdiadochokinesia in a schizophrenic patient being presented at grand rounds—that while this was not "characteristic," it did occur often enough so that one should be alert for it

7. Reactions, Reflections, Projections

in schizophrenia and not be misled into concluding that the patient had some sort of cerebellar lesion. In recent years, several investigations, some still unpublished (such as the work of Rosenthal, Nagler, and Kugelnass on children of schizophrenic mothers who are being raised apart from their mothers in Israeli kibbutzim), Barbara Fish (1972, and her papers cited therein), Pollack and Krieger (1958) suggest that Paul Hoch's postulated "integrative neural deficit" in the schizotype may shortly be detectable by suitably refined (= instrumental + quantified + cut-optimized) neurological measures. My own clinical experience over the past 25 years has convinced me that the majority of schizotypal patients, if seen over long time periods, will spontaneously report various kinds of soft neurology (chiefly as "episodes" of diplopia, disturbances of balance, vertigo, gross eye-hand discoordination, spatial disorientation, one-sided tremor, numbness), and that the experienced clinician can elicit them from others by systematic questioning. I have, therefore, been slowly collecting a set of such complaints and observations suitable for framing in the form of a patient's verbal report. Any psychometric job aimed at detection of the compensated schizotype with an MMPI-type test should include items with this content.

Having used the schizotype as an example, I cannot refrain from a cautionary comment about Dr. Norman's (otherwise sound and helpful) contribution, where he permits himself the usual psychologist's dogma that the old Kraepelinian nosological categories are not worth anything. This statement is constantly repeated by psychologists and it is, so far as I am aware, not satisfactorily documented. Contrariwise, a fair-minded reading of the literature should convince Dr. Norman that the prognostic and treatment-selective power of our major nosological rubrics is at least as good as that of any existing "psychodynamic" assessment (by clinical interview) or any existing psychometric device, structured or projective. If Dr. Norman finds that an astounding statement, I herewith challenge him to show the contrary. Neither the Rorschach, nor the MMPI, nor psychodynamic interview assessment has been shown to predict long-term outcome, to forecast what kinds of symptoms a person is likely to be showing five years hence, to select between electroshock and phenothiazines, to indicate suicide risk, etc., with the accuracy achievable through formal diagnoses of "schizophrenia" or "psychotic depression." In fact, not even the usual statement that "psychiatric diagnoses are notoriously unreliable" is adequately supported by the research evidence, provided the reader can distinguish between a half-baked, meaningless study done under preposterous circumstances and the more carefully carried out investigations such as those that are likely to emerge from well-trained and British or continental clinicians. For references and discussion in support of these remarks, which will doubtless shock many of my readers (due to their antinosological undergraduate brainwashing), see the excellent review of this literature in Chapter 5 of Gottesman and Shields (1972) and my epilogue (Meehl, 1972b). Here I must content myself with a single example: Schmidt and Fonda (1956) found an interclinician "reliability" of .95 for the very important dichotomous decision schizophrenia/nonschizophrenia, a coefficient equalling that for a good individual intelligence test, and, let it be emphasized, much better than that of Rorschach interpretations or interview judgments.

Furthermore, statements about the unreliability of psychiatric rubrics are statements about the behavior of clinicians rather than statements about the intrinsic merits of the rubrics. As is well known to anyone familiar with the American tradition, most American psychiatrists and clinical psychologists are not only poorly trained in formal clinical diagnosis, but have been actively brainwashed by the "psychiatric establishment" to believe that it is an enterprise not worth undertaking. It is significant that despite this "dynamic psychiatry" prejudice, one almost never meets a clinical practitioner who is able to refrain from employing the major nosological rubrics—the reason for this being (what very few are willing to admit) that he has no competing set of constructs of comparable summarizing and prognostic power. In order to find out how much there is in favor of a nosological category, one does not, of course, merely "count noses" among a heterogeneous mess of badly designed studies. One takes those studies which are done by clinicians who believe in the meaning of the major categories, which involve adequate clinical exposure to the patient, large numbers of cases, and so forth. The interjudge reliability of a diagnosis of "schizophrenia" (even by American psychiatrists), compares favorably with that of other branches of medicine, and is definitely superior to the interjudge reliability of interpretation of the favorite instruments of American clinical psychology.

Of course the strongest evidence for the meaning of these nosological labels is the genetic evidence. I am surprised that Dr. Norman writes off formal nosology without feeling any obligation to explain the impressive mass of genetic evidence, since if "schizophrenia" and "manic-depression" and "unipolar psychotic depression" are arbitrary, unreliable rubrics without objective reference, the genetic data on concordance present us with some rather remarkable coincidences! Nobody who asks himself whether the existing rubrics "schizophrenia," "manic-depression," or "compulsion neurosis" have a substantive meaning can address himself intelligently to this question

7. Reactions, Reflections, Projections

without a detailed consideration of the genetic data. What the genetic data show, to an unprejudiced mind, is that these entities do have a real existence and are not merely "arbitrary pigeon-holes" (to use the favorite phrase of antitaxonomists) imposed by the clinician.

I may say in passing that psychologists have a tendency to be obsessed with reliability (although I do not attribute this obsession to my ex-student Norman) and an insufficient concern for what might be called the intrinsic or qualitative validity (i.e., before attenuation by unreliability) of a construct or judgment. This is a large and difficult subject, deserving a paper of its own. The "test-retest reliability" (I use the older terminology deliberately to highlight the point) of blood pressure readings is considerably below the figure ($r \geqslant 0.80$) commonly said in traditional psychometrics to be a "minimum value for application to individuals." Interjudge reliabilities of blood pressure readings, while somewhat higher than test-retest, are also unsatisfactory by this standard. On the other hand—to use a nice example I heard thirty years ago in one of Dr. Hathaway's classes—anthropometric measurements yield an extremely high reliability for such physical dimensions as wrist-width. Why is it then, that when you go to your physician for a general checkup or with a specific complaint, he insists upon taking your blood pressure (a measure with reliability of say, .65) and does not measure your wrist width, a measure with a lovely reliability of say, .98? This sounds like a dumb question, but given the way some psychologists think about diagnostic reliability in relation to construct validity, it seems a perfectly sensible question to ask, and everybody knows the answer. The point is that blood pressure has an intrinsic qualitative "validity" (i.e., is an indicator of certain inferred pathological conditions of the organism) so important that we want to measure it even after its net operational validity has been greatly attenuated by unreliability. It is simply more useful clinically to know a patient's blood pressure with a reliability of .65 than it is to know the width of his wrist with a reliability of .98. Nor do we have to depart from the realm of psychometric thinking to understand this. The fact that reliability sets an upper bound on net effective construct validity is not terribly important in practice when we are comparing two such clinical measures because (1) that upper bound is a square root and (2) the variation among indicators in intrinsic (attenuation-corrected) validities ranges over a region well below that upper bound. We are rarely anywhere near pushing the square root of a test-retest or interjudge reliability coefficient with most clinical measures. Consequently, the existence of this theoretical psychometric bound on "net effective (attenuated) construct validity" is rarely of practical importance.

The most important and discouraging thing I have to say may appear grandiose and perfectionistic. I urge reliance on a vast embedding context for such research, to wit, the availability of a complex, multistrand, interlocking multivariate system, a network of "criteria," both positive and negative. This perhaps sounds like the kind of bootless "gathering of a big mess of all kinds of data" that Dr. Loevinger decries, and I suspect I am actually in favor of something rather closer to that than she would think fruitful. (It may be that I am unduly influenced by the "medical model" in thinking along these lines.) However, my main reason for wanting this big mess of diverse data, both clinical and demographic (including interclinician consensus measures), is my growing belief that in scale construction *negative psychometric properties are likely to be as important in item-selection as the usual positive ones.*

As I now think, the "ideal item" in a structured test key ought to possess all of the following delightful properties:

1. Strong correlation exists with an "external criterion" of (accurately estimated and bounded) high construct validity. (Usually this "criterion" will itself be a carefully bootstrapped multivariate composite.)

2. The item's external criterion validity persists, and is only slightly reduced, when each of a long list of known and suspected nuisance variables—better, the whole set collectively when optimally weighted to predict "bad" variance—is held constant.

3. The correlation with each of the nuisance variables is negligible when the external "criterion" is held constant.

4. The item makes content-theoretical sense to a sophisticated theorist, at least *ad hoc* and preferably more than *ad hoc*. In this respect I not only have ceased to push my 1945 position but view it, insofar as it was consistent, as undesirable. An expansion of this point follows in the text *infra*.

5. However, despite (2), what the item "means" or "reveals" psychologically is either,

    (a) Not obvious to the nonsophisticated examinee or, if fairly obvious in its meaning,

    (b) Reports a kind of content that most persons tend to be willing, even eager, to report if they are the kind of person we are trying to detect. Example: In research with Clark and McClosky on political behavior (McClosky, Meehl, & Clark, unpublished) we were frequently surprised that one did not have to worry terribly much about "disguising" the punitive, Pharisaical, legalistic attitudes of certain extreme political types—for the simple reason that persons of this type tend to be

7. Reactions, Reflections, Projections 161

remarkably undefensive about the expression of what to others appear as malignant or absurd opinions.

6. The item's internal-consistency properties are appropriate to the psychometric model that flows from the psychological-causal structure postulated. I do not, alas, know how to say this with less generality, pending resolution of still unsettled psychometric issues. But as an example of what I mean here, once a group of items has been provisionally identified as possessing the external keying, content, and nuisance-independent properties that justify their continued inclusion in the set, I should think that item's factor loadings on the first factor permeating the set would be a legitimate basis for item selection.

7. The item's validity, its systematic invalid components, and its internal-consistency psychometric structural properties are not markedly influenced by moderator variables. (Roughly, the item holds up well not only on straight cross-validation but in the broader sense of validity generalization.)

I am only too well aware that an appropriate response to this list of desiderata is "Well, best of luck—but of course there aren't any such perfect items." I am afraid that will turn out to be true. But I do not think we should abandon the search without a few more years of systematic work within a sufficiently ambitious framework, especially on the nuisance variable and criterion side. Furthermore, there is no harm in adopting this list as a set of idealizations against which the empirical properties of potential items can be compared, with an eye to increasing net effective construct validity beyond where it presently lies.

The requirement in the above set which is most likely to be ignored, because it takes too much trouble on the part of the test builder, is the (joint positive and negative) requirement concerning the influence of numerous nuisance variables, but this requirement is extremely important, perhaps crucial. Ideally, if we have an item which purports to measure, say, "thought-disorder," we want to show that the item discrimination functions remain fairly steep when we move from the unselected (mixed) population to various subpopulations homogeneous with regard to age, sex, religion, education, IQ, race, social class, formal diagnosis, a variety of clinical variables other than thought disorder and all other provisional keys in the multivariate inventory. This requirement is, both as to conceptualization and cost (= time + money + personnel + sample size + quality of clinical judgments) one of the two most important factors—the other being still unresolved puzzles concerning the appropriate psychometric-structural model to mathematicize—in analogizing Einstein's dictum. I am arguing that an empirical showing that an item does not have certain undesirable properties, namely, systematic loadings on nuisance variables, is just as important as an empirical showing that it possesses the desirable properties of criterion discrimination and internal consistency. We must begin routinely to design our test-construction and test-validation research with an eye to negative properties. What makes this such a methodological and logistical pain in the neck is, of course, that the list of undesirable properties is considerably longer than the list of desirable properties! That is to say, given the structure of the human mind (a fact of the world and not a mere weakness of psychometric method or theory), during the course of scale-construction we may have to spend more time, money, brains, and energy measuring things we do not want the item to reflect, than we do measuring things we do want it to reflect. I put it perhaps more strongly than I fully intend, but I want to be sure to get the message across about this positive-negative property paradox.

One of the respects in which we have traditionally thought that (or at least acted as if) test construction was easier than could plausibly be supposed is in our easy, nonparametrized assumption that if an item "discriminates" then it should go into the key. Even before Campbell and Fiske (1959) developed the beautiful argument in their classic paper "Convergent and Discriminant Validation by the Multitrait-Multimethod Matrix," varying theoretical recognition of the importance of ruling out heavy nuisance contributions was combined with varying amounts of implementation in the practice of item-building, key construction, and validation. I am, of course, not suggesting that everybody up until the 1950's was naive about this. But I am insisting that few of us had a sufficiently acute awareness of its quantitative impact, and that none of us (can the reader come up with any exceptions?) came anywhere near employing the effort and technology required to take adequate account of it. But there were some admirable efforts made. Example: In constructing their test for three kinds of introversion (social, emotional, and thinking) Evans and McConnell (1941) combined their theoretical interpretation of previous research on the components of introversion-extraversion with face-valid item content and internal consistency, and with negligible external criterion keying at first publication, to build a rather interesting psychometric instrument. And, if I recall correctly, an important phase in that construction was the elimination of an item from any of the three introversion keys if the item showed a significant biserial correlation with either of the other two introversion keys. Example: Even Hathaway and McKinley, in the late 1930's, despite their acceptance of the SVIB tradition of (remarkably successful) "blind empirical criterion keying," departed from it on occasion, although these departures are mainly known through local

7. Reactions, Reflections, Projections

lore, being only faintly and passingly mentioned in most of the early MMPI literature. In the development of the Hysteria scale, for instance, it was noted (a finding subsequently corroborated by Meehl, 1945b and by Meehl & Hathaway, 1946) that the Hy nonsomatic items—partly (but not wholly) the so-called "subtle" or "0" items—tended to be scored not only by the diagnosed "criterion" cases of conversion hysteria, who were, by and large, middle and lower class patients both by virtue of their appearance in a charity clinic and by virtue of their diagnosis, but that college and precollege students also tended to respond in the "hysteroid" direction. Not knowing exactly what to make of this demographic correlation, but realizing that hysteria was not clinically characteristic of more intelligent and educated persons (a statistical finding that went back as far as World War I), and yet not wishing to eliminate what might be called the "characterological" or "defense-mechanism" component of the proposed hysteria key, Hathaway and McKinley compromised by using some of the "0" items that discriminated conversion hysterics but not all of them, giving preference to those that showed a somewhat lesser degree of demographic nuisance-variable correlation (and, maybe, a smidgeon of "theoretical" difference?). I don't mean to say that this was or was not the right thing to do; that is not the point here. The point is that they did it despite their over-all emphasis on pure criterion empirical keying. It would be rather hard to say today whether or not that was a good maneuver, since the Hy-0 items are theoretically interpretable and do reflect one component that enters the hysterical potential, namely, the use of repressive-denying-dissociative defense techniques; and, as Freud pointed out a long time before anybody started building personality inventories, this hysterical character structure contributes but does not suffice to produce conversion hysteria as a clinical syndrome, in the absence of another factor Freud called (constitutional?) somatic compliance. Furthermore, it is still not clear to what extent the "defensive" components found in keys like Hy-0 and K ought to be viewed as "healthy" and "unhealthy." Neither clinical evidence nor psychodynamic theory can tell us yet to what extent it is desirable for an individual to have unlimited access to painful truths about his own mind and about the external world (cf. Ibsen, *The Wild Duck*). "Failure of defense" is a complicated notion, as is "successful defense." What appears in some as a manifestation of defensiveness (K) or outright lying (L) seems to appear in other individuals as a characterological rigidity that is, however, not associated with clinical pathology or social maladaptation, and in still other individuals as a form of healthy-mindedness that is a "defense-mechanism" only in the technical (and artificial) sense that every automatized id-handling technique which gives rise to aim-inhibited derivatives, or any perceptual gate or filter that buffers harsh reality-inputs, is strictly speaking, a "defense." Example: Many psychologists, even including some habitual MMPI users, are unaware of the quiet transition (sometime in the early 1940's) between the first published form of the hypochondriasis scale and the one that is now scored. The old hypochondriasis scale was $(H - C_H)$ and made the first MMPI use of a suppressor key. (The suppressor of key D was not obvious to the uncurious user because the suppressor items were themselves included, scored backward, on the scoring template.) The reason for introducing this suppressor key C_H was Hathaway and McKinley's early finding that when they applied this original raw scale H to miscellaneous psychiatric patients, a sizable number who were not diagnosed in the chart as "hypochondriasis," or even as "symptomatically hypochondriacal," obtained elevated scores, often as elevated as patients for whom hypochondriasis was the formal nosological label. There was also a problem with college students, and the authors specifically mention having excluded some items on that basis.

> In a few of these items, percentage of occurrence of the college group equaled or exceeded that of the hypochondriacal group, though both were significantly different from the adult normals. Such items were deleted on the basis of no differentiations between college students and hypochondriacal individuals. Where differences appeared to be obviously on such bases as marital status, or attitudes towards one's children, the items were excluded on the grounds that they did not apply generally in the population. Through similar reasoning a few more items were rejected on inspection of the list. [Sic!]

Minnesota lore has it, although it is not stated in the original article, that the biggest source of this undesired "nuisance variable validity" was patients who were labelled as schizophrenic. The desirability of having multiple positive and negative "criteria" is indicated already by the introduction of the "correction key," C_H. I put the word "criteria" in quotes not ironically but to emphasize that, from my construct-validity standpoint, almost every criterion is only a quasicriterion from a sophisticated standpoint—except in those very rare instances in which we are literally concerned with a simple straightforward forecasting job, such as predicting whether somebody will or will not wash out of flight training, or how many pounds of butter he will pack per hour. The authors write,

> The preliminary score (H score) as above determined was obtained on all the hospitalized psychiatric cases to whom the complete schedule had been administered. As one would expect on clinical grounds, many cases of frank psychosis (depression, for example) obtained high hypochondriacal scores. Contrary to expectation, however, a fair number of cases obtained high scores although the psychiatric staff had failed to elicit adequate evidence for the presence of hypochondriasis. On this basis, a correction scale seemed indicated and the following approach was undertaken for its construction.

7. Reactions, Reflections, Projections

It is pretty difficult to interpret the scale C_H by inspection of its item content, although one notes especially some rather serious psychotic-like complaints such as "People say insulting and vulgar things about me," and there is quite a bit of schizoid-like content which is reflected in item overlap with Scale 8. McKinley and Hathaway recognized the likelihood that getting a "corrected" $(H - C_H)$ score at a given point on the distribution in two different ways is hardly likely to reflect identical psychology on the part of two examinees, and they write:

> Although we do not hold that two persons are alike whose final $H - C_H$ scores are both 20, the one with $H = 20$ and $C_H = 0$, the other with $H = 40$ and $C_H = 20$ we have been unable to disclose any difference between them related to hypochondriasis.

No further speculation or empirical research on the psychological nature of the hypochondriasis correction keys C_H was undertaken until 1945. In my doctoral dissertation research, commencing with a search for a psychiatric "normalizing" or "control" factor, but shifting (on the basis of my data) to a conceptualization almost wholly in terms of test-taking attitudes—a swing which subsequent research showed to have been overdone, since the truth of the matter seems to lie somewhere between these two interpretations— I had derived a "control" scale. It was labelled N (= normality) being derived on the records of persons in the normal Minnesota population whose profiles had significant elevations on the neurotic triad and who were matched individually by age, sex, and, as closely as could be found by going through nearly 400 records, the profile of a patient whose psychiatric decompensation had been sufficient to bring him into the University of Minnesota Hospital psychiatric service. I found to my surprise that the N-scale correlated with the old C_H (already discarded by that time) almost as strongly as the reliabilities would permit (0.79 in the male normals, 0.78 in the female normals, 0.82 in the male abnormals, and 0.78 in female abnormals). What to make of such a thing? It is noteworthy that in Table 13 of my doctoral dissertation (Meehl, 1945b, p. 44) the correlations of N with clinical scale S_c are 0.71, 0.72, 0.74, and 0.69, and with clinical scale P_t (built partly on internal consistency grounds) they run in the low .80's. In subsequent work on test-taking attitudes, developing out of my thesis research and some valuable unpublished studies by Howard Hunt of experimental manipulation of "fake" (good or bad) instructions, Hathaway and I pursued the construct further in research that led to the introduction of routine "K-correction" on clinical scales H_s, P_d, P_t, S_c and M_a. The suppressor scale L_6, immediate predecessor of the finally adopted suppressor scale K, was derived by studying responses of clinically abnormal patients with normal profiles rather than, as in the case of scale N, by the study of records of normal persons with deviant profiles. But we found that L_6 turned out to be relatively effective in discriminating experimentally manipulated fake-good and fake-bad records produced by "normals" (college students). The most interesting and hard to interpret finding about K was its extremely high correlations with several other variables derived in a variety of ways, including the hypochondriasis correction scale C_H (see Table 2 of Meehl and Hathaway, 1946). Factor analysis of a six-variable matrix including scale K, +, G, N, C_H and Hy-S (mostly "subtle" items scored "0" on the hysteria key template) showed that one common factor sufficed to account for all these intercorrelations, the factor we christened *"K."* The remarkably large intercorrelations among the suppressor keys and "test attitude" keys derived in such diverse ways were not appreciably due to item overlap (see Table 3 of Meehl and Hathaway, 1946). As is well known, subsequent research has rendered it doubtful whether we should have emphasized so strongly the purely psychometric error features (that is, "test-taking" attitudes) in our interpretation of the K factor. I gather, although I am no expert on the latest state of this literature, that it still remains ambiguous to what extent the K factor should be given an important personological significance in its own right. It seems to be related to certain aspects of ego strength, an adequate defensive system, and a reasonably secure self-concept (even if perhaps the price is some amount of "healthy self-deception"). This component is actually somewhat closer to the interesting "control factor" which I was initially searching for in my Ph.D thesis work but abandoned too easily in favor of a nearly exclusive emphasis on what shortly became widely researched under the rubric "response set."

My point in this brief and selective sketch of an important sector in MMPI history is that there were several choice-points, whether of research direction ("What to try next?"), item rejection, competing scale selection, and, perhaps most importantly, psychological interpretation, at which we were choosing options upon evidence that, in the light of subsequent developments, must be considered grossly inadequate in both quality and quantity. I will not delineate all of the choice points, which will be evident to the reader on the basis of the above, but let me give a couple of obvious and important examples: Discussing the correction scale C_H for the original hypochondriasis key H in relation to "false (test-) positives," McKinley and Hathaway do mention the clinical presence of considerable hypochondriasis in many patients not formally so diagnosed. That is to say, some false positives are only pseudo-false-positives! As is well known, hypochondrical concerns are extremely common in psychotic depressions, especially those of the involutional period, and they are also part of the clinical picture in many schizo-

7. Reactions, Reflections, Projections

phrenics—so much so that the old "Magnan sequence" for the development of what was then called simply paranoia (many of these patients being what we would now call "paranoid schizophrenia" of a relatively more intact variety) had the textbook course: Hypochondriacal phase → phase of ideas of reference → phase of persecutory delusions → phase of grandiose delusions → phase of dementia. While nobody today believes in the strict Magnan sequence, any experienced clinician can easily understand why Magnan came to formulate such an "ideal type." (I believe most of the idealized syndromes and sequences of the old nosologists are like this. You don't buy the exact "standard pattern" described—but unless you have wax in your ears and blinders on your eyes, clinical experience shows you why they did.) Clinical experience discloses an important component of somatic concern in the prepsychotic history of a sizeable fraction—well over half, I think—of our paranoid schizophrenic patients. And I venture to suggest, on the basis of my experience as a psychotherapist, that there is almost no case of developing schizophrenia in whom at least some degree of hypochondriacal thought, behavior, or feeling is totally absent, if it only takes the form of a short-term episode of food faddism, or drinking 20 glasses of water daily "to flush my kidneys out," or some such minor manifestation. (In my practice I have never come across far-out food fads in physically healthy individuals without becoming aware of other evidence of a schizophrenic process. I daresay there are such, but I have yet to see one.) One main difficulty that was probably responsible for the necessity to develop the hypochondriasis correction subkey C_H (and here Dr. Norman's strictures upon diagnosis have, I suspect, considerable validity) was the presence of a nonnegligible subset of mild or early schizophrenias in the criterion group officially labelled "hypochondriasis" by the University of Minnesota Hospital staff in the period 1937-1940.[I remind the reader that Hoch and Polatin's classic paper on pseudoneurotic schizophrenia was not yet published (Hoch & Polatin, 1949), nor was Eisenstein's on borderline states (Eisenstein, 1951) and—*mirabile dictu!*—Bleuler's 1911 classic was still untranslated.] Nobody knows how big this group was, but it was surely a sizeable minority; it could conceivably have been a majority. I find that many American clinicians are unaware of the great Eugen Bleuler's view that almost all patients presenting textbook hypochondriasis as their clinical syndrome are in fact cases of schizophrenia. Although Bleuler's definitive work on dementia praecox was not translated into English until 1950, the stronger statement on his part can be found in his *Textbook of Psychiatry* (1924).

This is not the place to enter into a disquisition on that question, although I will permit myself some observations that I find illuminating and highly relevant to the construct validity problem. Many so-called hypochondriacs do present a pattern of characterological factures that differentiate them from either psychosomatic (psychophysiological, respondent-based) "organ neuroses" or the histrionic, manipulative (operant-based) striped-muscle somatic conversions of the (rare) hysteric—features which collectively remind one of schizophrenia. It has, for instance, been long recognized that the "pure, chronic hypochondriac" has a malignant prognosis, with or without psychotherapy, that part of the reason for this dim outlook is his failure to develop adequate rapport and transference to the psychotherapist, that his general life style commonly involves a massive, diffuse, and rigid withdrawal from normal social, sexual, vocational, and avocational life typically rationalized in terms of his "illness," that even though he does not have florid paranoid delusions, the "paranoid flavor" (including a good deal of hostility to professional helpers generically, especially physicians) is almost always in evidence—many of these people are "injustice-collectors"—and unlike most hysterias and psychophysiological neurotics, these people typically look ill, so that the medical student may find it hard to believe that there isn't something organically wrong with them. Furthermore, a fixed irrational conviction that one has an organic disease, completely resistive to modification by medical evidence and assurance from a long string of competent diagnosticians, has a reality-distorting quality that is quasi-delusional, does it not? If I am firmly convinced that I have syphilis or cancer or "some terrible disease that the doctors can't find," and no amount of medical reassurance can shake this conviction, it is hard to see, philosophically speaking, why such a belief should not be considered "delusional." Such a fixed false belief is *prima facie*, in the same broad category of ego-malfunction, a failure of reality testing, as is, say, a delusion that the Jesuits are plotting against me or that I have invented a perpetual motion machine. Whereas in ordinary psychiatric practice, at least in the United States, fixed false ideas about one's own bodily health are not typically classed as delusional unless (1) they occur in a syndrome context with other corroborating evidences of psychotic distortion or gross loss of control, or (2) the content is, as we say, "bizarre," which means (roughly) that the false belief about one's bodily state is not only false but is somehow outlandish or absurd. People do get cancer and syphilis, and people do suffer from mysterious organic diseases that physicians sometimes fail to diagnose or treat successfully, but it just happens that this particular hypochondriacal patient is wrong about this hypothesis in his own case, whereas people do not ever have empty insides, or a glass liver, or a little mill wheel turning in their heads.

Let us suppose, for the sake of argument, that there is a subgroup of psycho-neurotic patients who are not schizotypal and whose neurosis is

7. Reactions, Reflections, Projections

hypochondriacal (rather than conversion hysterical or "organically psychosomatic"). This subset of patients was not adequately separated from the others in the original H scale construction, and the point is that only by use of a quantitatively expensive and qualitatively superior set of multiple positive and negative criteria for item analysis could the necessity for a correction key like C_H have been avoided, if at all. Subsequently, of course, it was avoided by eliminating those items from the original scale H that were contributing the undesired score elevations in "nonhypochondriacal" individuals. The relevant distinctions involved in cleaning this up include a congeries of clinical criteria such as (to mention only a few of them): a distinction between somatic concern and psychosomatic phenomena; a distinction between each of these and conversion phenomena; a distinction between hypochondriacal delusions and free-floating concern about one's health; a distinction between neurotic hypochondriasis as a syndrome and Hoch-Polatin schizotypal pseudoneuroses with predominantly hypochondriacal concern as presenting complaints; and a distinction between hypochondriacal concern and reaction to organic disease (which was, as the original papers and subsequent research indicate, fairly well achieved by the methods used). Of course I am again open to the objection that if all these nuisance variables and clinical distinctions had been studied in the item analysis, there wouldn't have been enough items to make a scale! That may be and, if true, suggests that the enterprise is just not feasible. My point is that in order to find out whether it is feasible and, if so, to carry it out properly, it is necessary to have available a rich network of nonpsychometric and other psychometric dimensions available on one and the same group of carefully studied patients.

An important consideration with respect to nuisance variables that is easily forgotten in the pure criterion keying tradition is the possibility (I should say likelihood) of numerous items ending up on a scoring key for psychometrically bad reasons. Ideally, we would like an item to reflect as "directly as possible" the psychological factor after which the scale is named. We would like the item, so to speak, to be relatively close in the causal chain to some feature of the patients' phenomenology (or impulse, or defensive structure, or fantasy themes, or whatever) whose "psychological nature" is what gives the test score its interpretative name. Now one difficulty with an unqualified blind criterion keying is that it does not provide even a weak guarantee—unless done in a context of multiple exclusionary criteria along with the positive one—that it is "causally close" to the psychological variable of interest. Example: MMPI scale 4(P_d = psychopathic deviate) is one of the better validated clinical keys; when its elevation is found together with an elevated 9 (M_a = Hypomania) and a relative absence of either neurotic or psychotic elevations—especially with a normal or supernormal pattern on the "neurotic triad"—it is a pretty powerful identifier of the broadly "sociopathoid" type. But every clinician experienced with the MMPI has learned that, taking the P_d scale alone, there are some important clinical differentiations which we would like to make better than we can, one of them being the distinction between a young psychopathic deviate of the "hard core variety" (I think myself that these make up less than half of the patients officially labeled "sociopathic personality," but that is another matter) and a neurotically conflicted young adult or teenager—particularly one embroiled in an identity crisis involving rebellion against rejective, authoritarian, straight-laced parents. Looking at these two sorts of individuals superficially, where we note a kind of "chip-on-the-shoulder" attitude and an objective life history documentation showing that the person has gotten into trouble with the school system, or with the law, or with other authority figures, it would be helpful if the MMPI were a sharper instrument than it is for telling them apart. Unfortunately, one can achieve a moderate and sometimes rather high elevation on Scale 4 without being a sociopath—not surprising when we look at the items scored for this variable. Life-history type admissions about family strife, school disciplinary problems, getting in trouble with the law, "social alienation," and the like are characteristic of sociopaths, and that is why such item content shows up on Scale 4 as a result of pure external criterion keying; but they are, alas, also found in nonsociopathic "acting-out neurotic" teenagers with family trouble. Items like "In school I was sometimes sent to the principal for cutting up," "There is very little love and companionship in my family as compared with other homes," "My parents have often objected to the kind of people I went around with," "My parents and family find more fault with me than they should," if answered honestly and with accurate recall, are reflective of the social facts of family strife or legal delinquency. Now these two kinds of facts, while they can follow causally from the basic dispositions of sociopathy, can follow also from nonsociopathic acting out of neurotic, family conflict, or identity crisis teenage problems. There is nothing in the item content, and nothing plausible about the psychodynamics of answering the item honestly or not, that would lead us to expect any of such items to discriminate the sociopathic from the nonsociopathic delinquent teenager or young adult. At an increment of two or three T-score points per raw score item shift, it takes less than ten items in the combined areas of family strife and "institution troubles" to achieve a T-score at $T = 70$. We all recognize today that this kind of thing happens, and is one source of error which we attempt to "correct for" mentally by taking the patient's situation into account as well as looking at the rest of his profile. But it would be nicer

7. Reactions, Reflections, Projections

if such error were eliminated from the P_d key entirely. As a factor analyst once complained to me during a heated discussion on criterion keying, internal consistency, scale "purity," and related topics, "If you Minnesotans are going to eyeball the profile and do a subjective factor analysis in your head that way, why not let the computer do it better, at the stage of key construction?" Not an easy argument to answer.

Matters get more complicated when an item reflects a nuisance variable that is not even a link, however remote, in the causal chain leading from the dimension of interest to the verbal response, but is merely a statistical correlate (in our society) of that dimension. I don't know how many items are like this, but I am pretty sure that some of them are. We know that there are class, age, and race differences on scales and on individual items. Consider, for example, an item that reflects some aspect of "social fear," a kind of lack of self-confidence in interpersonal relations that can be generated (1) by schizoidia, (2) by "garden-variety social introversion," and, for reasons not entirely clear but presumably related to authoritarian child-rearing practices and to the status-hierarchy ethos of our society, (3) by being "lower class" in social origin. [See, for instance, the item content of MMPI Scale S_t (= Social Status), Gough, 1948; see also Gough, McClosky & Meehl, 1951, 1952.] Accept, for the moment, the evidence, fairly good although in some dispute, for a higher incidence of schizophrenia in the lower classes. Accept further my speculation that "garden-variety social introversion"—probably largely a polygenic trait orthogonal to schizoidia (see, e.g., Gottesman, 1963; Scarr, 1969)—is one of the potentiators of clinical schizophrenia among some schizotypes. Then when we do an item analysis contrasting schizophrenics with normals, the item shows up as a fairly strong statistical discriminator on one or more of these three grounds, most often on all three. That is, the item reflects schizoidia, it reflects nonschizoid social introversion (because high values of the latter have raised the probability that a schizotype will decompensate clinically and thus show up in a criterion group of diagnosed schizophrenias, Meehl, 1962, 1964), and, finally, unless I control for it as one of the standard nuisance variables in a huge criterion network as proposed above, because it is directly correlated with lower class membership, psychopathology aside. Suppose we put into a scoring key all of the items that show as low as a 20 percent or even 15 percent difference between the standardization normals and the diagnosed schizophrenic group. (We probably should avoid these weak discriminators, see argument *infra*, but we typically do not.) It could easily happen that only a portion of even that 15-20 percentage difference is schizo-specific, the rest reflecting nonschizoid introversion and the nuisance variable correlates of social class. There is nothing about traditional item analytic procedures—unless we are lucky enough to get items that show whopping differences between the two groups, differences so large that we could almost use the items as the physician uses quasi-pathognomonic signs (instead of combining them additively into a psychometric "key")—that assures us that because an item "discriminates the criterion," therefore it is more heavily loaded with the criterion than it is with something else. This is one of the straight statistical difficulties with blind empirical criterion keying that I failed to recognize in 1945. Unless I am mistaken, it is really a very simple point: That an item discriminates a criterion "significantly" does not tell us whether it might be discriminating something else even more. And if it happens further that the criterion of interest is correlated with a variable that runs through a whole batch of items, it is possible statistically that I should construct a key which, while admittedly "valid for the criterion," is even more valid for some nuisance variable that got dragged along in the process. While one cannot confidently exclude the whole (unknown) class of such potential nuisance variables in a utopian fashion, the longer the list of such nuisance variables we have available in the stage of scale building (for "negative property" analysis) the better chance we have of ruling out this untoward result. It would be interesting for someone to work out, analytically or by Monte Carlo methods, given plausible assumptions about the factorial composition of typical structured personality test items, how large a percent difference between the original criterion groups (using samples so large that sheer random sampling fluctuation plays a minor role in psychometric instability) will have to obtain "on the average" before we can have reasonable assurance that the item thus identified can be expected to have a higher loading with the factor of interest than it does with any other single uncorrelated (or low correlated) factor that we do not wish to measure.

In this connection, it is worth mentioning—because, although it is something we all officially know, we find it easy to forget in practice—there is no mathematical justification for assuming that every item that "differentiates" should be added to a key when, as is customary, the key is based on unit weights and does not attempt to take account of item intercorrelation. It is, of course, easy for an item to contribute more to the intragroup variance (by virtue of its distribution of covariances with other items, see Kuder-Richardson formulas) than it does to the separation of the group means. This is another matter that ought to be looked into more thoroughly by both analytic and Monte Carlo methods than has been done as yet. If I may commit the minor sin of relying upon an unpublished study (which, so far as I know, had nothing wrong with it) I may mention an empirical investigation carried out by Dr. Grant Dahlstrom and myself some 25 years ago in the

7. Reactions, Reflections, Projections

discrimination of psychotic from neurotic patients. Confining ourselves to MMPI items that showed statistically significant differences ($p < .01$) between the two groups, we then set aside the significance test itself and simply arranged all of the discriminating items in the order of their absolute percent differences between the two groups. Dividing them into six blocks of ten items each, we thereby generated six progressively longer keys, each of which contained the preceding blocks of items and which were longer keys by virtue of including progressively "weaker" (while still significantly discriminative) items. Plotting several measures of discrimination against key length, we found that on the criterion cases the success of discrimination, while decelerated in form, continued to rise and was still rising slowly when we reached the longest (60-item) key. However, upon cross-validation we found, to our surprise, the curves of discrimination-efficiency peaked at somewhere between a scale length of 15-20 items, that is, the progressively weaker items in the next four blocks had the effect of reducing group differentiation in the cross-validation sample. Similar results may have been reported in the literature, but it is important to look into this question thoroughly.

If measures of the collection of external and intratest nuisance variables are not readily available, and the test builder is determined to do his best without them, then situations in which he is unable to understand the item's apparent discriminating property even after the fact and in the light of the relations between its psychological content and that of other "mysterious" items that show up in the item analysis, should give him pause. An item which does not "make psychological sense" under these unhappy circumstances is presumably more likely to be manifesting psychometric validity via its loading with some correlated nuisance variable than one which a skilled clinical interpreter can understand once he puts his mind to it. If the sample sizes are such (= usual = less than gigantic) that we can be statistically confident before the fact that at least some items from a large heterogenous item pool will pop up as "upward" sampling fluctuations (when this random component is added to a small-to-moderate valid discrimination of the factor of interest), then psychologically uninterpretable items become further suspect. The research literature on the MMPI provides some probable examples of this in regard to "subtle" or "nonpathological" items that do not hold up well on cross-validation or validity generalization. But I would armchair this argument even without such data, the reasoning being so straightforward: "Given that some items from a large candidate pool will appear to discriminate because of upward sampling fluctuations and nuisance variable loadings, it's a reasonable bet that the psychologically uninterpretable ones are, on the average, more often of that kind." But one must not be overly fussy about what constitutes an acceptable "explanation" in this strategy of test-construction. Allport's famous horrible example (scoring response "green" to stimulus "grass" for variable *loyalty to the gang*) has always seemed to me badly chosen for his purpose. It would not distress me much because a kind of conformity-conventionality flavor provides a quite plausible linkage.

With regard to my listing of condition (6) internal consistency as a desirable item property, I have neither the time, the space, nor the mathematical competence in recent developments of psychometric models to enter into that in technical detail. I confine myself to three observations. First, it seems to me that we ought to feel under a continual burden to relate the formalism of those psychometric models that generate search techniques and scale constructing methods to one or more plausible causal "models of the mind." Dr. Hathaway thinks this is premature—or perhaps I should read him as saying it is permanently impossible? Recognizing the arguments in favor of his pessimistic position, I prefer, perhaps foolishly, to bet on the other horse. Second, it no longer seems sensible to me to oppose internal consistency approaches to empirical criterion keying approaches, especially in the light of what I have said above about the necessity of having available an extended and qualitatively "good" network of interlocking "negative criterion" and other psychometric variables, even when we aim to measure only a single important clinical dimension. The existence of these multiple criteria, especially for purposes of ascertaining whether an item has the desired negative (nondiscriminating) properties, would imply, it seems to me, that the postulated casual model giving rise to our choice of psychometric method should be empirically interlocked with this set of available criteria in the process of scale construction. Third, in the development of new statistics appropriate to various causal-psychometric mind models, I would deemphasize the traditional Fisherian insistence on analytic derivation of exact studentized random sampling distributions in favor of an emphasis upon search for relatively stable item-parameters, even if their sampling fluctuations have to be handled by a combination of Monte Carlo and huge-sample approaches. I think this is particularly true in the case of taxonomic problems, on the following line of reasoning (suggested by remarks of a mathematical statistician whose name I unfortunately cannot recall, at the 1970 meeting of the Classification Society): In most taxonomic-typological problems, the multivariate complexity is such that we are unable to generate studentized random sampling distributions analytically without making extremely strong assumptions in the formalism. But when we make such strong assumptions, we know in advance that the state of nature ("how the psyche is organized") will not

7. Reactions, Reflections, Projections

satisfy the mathematical idealization. Consequently, when we rely upon this idealization in our psychometric technology, we are immediately confronted with the problem of robustness. But, even for less strong models, it will usually turn out that no rigorous analytical solution of the robustness problem is possible, either because no exact solutions exist or because our mathematical ingenuity is insufficient to derive them. Hence our examination of the robustness question has to be done by Monte Carlo methods. But if we can foresee that we will eventually have recourse to the Monte Carlo method, we might as well utilize the computer for this purpose in the first place, bypassing tedious manipulation of equations in the (possibly vain) effort to generate exact studentized sampling distributions.

In general, I believe it is far more important to have fairly stable point-estimates of an item-parameter in a huge sample, along with a distribution of such point-estimates for groups of patients sharing a certain criterion property (whether taxomic or dimensional) but differing on an extended set of nuisance variables, than it is to have an "exact significance test." [Ask a physicist, chemist, or geneticist which he would prefer to know: that a theoretical parameter has (approximately) such-and-such value, or that the conditional probability of observing a stated difference between two estimates would be exactly so-and-so, if the parameters did not differ. I have not met any physical or biological scientist yet who would prefer to have the second kind of information (see Hogben, 1957).] Of course this methodological advice is almost pointless since if the N is gigantic we are not worrying about statistical significance anyway. Example: In my own current research on the compensated schizotype, I am aiming for a "criterion sample" of at least 2000 male and 2000 female schizotypes (and around 10,000 psychiatric patients altogether), partly because I want an N large enough to tell me within a few percentage points what the item difficulty level is but, more importantly, because I want to be able to look at the spread of an item's percentages over the various subdivisions within the schizotypal group, with an eye to eliminating those items that are too closely tied to a particular clinical aspect (e.g., predominance of catatonic over paranoid symptoms, or whether the patient is an inpatient or sufficiently compensated socially and economically to have been seen in the outpatient service). But I am not going to eliminate an item on the ground that it "discriminates significantly" among the diagnostic subtypes because I am confident that if my N were, say, 10,000 diagnosed schizotypes, every single item in the MMPI pool would show a "statistically significance difference" over these subtypes of that diagnosis (see Lykken, 1968; Meehl, 1967a; Morrison & Henkel, 1970). I am, therefore, prepared to settle for items that show the least obtainable dispersion of percentages over the clinical subtypes. The smaller, the better, if not small enough to make a scale relatively schizo-specific but not specific to (1) nosological subtypes or (2) clinical status, the enterprise will be abandoned as psychometrically unfeasible with this item pool.

In my current work on taxonomic search methods (Meehl, 1965b, 1968, 1970b, 1973a; Meehl *et al.,* 1965; Golden & Meehl, 1972a,b) I have become preoccupied with the development of "model consistency tests," that is, multiple statistical consequences of the formalism's postulates about the latent taxon/indicator structure. If these consistency-tests are unsatisfied by the data, either the postulated model is discorroborated, or the instant sample is aberrant, or both. I see no reason why the demand for consistency-tests should be restricted to the taxonomic situation, although this problem happens to hold my own research interest at present. The statistician customarily distinguishes between "statistical hypotheses" and "statistical assumptions." The former (such as homogeneity of variance or linearity of regression) are subject to fairly direct empirical tests within one's data. The latter are more or less plausible postulates (frequently only pious hopes) that do not have the possibility of strong discorroboration within one's data. Thus, for instance, if I normalize test scores by an area transformation because I believe the hypothetical underlying dimension to be Gaussian, this assumption about the state of Nature may or may not be correct, and, usually, it will not be susceptible of any direct test. I think that even rather crude and inexact consistency tests—again relying upon Monte Carlo methods to set appropriate cutting scores as strong evidence of "model inconsistency"—are more important than "exact" statistics which, however, presuppose that the postulated latent structure is satisfied or (more precisely and realistically) that the departure from this idealization is small enough to permit us to proceed with our technological development. We ought to be exercising a combination of psychological and mathematical ingenuity in developing consistency tests that will prevent us from psychometrizing on the basis of a psychometric model that is too far from the actual psychological structure.

One aspect of internal consistency that should be vigorously pursued (I am about to embark upon such an investigation myself with the MMPI *D* scale—an obvious candidate, given my clinical impression that there exist a half-dozen "kinds" of depression) was suggested, almost as an afterthought (and I believe he himself never attempted to implement it) by Guttman in his classic paper on reproducibility (Guttman, 1944). While he was mainly oriented toward item selection and scale construction, and, connected with that psychometric job, ascertaining whether there existed a "unidimensional"

7. Reactions, Reflections, Projections

variable in a given item-person joint domain, at the end of the paper he suggested that it might be useful for the clinician to have a more intensive look at those individuals who were largely responsible for producing the undesired departures from Guttman scaleability. The subsequent emphasis upon scale-building (and the associated progressive lowering of the required reproducibility coefficient to handle recalcitrant domains) rather than upon looking at persons who were the nonscalable culprits, has perhaps been unfortunate. It is, after all, fundamentally the actual psychological characteristics of persons (in their interaction with items) that renders a batch of items nonscalable Without going into details about my own projected investigation of D, I suggest that what is needed is a kind of shuffling back and forth between the elimination of various subgroups of persons and the elimination of various subgroups of items, hoping that after several steps in such an oscillation process, we are no longer asking of a certain item that it "do the impossible" because we will have eliminated those patients who make the dimension unscalable. Here, again, the necessity for very large samples is obvious, there being grave danger that we capitalize upon random sampling fluctuations in squeezing all of the juice out of the psychometric turnip. An extreme case is, of course, the possibility of achieving perfect scalability on each of a very large number of alternative, partially overlapping "depression" keys where we have, in effect, tailor-made our "dimensions" to map a congeries of pseudonomothetic unidimensional variables that would all fade completely away on cross-validation.

Finally, I cannot resist the impulse to add a suggestion that may appear somewhat disharmonious with my earlier suggestion that we seek items "causally close" to the variable of interest. Whenever we have a respectable body of evidence indicating the existence of a sizeable genetic contribution to a personality variable, one solution to the rotation problem in an internal consistency analysis, or even for an ordinary item-analytic procedure, might be to rotate the factor (or choose the items) so as to maximize the resulting scale's genetic loading. This criterion cannot, unfortunately, be translated directly into a statistical prescription to "maximize the heritability coefficient," because of certain unresolved and messy problems about that statistic's properties (Roberts, 1967; Hirsch, 1967). Although it may seem that a person's response to a structured verbal test item is too many causal steps removed from, say, a dominant schizogene, in identifying the adult schizotype it might, nevertheless, pay off to select items on the basis of MZ-DZ trends (a suitable optimizing function being adopted). If the verbal behavior is too remote in the long causal chain to be statistically powerful, then such a procedure will fail. Example: If schizotypal anhedonia (Rado, 1956, 1960; Rado and Daniels, 1956; Meehl, 1962, 1964) is a "close causal consequence" of the gene-controlled neurological defect, as it is in my theory, does the MMPI item "I wish I could be as happy as others seem to be"—empirically known to be a powerful concurrent-validity schizotypal indicator—really seem so remote? The causal remoteness or closeness depends partly on how we formulate matters. Learning the English language was a long and complicated process for the patient. Yet, having learned it, the verbal report of phenomenological "unhappiness" may be linked very closely to the relevant CNS state of anhedonia, and, hence, be only a link or two in the causal chain from the gene-controlled biochemical defect. In order to find out that such an approach is doomed to failure, it would seem obvious that the game has to be played fairly. One should use the genotype as his criterion rather than something else which, like the candidate item, is also many steps removed from the etiological agent of interest. Roughly put, "If you can't build a schizotype key relying upon data from subjects who have remained clinically compensated despite having a schizophrenic MZ twin, then you will not find items adequate for this purpose by item analyzing against some other remote criterion such as clinical status." The findings of Gottesman and Shields (1972) on S_c scores of compensated MZ twins of schizophrenic probands leave us in doubt as to this question.

Today one is frequently asked, "When are you going to make a new MMPI?" While I confess experiencing transitory impulses to have a try at it, I am not likely to do it. Although I am more confident than Dr. Hathaway that we could do it better, I suspect only slightly better, despite the advancements in psychometric thinking since 1937 and the tremendous body of evidence (over 5000 titles) that has accumulated about the present instrument. I would consider it unwise for a psychologist to invest what would amount to a decade or more of his professional life in this Herculean task without first resolving certain methodological and substantive issues that remain (unaccountably) *sub judice* at this time. For example, whether one should employ a psychometric construction-and-validation procedure predicated upon a "class" (taxonomic) model or a Galileian one cannot be answered from the armchair (although one is struck by how many psychologists think they can do it this way, cf. Meehl, 1972a) but would appropriately depend upon whether or not the research data corroborated a taxonomic model. Furthermore, there is no guarantee that the answer to this taxonomic/dimensional question would be the same for each "variable" that might go into a new MMPI profile; rather, the contrary is rationally expectable. Thus, for example, we might want to make an anxiety scale or a depression scale aimed at

7. Reactions, Reflections, Projections 179

dimensions of mood (or mood-disposition), but we might also want to make a manic-depressive, psychopathic deviate, or schizotypal scale aimed at taxonomic classification. I cannot imagine myself starting to "build a new MMPI" without having tentatively settled this kind of question for at least the major variables of clinical interest.

Another issue which would seem very important, and premature to freeze at present, is what kinds of item content, and what kind of a psychometric model, are appropriate for assisting in treatment choice among the psychotropic drugs. As everyone knows, it is impossible for the present combination of animal research plus large scale quantitative research plus "clinical trials" to keep up with the pharmaceutical industry's biochemical ingenuity. Any clinical practitioner who is honest with himself knows that for many patients his selection among the current armamentarium of major and minor tranquilizers and antidepressants (and perhaps thought-disorder alleviants?) is more of a base-rate procedure (and a sheer trial-and-error matter) than a rational method for confidently picking the best drug for this particular patient's "diagnosis" and "personality type." Now the choice of optimal psychotropic medication—with or without traditional psychotherapy or other kinds of behavioral intervention—is, in my opinion, one of the most important functions that psychometrics (along with quantitative life-history and quantitative Mental Status methods) should contribute to clinical practice. Suppose, for instance, that I am right in my belief that there are a half dozen different "kinds" of depression. It would require at least five years, and probably more, of well-subsidized, large-scale, high-quality clinical, experimental, psychophysiological, and genetic research to test that impressionistic notion. I strongly suspect that there are psychopharmacological differences of great clinical importance related to this matter of kinds of depression. (Example: Current popularity of well-advertised antidepressants developed over the last decade and a half has markedly reduced the clinical use of an "old stand-by," dexamyl, which I believe to be excellent therapy for one type of mild, episodic depression-prone patient in whom a short-term downward mood swing, situationally elicited, produces an immediate performance-decrement and consequent intropunitive "self-talk," hence an autocatalytic process that spirals downward for weeks when the drug could have interrupted it in a few hours.) If one of the main jobs we want to do with a personality test for clinical use is help the physician pick an optimal drug, major test revision should perhaps wait upon a more thorough exploration of the dimensions and taxonomy in psychopharmacology.

The most important single question I would want to answer before embarking upon such a huge test-building job would, I think, be one that (incredible though it may seem) is still not answered. That question is this: Just how much blood is there in this particular psychometric turnip when we do the kind of souped-up research that is necessary to squeeze all of it out? I maintain that we do not know at the present time how well the present MMPI profile does as a characterizer of the patient! Fortunately it is possible—and my colleague Schofield and I plan to embark on such a project, relying on the unique set of therapist rating data we now have available in connection with the development of the Minnesota Hartford Personality Assay (MHPA) (Glueck, Meehl, Schofield, & Clyde (2 articles); Glueck, Meehl, Schofield, & Clyde 1964; Meehl, Schofield, Glueck, Studdiford, Hastings, Hathaway, & Clyde, 1962; Melrose, Stroebel, & Glueck, 1970)—without first solving the dimensional/taxonomic dilemma. It might be supposed that one could not answer the question "How well at best?" without first answering the question, "Proceed typologically or dimensionally?" But I think this is a mistake. In my "Wanted—a Good Cookbook" (Meehl, 1956b) I made the point that the kind of MMPI-type analysis employed by my student Halbower (with what turned out to be unexpectedly high-valid results) operated under certain opposing constraints (see also Meehl, 1959a). If we proceed typologically, the dilemma forced upon us is obvious; but I think it is present (although sometimes latently) no matter what our procedure and model. There are two undisputed general facts working against us whenever we attempt to concoct a personality description applicable to future patients presenting a given MMPI profile.

Bad Fact Number One: The MMPI is fallible, both in the sense of incompleteness and invalidity; hence individuals having similar or identical profiles will differ from one another.

Bad Fact Number Two: The more dissimilar two patients' profiles are, the more dissimilar the patients are likely to be.

Even if there were no problem of validity generalization in moving from say, inpatient to outpatient populations, or into any new population differing in demographic variables or in base-rates of various clinical entities (i.e., if we confine ourselves solely to strictly "random sampling fluctuations"), these two unblinkable and permanently unavoidable facts set limits upon what we can accomplish. Unfortunately, the two tend to push us in our "search technique" and "cookbook construction" in opposite directions procedurally. Bad Fact Number One means that we cannot assume that a cross-validative patient will be closely similar personologically to a single patient, however well-described, in our criterion study. He is likely to be more similar to an average of two patients, probably to be still more similar to an average of three criterion patients, and so on. That is, consideration of random

7. Reactions, Reflections, Projections

sampling fluctuation (putting it another way, the existence of real residual differences among patients psychometrically indistinguishable) should rationally impel us to increase the number of cases upon which any cookbook characterization of a given MMPI profile (or profile subtype) is based. But with only as many variables as appear on the usual minimum MMPI profile (say, around a dozen, including the validity scales, *Si* and *Es*), it is impossible to locate even a small number of identical profiles for the purpose of constructing a mean or modal personality description—unless one begins with a sample that is not merely large but gigantic. An idea of the difficulties can easily be discerned by considering how many cases one would need in order that every two-digit primed code type would be represented in an outpatient sample by at least two dozen criterion cases. Look for instance, at Figure 1 in the Hathaway-Meehl *Atlas* (1951) showing the relative frequencies of various high point codes from a sample of adult male Psychiatric Unit patients at the University of Minnesota Hospital. How large a sample would we need in order to have, say, the code type 17 represented by a couple of dozen cases for cookbook construction? We would need something like 4000 male patients; and in picking code type 17 I have not gone out of my way to find one of unusual rarity. Suppose one considered the (psychologically interesting) two-digit code 97. He would need a clinical population of 10,000 male patients in order to find even 10 cases for cookbook construction purposes! And, mind you, this is treating as "psychometrically equivalent" all individuals whose peak scores are M_a and P_t with both running over 70, ignoring all other information in the profile except that the remaining scores rank below these two. The problem is worsened by the fact that the profiles for which ordinary nonactuarialized clinical experience is less likely to build up "lore" (because the given pattern is so rarely seen in any clinician's experience) are the ones where there is the greatest necessity for an actuarial finding to rely on. Nor can we avoid this stomach-ache simply by rejecting the typological model in favor of the regression model, even if Professor Goldberg is wholly right. I daresay neither he nor anyone else wants to maintain that two persons having identical regression scores are psychologically identical with regard to all clinically important characteristics—a question that cannot be answered by studies of the infamous Meehl-Dahlstrom data on psychosis-neurosis.

Despite Professor Lewis Goldberg's documentation that complicated step-wise, successive hurdles, code-oriented techniques like the Meehl-Dahlstrom Rules are not better, and may be significantly worse, than a suitable linear combination (Goldberg, 1969), I remain unconvinced that in all situations we can expect linear functions to do the job. I dislike to find myself in this position, because it sounds too much like a typical fuzzy-headed clinician invoking his "clinical experience" in defiance of a clear research contradiction. However, I doubt that Professor Goldberg wants to maintain that a strong anticonfigural generalization can be safely made at this time, except in the cautious way in which he makes it, that is, there is no satisfactory positive evidence for significant configural effects. I will bravely record my prophecy that with (1) sufficiently large N and (2) adequate criteria, there will be found (3) some significant configural effects in accord with the clinical lore of experienced MMPI-users. But it may well be that any such found (while statistically significant) will be so small that they are not worth the trouble. The kind of consideration which makes me nervous about a strong Goldberg-type negative generalization, on which I daresay most clinicians experienced with the instrument would agree with me, is exemplified by the following: suppose we have a linear assessment function (to make it easy, I will consider only the three variables of the "neurotic triad"):

$$y = 0.5H + D + 0.5Hy$$

Now we consider two neurotic patients, with no psychotic elevations, one of whom has T-scores: (Hs = 65, D = 85, Hy = 65) and the other T-scores: (Hs = 85, D = 65, Hy = 85). Since these two patients will both yield weighted sum y = 150, the linear function will not tell them apart. Now I doubt that any MMPI using clinician can believe it to be literally true that there is, on the average, no difference in the psychology of patients with a (marginal) neurotic triad "D-spike" and patients with a "hysteroid valley." And of course it is a simple matter of the algebra of simultaneous equations that we can work with the elevations on the D-spike or the D-valley to match up any pair of multiple regression scores in this situation. On the other hand, Professor Goldberg could point out that if one reads through the Q-sort descriptions of the Marks-Seeman codes 231 versus 31, they are disconcertingly similar. Having a deep-seated cynicism about quantitatively unsupported "clinical experience" (claims made for some contemporary psychotherapies are an even better illustration of this), and since I do not find it much to my taste when a fervid Rorschacher tells me that, despite the largely adverse evidence of significant Rorschach validity for most situations, he "knows" that it "works" because "we rely on it a lot in our clinic," I am not about to make a federal case against Professor Goldberg and other linearists! I shall be surprised, but not thunderstruck, if we find that configural effects, when carefully sought in a variety of contexts with adequate criteria, still remain undetectable. My present position, speaking in terms of what horse one is willing to bet on pending further evidence, is that linearizing within Hathaway code type will turn out ultimately to be worth doing. Using this

7. Reactions, Reflections, Projections

strategy, one first classifies the MMPI profile by, say, its two-digit (or possibly for some of them, three-digit) code, plus maybe one or two additional "coarse" successive-hurdles criteria a la Marks and Seeman. Then, within that coarse grouping by "supplemented Hathaway code," one fits linear regression equations for predicting each element of the Q-array. That is to say, except for "entities" (I use the term in its generic, logician's sense!) that are pretty clearly shown to be taxonomic, such as the manic-depressive or unipolar depressive psychosis (or, as I read the record, schizoidia) I expect that the linear prediction of each single phenotypic or genotypic trait of interest, with separate equations fitted within code types, will be more effective than mediation of trait-attributions by a set of taxonomic-typological profiles as was done by Gilberstadt and Duker (1965), Marks and Seeman (1963), and others.

With anything like the sample sizes available to us for research, some compromise is unavoidable between (1) psychometric indistinguishability among criterion patients used to concoct the cookbook and (2) sampling stability requiring each "set of equivalent profiles" to be represented by at least a dozen or two criterion individuals. Even with several thousand cases to dip into, what happens is that we can generate a half-way respectable sample size of criterion patients only by increasing the tolerance within a batch of profiles that are being lumped together as "psychometrically indistinguishable." We pay the price of decreasing the psychometric homogeneity of the patients in order to get enough of them to have some statistical faith in the average of modal placements. It stands to reason that these two curves must cross at some point, that there is some optimal sample size which generates sufficient statistical stability for cookbook purposes without sacrificing too much homogeneity by lumping together patients that do not "belong together" even from the information in the MMPI profile alone. To the best of my knowledge, nobody has investigated where this optimum is. I think it is extremely important, partly because by knowing the (approximate) answer we can justify spending taxpayer money on obtaining the right kind of cookbook sample which would have to be of fabulous proportions. The expense would be enormous, since there is little point in doing such a study with qualitatively feeble criteria (e.g., inexpert raters, inadequate patient contact, no interjudge reliability estimates, insufficient diversification of demographic sample characteristics).

Of course, even with smaller samples, some idea of these numerical questions can be gained, namely, by working back from a cross-validative profile chosen because it represents a code type that we know is observed in our sample with sizeable frequency and then arranging "criterion" profiles in order of their closeness to this profile (which is going to be used as cross-validative). Beginning with a batch of profiles all of whose scores are within, say, one standard error of measurement of the cross-validative profile, we progressively increase the psychometric tolerance (and therefore decrease the presumed psychological homogeneity) and see where we get. It would be worth spending some time and money on this project in order to answer the methodological question: suppose we had literally thousands and thousands of MMPI records on patients who had been carefully rated on a standard set of phenotypic and genotypic variables by conscientious, well-paid clinical judges on the basis of extensive and qualitatively intensive clinical exposure (e.g., in psychotherapy with the patient), so huge a batch that random sampling fluctuation was reduced to a negligibly important factor. Then, looking at a new patient's profile, we would be able to say, "Here in the Super-Atlas, is the mean cookbook description of 100 patients having MMPI profiles indistinguishable, score-by-score, from this one." How valid (whether measured by Q-correlation, or distance function, or whatever you please) would this description be? Of course, if you are going to take the trouble to answer that question, it would probably be desirable to have multiple ratings by skilled clinicians on the criterion side, so that at least some approximate attenuation-correction for "criterion unreliability" could be built in. I will play the prophet here and predict that when this kind of investigation is done, the validity of the MMPI profile as optimally interpreted—squeezing all of the blood out of the psychometric turnip—will be considerably higher than the more pessimistic comments of its author, and others in this volume, seem to suggest.

REFERENCES

Allport, G. W. *Personality, a psychological interpretation.* New York: Holt, 1937.
Beck, A. T. *Depression.* New York: Harper & Row. 1967.
Bunge, M. (Ed.) *The critical approach: Essays in honor of Karl R. Popper.*
Campbell, D. P., & Fiske, D. W. Convergent and discriminant validation by the multitrait-multimethod matrix. *Psychological Bulletin,* 1959, 56, 81-105.
Castleman, B., & Dudley, H. R. Selected Medical Cases, *Clinicopathological conference of the Massachusetts General Hospital.* Boston, Massachusetts: Little, Brown, 1960.
Castleman, B., & Richardson, E. P. *Neurologic clinicopathological conferences of a Massachusetts General Hospital.* Boston, Massachusetts: Little, Brown, 1968.
Cleckley, H. *The mask of sanity.* St. Louis, Missouri: Mosby, 1964. (4th ed.)
Cronbach, L. J., & Gleser, C. G. *Psychological tests and personnel decisions.* Urbana, Illinois: University of Illinois Press, 1957.

7. Reactions, Reflections, Projections

Cronbach, L. J. *Essentials of psychological testing.* (2nd ed.) New York: Harper & Row, 1960.
Cronbach, L. J., & Meehl, P. E. Construct validity in psychological tests. *Psychological Bulletin,* 1955, **52,** 281-302.
Eisenstein, V. Differential psychotherapy of borderline states. *Psychiatric Quarterly,* 1951, **25,** 379-401.
Evans, M. C., & McConnell, T. R. A new measure of introversion-extroversion. *Journal of Psychology,* 1941, **12,** 111-124.
Evans, M. C., & McConnell, T. R. *Minnesota T-S-E inventory.* Princeton, New Jersey: Educational Testing Service, 1947.
Fish, B. Infants at risk for schizophrenia: Developmental deviations from birth to ten years. *Journal of the American Academy of Child Psychiatry,* 1972, **11.**
Gilberstadt, H., & Duker J. *A handbook for clinical and actuarial MMPI interpretation.* Philadelphia, Pennsylvania: Saunders, 1965.
Glueck, B. C., Meehl, P. E., Schofield, W., & Clyde, D. J. *Minnesota-Hartford personality assay: doctors subset.* Hartford, Connecticut: Institute of Living.
Glueck, B. C., Meehl, P. E., Schofield, W. & Clyde, D. J. *Minnesota-Hartford personality assay: Forty factors.* Hartford Connecticut: Institute of Living.
Glueck, B. C., Meehl, P. E., Schofield, W., & Clyde, D. J. The quantitative assessment of personality. *Comprehensive Psychiatry,* 1964, **5,** 15-23.
Goldberg, L. R. The search for configural relationships in personality assessment: The diagnosis of psychosis versus neurosis from the MMPI. *Multivariate Behavior Research,* 1969, **5,** 523-536.
Golden, R., & Meehl, P. E. Detecting Latent Clinical Taxa, IV: Empirical study of the maximum covariance method and the normal minimum chi-square method, using three MMPI keys to identify the sexes. *Reports from the Research Laboratories of the Department of Psychiatry, University of Minnesota,* Report No. PR-72. Minneapolis, Minnesota, 1972. (in preparation)   (a)
Golden, R., & Meehl, P. E. Detecting Latent Clinical Taxa, V: A Monte Carlo study of the maximum covariance method and associated consistency tests. *Reports from the Research Laboratories of the Department of Psychiatry, University of Minnesota,* Report No. PR-72. Minneapolis, Minnesota, 1972. (in preparation)   (b)
Gottesman, I. I. Heritability of personality: A demonstration. *Psychological Monographs,* 1963, **77,** No. 9 (Whole No. 572).
Gottesman, I. I., & Shields, J. *Schizophrenia and genetics: A twin study vantage point.* New York: Academic Press, 1972. (in press)
Gough, H. G. A new dimension of status: I. Development of a personality scale. *American Sociological Review,* 1948, **13,** 401-409.
Gough, H. G., McClosky, H., & Meehl, P. E. A personality scale for dominance. *Journal of Abnormal & Social Psychology,* 1951, **46,** 360-366.
Gough, H. G., McClosky, H., & Meehl, P. E. A personality scale for social responsibility. *Journal of Abnormal & Social Psychology,* 1952, **47,** 73-80.
Guttman, L. A. A basis of scaling qualitative data. *American Sociological Review,* 1944, **9,** 139-150.
Hare, R. Acquisition and generalization of a conditioned fear response in psychopathic and nonpsychopathic criminals. *Journal of Psychology,* 1965, **59,** 367.   (a)

Hare, R. Temporal gradient of fear aroused in psychopaths. *Journal of Abnormal & Social Psychology*, 1965, **70**, 442. (b)
Hare, R. Psychopathy and choice of immediate versus delayed punishment. *Journal of Abnormal & Social Psychology*, 1966, **71**, 25.
Hathaway, S. R. A coding system for MMPI profiles. *Journal of Consulting Psychology*, 1947, **11**, 334-337.
Hathaway, S. R., & Meehl, P. E. *An atlas for the clinical use of the MMPI.* Minneapolis, Minnesota: University of Minnesota Press, 1951.
Hirsch, J. Behavior genetic analysis. In J. Hirsch (Ed.), *Behavior genetic analysis.* New York: McGraw-Hill, 1967. Pp. 416-436.
Hoch, P., & Polatin, P. Pseudoneurotic forms of schizophrenia. *Psychiatric Quarterly*, 1949, **3**, 248-276.
Hoering, W. Indeterminism in classical physics. *British Journal of Philosophy of Science*, 1969, **20**, 247-255.
Hoffman, P. J. Cue-consistency and configurality in human judgment. In B. Kleinmuntz (Ed.), *Formal presentation of human judgment.* Chapter 3. New York: Wiley, 1968.
Hoffman, P. J., Slovic, P., & Rorer, L. G. An analysis of variance model for the assessment of configural cue utilization in clinical judgment. *Psychological Bulletin*, 1968, **69**, 338-349.
Hogben, L. *Statistical theory.* New York: Norton, 1957, 1968 (Revised Ed.).
Jackson, D. N. The dynamics of structured personality tests: 1971. *Psychological Review*, 1971, **78**, 229-248.
Kemeny, J. G., Snell, J. L., & Thompson, G. L. *Introduction to finite mathematics.* Englewood Cliffs, New Jersey: Prentice-Hall, 1957.
Kleinmuntz, B. (Ed.) *Formal representation of human judgment.* New York: Wiley, 1968.
Kleinmuntz, B. (Ed.) *Clinical information processing by computer.* New York: Holt, Rinehart, & Winston, 1969.
Lakatos, I., & Musgrave A. (Eds.) *Criticism and the growth of knowledge.* Cambridge, Massachusetts: Cambridge University Press, 1970.
Langmuir, I. Science, common sense and decency. *Science*, 1943, **97**, 1-7.
Lester, D. Attempts to predict suicidal risk using psychological tests. *Psychological Bulletin*, 1970, **74**, 1-17.
London, I. D. Some consequences of history and psychology of Langmuir's concept of convergence and divergence of phenomena. *Psychological Review*, 1946, **53**, 170-188.
Lykken, D. T. A study of anxiety in the sociopathic personality. *Journal of Abnormal & Social Psychology*, 1957, **55**, 6-10.
Lykken, D. T. Statistical significance in psychological research. *Psychological Bulletin*, 1968, **70**, 151-159.
Manning, H. M. Programmed interpretation of the MMPI. *Journal of Personality Assessment*, 1971, **35**, 162-176.
Marks, P. A., & Seeman, W. *The actuarial description of abnormal personality.* Baltimore, Maryland: Williams & Wilkins, 1963.
Meehl, P. E. The dynamics of structured personality tests. *Journal of Clinical Psychology*, 1945, **1**, 296-303. (a)
Meehl, P. E. An investigation of a general normality or control factor in personality testing. *Psychological Monographs*, 1945, **59**, No. 4. (b)

7. Reactions, Reflections, Projections

Meehl, P. E. *Clinical versus statistical prediction: A theoretical analysis and a review of the evidence.* Minneapolis, Minnesota: University of Minnesota Press, 1954. (a)

Meehl, P. E. Comment on "Analyzing the clinical process." *Journal of Counseling Psychology*, 1954, 1, 207-208. (b)

Meehl, P. E. Clinical versus actuarial prediction. *Proceedings of the 1955 Invitational Conference on Testing Problems.* Princeton, New Jersey: Educational Testing Service, 1956. Pp. 136-141. (a)

Meehl, P. E. Wanted—a good cookbook. *American Psychologist*, 1956, 11, 263-272. (b)

Meehl, P. E. Symposium on clinical and statistical prediction. *Journal of Counseling Psychology*, 1956, 3, 163-173. (c)

Meehl, P. E. When shall we use our heads instead of the formula? *Journal of Counseling Psychology*, 1957, 4, 268-273.

Meehl, P. E. Some ruminations on the validation of clinical procedures. *Canadian Journal of Psychology*, 1959, 13, 102-128. (a)

Meehl, P. E. A comparison of clinicians with five statistical methods of identifying psychotic MMPI profiles. *Journal of Counseling Psychology*, 1959, 6, 102-109. (b)

Meehl, P. E. Structured and projective tests: Some common problems in validation. *Journal of Projective Techniques*, 1959, 23, 268-272. (c)

Meehl, P. E. The cognitive activity of the clinician. *American Psychologist*, 1960, 15, 19-27.

Meehl, P. E. Schizotaxia, schizotypy, schizophrenia. *American Psychologist*, 1962, 17, 827-838.

Meehl, P. E. *Manual for Use with Checklist of Schizotypic Signs.* Psychiatric Research Unit, University of Minnesota Medical School, Minneapolis, Minnesota: Copyright, 1964.

Meehl, P. E. Seer over sign: The first good example. *Journal of Experimental Research in Personality*, 1965, 1, 27-32. (a)

Meehl, P. E. Detecting latent clinical taxa by fallible quantitative indicators lacking an accepted criterion. *Reports from the Research Laboratories of the Department of Psychiatry, University of Minnesota*, Report No. PR-62-2. Minneapolis, Minnesota, 1965. (b)

Meehl, P. E. Theory-testing in psychology and physics: A methodological paradox. *Philosophy of Science*, 1967, 34, 103-115. (a)

Meehl, P. E. What can the clinician do well? In D. N. Jackson & S. Messick (Eds.) *Problems in human assessment.* Chapter 48. New York: McGraw-Hill, 1967. Pp. 594-599. (b)

Meehl, P. E. Detecting Latent Clinical Taxa, II: A simplified procedure, some additional hitmax cut locators, a single-indicator method, and miscellaneous theorems. *Reports from the Research Laboratories of the Department of Psychiatry, University of Minnesota*, Report No. PR-68-4. Minneapolis, Minnesota, 1968.

Meehl, P. E. Psychology and the criminal law. *University of Richmond Law Review*, 1970, 5, 1-30. (a)

Meehl, P. E. Nuisance variables and the ex post facto design. In M. Radner and S. Winokur (Eds.), *Minnesota studies in the philosophy of science*, Vol. 4. Minneapolis, Minnesota: University of Minnesota Press, 1970. Pp. 373-402. (b)

Meehl, P. E. Law and the fireside inductions: Some reflections of a clinical psychologist. *Journal of Social Issues*, 1971, 27, 65-100.

Meehl, P. E. Specific genetic etiology, psychodynamics and therapeutic nihilism. *International Journal of Mental Health*, 1972, 1, 10-27. (a)

Meehl, P. E. Epilogue. In I. I. Gottesman & J. Shields (Eds.), *Schizophrenia and genetics: A twin study vantage point*. New York: Academic Press, 1972. (b)

Meehl, P. E. Clinical issues. In S. S. Kety and S. Matthysse (Eds.), *Prospects for research on schizophrenia. M.I.T. Neurosciences Research Program Bulletin*, 1972, 10, No. 4. (c)

Meehl, P. E. Maxcov-Hitmax: A taxonomic search method for loose genetic syndromes. *Psychodiagnosis: selected papers*. Minneapolis, Minnesota: University of Minnesota Press, 1973. (in Press) (a)

Meehl, P. E. Why I don't go to case conferences. *Psychodiagnosis: selected papers*. Minneapolis, Minnesota: University of Minnesota Press, 1973. (in press) (b)

Meehl, P. E., & Dahlstrom, W. G. Objective configural rules for discriminating psychotic from neurotic MMPI profiles. *Journal of Consulting Psychology*, 1960, 24, 375-387.

Meehl, P. E., & Hathaway, S. R. The K factor as a suppressor variable in the Minnesota Multiphasic Personality Inventory. *Journal of Applied Psychology*, 1946, 30, 525-564.

Meehl, P. E., Lykken, D. T., Burdick, M. R., & Schoener, G. R. Identifying Latent Clinical Taxa, III: An empirical trial of the normal single-indicator method, using MMPI Scale 5 to identify the sexes. *Reports from the Research Laboratories of the Department of Psychiatry, University of Minnesota*. Report No. PR-69-1. Minneapolis, Minnesota: 1969.

Meehl, P. E., Lykken, D. T., Schofield, W., & Tellegen, A. Recaptured-item technique (RIT): A method for reducing somewhat the subjective element in factor-naming. *Journal of Experimental Research in Personality*, 1971, 5, 171-190.

Meehl, P. E., & Rosen, A. Antecedent probability and the efficiency of psychometric signs, patterns, or cutting scores. *Psychological Bulletin*, 1955, 52, 194-216.

Meehl, P. E., Schofield, W., Glueck, B. C. Jr., Studdiford, W. B., Hastings, D. W., Hathaway, S. R., & Clyde, D. J. *Minnesota-Ford Pool of phenotypic personality items*. (August 1962 ed.) Minneapolis, Minnesota: University of Minnesota Press, 1962.

Melrose, J. P., Stroebel, C. F., & Glueck, B. C., Jr. Diagnosis of psychopathology using stepwise multiple discriminant analysis. *Comprehensive Psychiatry*, 1970, 11, 43-50.

Morrison, D. E., & Henkel, R. E. (Eds.) *The significance test controversy*. Chicago, Illinois: Aldine, 1970.

Murphy, D. C. One cause? Many causes? The argument from a biomodal distribution. *Journal of Chronic Disease*, 1964, 17, 301.

Newell, R. R., Chamberlain, W. E., & Rigler, C. Descriptive classification of pulmonary shadows: A relation of unreliability. *American Review of Tuberculosis*, 1954, 69, 566-584.

Pollack, M., & Krieger, H. P. Oculomotor and postural patterns in schizophrenic children. *American Medical Association Archives of Neurology Psychiatry* 1958, 79, 720-726.

Popper, K. R. *The logic of scientific discovery*. New York: Basic Books, 1959.

Popper, K. R. *Conjectures and refutations*. New York: Basic Books, 1962.

Rado, S. *Psychoanalysis of behavior*. New York: Grune & Stratton, 1956.

Rado, S. Theory and therapy: The theory of schizotypal organization and its application to the treatment of decompensated schizotypal behavior. In S. C. Scher and H. R. Davis (Eds.) *The outpatient treatment of schizophrenia.* New York: Grune & Stratton, 1960. Pp. 87-101.

Rado, S., & Daniels, G. *Changing concepts of psychoanalytic medicine.* New York: Grune & Stratton, 1956.

Roberts, R. C. Some concepts and methods in quantitative genetics. In J. Hirsch (Ed.), *Behavior genetic analysis.* New York: McGraw-Hill, 1967. Pp. 416-436.

Rosen, A. Detection of suicidal patients: An example of some limitations in the prediction of infrequent events. *Journal of Consulting Psychology*, 1954, **18**, 397-403.

Scarr, S. Social introversion-extraversion as a heritable response. *Child Development*, 1969, **40**, 823-832.

Schachter, S. S. *The psychology of affiliation: Experimental studies of the sources of gregariousness.* Stanford, California: Stanford University Press, 1959.

Schmidt, H. O., & Fonda, C. P. Reliability of psychiatric diagnosis: A new look. *Journal of Abnormal & Social Psychology*, 1956, **52**, 262-267.

Schofield, W. *Psychotherapy: The purchase of friendship.* Englewood Cliffs, New Jersey: Prentice-Hall, 1964.

AUTHOR INDEX

A

Abelson, R. P., 81, *83*
Adler, A., 34, 55
Adorno, T. W., 46, *57*
Allport, G. W., 32, *42*, 148, 174, *184*
American Psychologist, 10, *17*
Ames, L. B., 3, *17*
Anthony, N., 8, *17*

B

Barker, H. R., 16, *17*, 96, *114*
Beck, A. T., 143, 183
Belleville, R. E., 105, *114*
Berdie, R., 118, 119
Berg, I., 72, *83*
Binet, 15
Bleuler, E., 156, 167
Block, J., 9, 13, 14, 15, 16, *17*, 34, *42*, 87, 112, *114*

Blum, G. S., 7, *17*
Bock, R. D., 9, *17*
Briggs, P. F., 98, *114*
Bunge, M., 151, *184*
Burdick, M. R., 149, 151, 175, 188
Buros, O. K., 3, 7, 13, *17*
Butcher, J. N., 3, 5, 10, *17, 18*, 132, 146

C

Caldwell, A., 105, *115*
Campbell, D. P., 3, 9, *18*, 38, 49, *57*, 162, *184*
Campbell, D. T., 3, *20*
Carr, J. E., 33, *42*
Carson, R. C., 3, *18*
Castleman, B., 149, *184*
Cattell, R. B., 3, 6, *18*, 96
Chamberlain, W. E., 146, *188*
Chapman, L. J., 2, *18*
Chapman, J. P., 2, *18*

Charms, N., 53
Childers, B., 33, *43*
Chodoff, P., 16, *18*
Clark, K. E., 68, 118, 160
Cleckley, H., 140, *184*
Clyde, D. J., 180, *185, 188*
Comrey, A. L., 96, 111, *114*
Cook, W., 79
Cronbach, L. J., 31, 32, *43,* 46, 70, *83,* 137, 139, *184*

D

Dahlstrom, W. C., 13, *18,* 86, 88, 96, 98-99, *114,* 146, 172, 181, *188*
Daniels, G., 178, *189*
Dicken, C., 9, *17*
DuBois, P. H., 48, *57*
Dudley, H. R., 149, *184*
Duker, J., 183, *185*
D'Zurilla, T. J., 6, *18*

E

Eber, H. W., *18*
Edwards, A., 8, 18, 46, 119
Eichman, W. J., 16, *18,* 111, *114*
Eichorn, D., 99, *114*
Eisenstein, V., 167, *185*
Ellsworth, R. B., 33, *43*
Elstein, A. S., 31, *43*
Endicott, N. A., 87, *114*
Ernhart, C. B., 51-53, *57*
Eron, L. D., 3, *20*
Evans, M. C., 162, *185*
Eysenck, H. J., 5, *18*

F

Fiddleman, P. B., 104-106, 109, 111, *114*
Fink, A., 10, *18*
Finney, J. C., 111, *114*
Fish, B., 157, *185*
Fisher, D. D., 105, *115*
Fiske, D. W., 49, *57,* 162, *184*
Fonda, C. P., 158, *189*
Foster, L., 33, *43*

Foulds, G. A., 87, 114
Fowler, R. D., 13, 16-17, 96, *114*
Frenkel-Brunswik, E., 46, *57*
Fuller, M., 105, *115*

G

Gheselli, E. E., 78, *83*
Gilberstadt, H., 183, *185*
Gleser, C. G., 48, *57,* 70, *83,* 137, *184*
Glueck, B. C., Jr., 146, 180, *185, 188*
Goldberg, L. R., 16, *18,* 23, *43,* 181-182, *185*
Golden, R., 176, *185*
Goldfried, M. R., 6, *18*
Gollob, H. F., 81, *83*
Gordon, L. V., *18*
Gorsuch, R., 87, *115*
Gottesman, I. I., 155, 158, 171, 178, *185*
Gough, H. G., 16, *18,* 119, 171, *185*
Grant, J. D., 53, *57*
Grant, M., 53, *57*
Gross, M. J., 10, *18*
Guilford, J. P., 96
Gunderson, E., 53
Guttman, L. A., 176-177, *185*
Gynther, M., 11, *18*

H

Haan, N., 99, 102-103, *114*
Halbower, C., 180
Hammond, K., 47, *57*
Hare, R., *185-186*
Hase, H., 16, *18*
Hastings, D. W., 180, *188*
Hathaway, S. R., 8, 10, 12, 15, *18-19,* 37, *43,* 46, 49, *57,* 98, 113, *114,* 132, 137, 139, 146-147, 150, 162-166, 174, 178, 180-182, *186, 188*
Havighurst, R. J., 53, *57*
Henkel, R. E., 175, *188*
Hirsch, J., 177, *186*
Hoch, P., 157, 167, *186*
Hoering, W., 154, *186*
Hoffman, P. J., 146, *186*
Hogben, L., 175, *186*
Hollingworth, L. S., 133

Author Index

Holt, R. R., 3, *19*
Holtzman, W. H., 27, *43*
Hugo, J. A., 15, *19*

I

Isaacs, K. S., 53, *57*

J

Jackson, D. N., 8, 15, *19,* 119, 131, *186*
Jones, H. E., 99, *114*
Jortner, S., 87, *114*

K

Kanfer, F. K., 6, *19*
Kemeny, J. G., 154, *186*
Kent, R. N., 6, *18*
Kincannon, J. C., 15, *19*
Kleinmuntz, B., 146, *186*
Kohlberg, L., 53, *57*
Kraepelin, E., 156
Kriedt, P., 69, *83*
Krieger, H. P., 157, *188*
Krocker, D., 33, *43*
Kuder, G. F., 172
Kugelness, S., 157
Kuhn, T. S., 55, *57*
Kunce, J. T., 122, *130*
Kurland, A. A., 105, *114*

L

Lakatos, I., 151, *186*
Langmuir, I., 154, *186*
Lanyon, R. I., 5, 15, *19*
LaPerriere, K., 50-51
Layton, W. L., 119
Lazarsfeld, 46, 151
Lebovitz, B. C., 105, *114*
Lester, D., 142, *186*
Levinson, D. J., 46, *57*
Lewis, O., 51
Loevinger, J., 3, 7, *19,* 47, 49, 53, *57,* 151, 155, 160

London, I. D., 154, *186*
Lorr, M., 36
Lushene, R. E., 87, *115*
Lykken, D. T., 149, 151, 175, *186, 188*

M

Macfarlane, J. W., 99, *114*
McClosky, H., 160, 171, *185*
McConnell, T. R., 162, *185*
McKinley, J. C., 8, 12, 15, *19,* 113, 156, 164-165
McReynolds, R., 3, *19*
Manning, H. M., 144, *186*
Marks, P. A., 144, 183, *186*
Masling, J. M., 8, *19*
Meehl, P. E., 4-5, 8, *19,* 46, *57,* 131, 137, 139, 142, 146-184, *184-188*
Melrose, J. P., 180, *188*
Messick, S., 8, 15, *19*
Mischel, W., 7, 8, *19*
Mooney, R. L., 5, *18*
Morrison, D. E., 175, *188*
Muench, G. A., 33, *43*
Munsterberg, H., 133
Murphy, D. C., 153-154, *188*
Musgrave, A., 151, *186*

N

Nagler, S., 157
Nettles, E., 53
Newell, R. R., 146, *188*
Norman, W. T., 75, 81, *83,* 157-159, 167

O

OSS Assessment Staff, 9, *19*
Ossorio, A., 50, 51
Ostfeld, A. M., 105, *114*
Owens, W., 47, *57*

P

Panton, J. H., 87, *115*
Paterson, D., 46, 132

Peck, R. F., 53, *57*
Pepper, L. J., 111, *115*
Peterson, D. R., 6-7, *19,* 105, *115*
Peterson, L. P., *16-17,* 96, *114*
Piaget, J., 53, *57*
Poffenberger, A. T., 12
Polatin, P., 167, *186*
Pollack, M., 157, *188*
Pomeranz, D. M., 6, *18*
Popper, K. R., 151, *188*

R

Rado, S., 178, *188, 189*
Redmore, C., 53, 55, *57*
Rice, F. A., 133
Richardson, E. P., 149, 172, *184*
Rigler, C., 146, *188*
Roberts, R. C., 177, *189*
Rogers, C. R., 4, *19*
Rorer, L. G., 146, *186*
Rosen, A., 69, *83,* 142, *188, 189*
Rosenthal, D., 156-157
Rosenwald, G. C., 3, *19*
Rotter, J. B., 47, *57*
Rundquist, R. M., 46, *57*

S

Sanford, R. N., 46, *57*
Saslow, G., 6, *19*
Saunders, D. R., 78, *83*
Savage, C., 105, *114*
Scarr, S., 171, *189*
Schachter, S., 9, *19, 189*
Schilder, P., 156
Schmidt, H. O., 158, *189*
Schoener, M. R., 149, 151, 175, *188*
Schofield, W., 87, 111, *115,* 141, 146, 149, 180, *185, 188-189*
Schopenhauer, 38, *43*
Schumer, F., 3, *20*
Schwartz, R. D., 3, *20*
Scriven, M., 36, 37, 41, *43*
Sechrest, L., 3, 9, *19, 20*
Seeman, W., 144, 183, *186*
Shaffer, J. W., 105, *114*
Sheldon, W., 139

Shields, J., 155, 158, 178, *185*
Sletto, R. F., 46, *57*
Slovic, P., 146, *186*
Snell, J. L., 155, *186*
Souri, A., 96, *114*
Spearman, D., 79, 80
Spielberger, C. D., 87, *115*
Stanley, J. C., 9, *18*
Starch, D. A., 133
Stein, K. B., 16, *19,* 96-98, *115*
Stevens, S. S., 36, *43*
Stroebel, C. F., 180, *188*
Strong, E. K., 68, 117, 122, 127
Studdiford, W. B., 180, *188*
Sullivan, C., 53, *57*
Sullivan, H. S., 53, *57*
Sweet, B., 47, 49, *57*
Swenson, C. H., Jr., 2, *19*

T

Tatsuoka, M. M., *18*
Tellegen, A., 10, *18,* 149, *188*
Thompson, G. L., 155, *186*
Thorndike, E., 133
Thorndike, R. L., 119
Thurstone, T. G., 49, 79, 80, 96
Tryon, R. C., 96, 97, *115*
Tukey, J., 61

U

Unger, S., 105, *114*
Ungerleider, J. T., 105, 115

V

Valentine, W. L., 133
Van Pelt, J., 9, *17,* 31, *43*
Visotsky, H. M., 105, *114*

W

Walker, C. E., 10, *20*
Wallace, J., 6, *20*
Wanderer, Z. W., 2, *20*

Author Index

Ward, J. 10, *20*
Ward, V. I., 53
Webb, E. J., 3, 9, *20*
Welsh, G. S., 16, *20,* 86, 88, 96, 98, 99, 111, *114, 115*
Wessler, R., 3, 7, *19,* 53, *57*
Whipple, G. M., 133
Whittenbough, J., 33, *42*
Whyte, W. H., Jr., 10, *20*

Wiggins, J. S., 111, *115*
Wittenborn, J. R., 36
Woodworth, R. S., 12, *20*
Worley, B., 122, *130*

Z

Zubin, J., 3, *20*

SUBJECT INDEX

A

Abdomen, 136
Aberrated behavior, 134
Ability tests, 48, 54
Achievement, 24
　motive, 55
　study of, 54
　test, 153-154
Acquiescence, 119
　interpretation, 16
　Response set formulation of, 8-9
Actuarial computer analysis, 12-13
　with MMPI, 14
Actuarial descriptions, validation of, 144
Actuarial prediction, 12-13, 145-146
　superiority of mechanical, 149
Adjective checklists, 155
Adjustment,
　to daily problems, 24
　to prison, 87
Affective level, 143

Alcohol, 138
Alcoholic, 89
Allport-Vernon Study of Values, 129
Alpha, 82
Alternation, of emotional status, 111
Ambivalence, 139
American psychiatrists, 158
American Psychologist, 10
American Psychology, 131
Analysis, MMPI-type, 180
Analysis of variance, 35
Analytic studies,
　factor or cluster, 16
Anamnesis, 141
　interviews for, 45
Anatomy, comparative, 132
Anger, 112
Anhedonia, schizotypal, 178
Animal grace, 135
Annual Review of Psychology, 5
Antidepressant medication, 134
Antitaxonomists, favorite phrase of, 159

Subject Index

Anxiety,
  derivative, 139
  indices of, 2
  manifest, 88
  over insanity, 29
  parameter of, 139
  scale, 82
  trait of, 87
Anxiety-avoidance reinforcement, 139
Anxious intropunitiveness, 31
Apperception, 2
Aptitudes,
  for survival, 29
Archival techniques, 9
Asch, 146
Asocial, moral type, 140
Assessment, 1-20
  of change, 32
  computer based, 85
  credibility of, 7-9
  criticism of, 7
  flaws in clinical, 7
  methods of personality, 2
  proper role of, 6
  single stage, 66
  utility of, 4
  validity of, 7
Atlases,
  cross-validation, 34
  problem for makers of, 34
Attitudes, 1, 138
  research, 46
  sexual, 16
  test taking, 10
Augean stables, 137
Authoritarian family ideology, 49-50, 53
Autism, 98
Automated interpretation systems, 13
  ethical issues in, 145
Automation, 136

B

Bad trips,
  absence of, 105
Bandwidth, 137
Base-rates, 152
  procedures, 179
Baye's formula, 142, 144

Behavior,
  diagnostic, 135
  prediction of, 36
  social, 27
Behavior genetics, 150
Behavioral analysis, 6
Behavioral consistency, 33
Behavioral intents, 30
Behavioral modification, 5, 135
Behavioral modifiers, 5
Berkeley F Scale, 47, 54
  response bias in, 56
Bernreuter scale, 40
Binet, 79
Biochemical defect,
  gene controlled, 178
Black-white,
  differences on tests, 11
Blackie pictures, 7
Bodily health, 68
Bootstraps effect, 25, 40, 140, 148
Boundary conditions, 79
Branching, 69
Bridge players, 153
Building tests, 132

C

C_H, 164, 166-167, 169
CNS,
  parameters of, 134
  state, 178
CPI, see California Psychological
  Inventory
California Personality Inventory, 119
California Psychological Inventory, 132,
  146
Cancer, 168
Cardiac arrest, 136
Case conference, 132
Catatonic, 175
Causal model,
  taxonomic versus nontaxonomic, 155
Cerebellar lesion, 157
Character, 38
  development, 53
  disorder, 66, 69
Characterizations, 63

Subject Index

Characterological features,
    measures of, 96
Characterological rigidity, 163
Chemistry, 134
Classification,
    errors, 152
    diagnostic problem, 64
    pseudonosological, 30
    systems at, 39
Classification Society, 153, 174
Clinical diagnosis,
    instrument for, 50
    problems of, 71
    subjectivism in, 22
"Clinical experience,"
    nonactuarialized, 181
Clinical judgment, 113, 135, 149
Clinical work up, 149
Clinical status, 90
Clinical psychology,
    rise in, 133
Clinical training programs, 21
Code of professional ethics, 23
Code type, 12, 181
    (*See also* Cookbook)
Code-oriented techniques, 181
Codes,
    profile, 31
Cognitions, 31
Cognitive abilities, 81
Communal animal, 24
Community,
    consultant, 5
    health, 15
    mental health approaches, 5
Compulsion neurosis, 158
Computer,
    analysis with, 12-13
    facility, 42
    with MMPI, 14
    technology, 17
    utilization, 175
Configural effects, 182
Configurations, 66
Congressional hearings, 10
Connections,
    phenotypic versus genotypic, 139
Consensus measures, 160
Construct, clue of the elusive, 24
Construct validity, 164
    problem, 167
Constructs,
    Galilean, 151
    taxonomic, 151
Content, 72
    measures, 111
    theoretical sense, 160
Context, 79
Contrasted-group method, 72
Control, 87
    authoritarian, 51
    factor, 165-166
    styles, 112
Conversion reaction, 67
"Cookbooks," *see also* Code type,
    144-145, 183
    construction, 149, 180
    description, 145
    rules, 145
Correction key, 75, 164
Correctional populations, 13
Counseling, 11, 22
    the assessing of, 33
    rehabilitation, 15
Criminal, 28
Crisis-oriented, 5
    settings, 15
Criteria,
    multiple positive, 164
    multiple negative, 164
Criterion, 149
    discrimination, 162
    external, 160
    negative, 174
    unreliability, 184
Criterion groups, 16, 30
Criterion keying, 155, 162-163, 169, 171-172
    difficulties with blind empirical c.k., 172
    emphasis on, 163
Criterion patients, 140
Criterion problem,
    discouraging state of, 32
    change sensitive criteria, 32
Cross-validation, 154
Culture of poverty, 51
Curve "types,"
    multiple criteria for, 144

D

D (Depression) scale, 87, 143-144, 177
Data banks, 55
Data processor, 135
Death, threat of, 27
Decision,
 clinical, 136
 diagnostic, 56
 making, 135
 rules, 71
Defense,
 mechanisms, 73, 163
 failure of, 163
Defensive structure, 166, 169
Defense techniques, 163
Defensiveness, 8, 46
Delinquency, 139
 legal, 170
Delusional, 168
Delusions, 167
Dementia, 153
Dementia Praecox, 156, 167
Denial mechanism, 83, 103, 142, 144
Depressed mood, 141
 depth of, 151
Depression, 88, 112
 endogenous, 143
 kinds of, 134, 176, 179
 post partum, 90
 psychotic, 152
 severity of, 142
"Depression" key, 151, *see also* D scale
Derivatives,
 aim-inhibited, 163
Description,
 difficulties of, 36
 global personality, 5
 of personality, 131
Desensitization, 135
Developmental theory, 150-152
Deviate,
 psychopathic, 179
Dexamyl, 179
Diagnosis, 69
 decision theoretical
  formulation of, 70
 formal, 161
 identification sought in, 67
 modifying our approach to, 62

 psychological, 4, 134
 purpose of, 66
 of schizophrenia, 25
Diagnostic, 134
 battery, 66
 behavior, 135
 categories, 46
 decision, 56
 interview, 45-46, 135
 problem, 138
 system, 66
Dilettantism, 137
Dimension, 137, 151, 153
Diplopia, 157
Discomfort, patient, 142
Discrimination,
 item, 161
 unfair, 22
Discriminatory practices, 11, 22
Disease entity, 152
Disorders, mental, 30
Dissimulation, 8, 61
Distance measures, 144
Divergent causality, 154
Double-centering, 81
Down phase, 143
Draw-a-Person technique, 2
Drinking, habitual, 138-139
Drug, selection of, 134
Dustbowl empiricists, 149
Dyadic rating problem, 33
Dynamics, 5
Dysdiadochokinesia, 156

E

Edwards Personal Preference Scale, 132
EEG, 1, 146
Edward's Personality Inventory, 119
Ego, 55
 defense mechanism, 99
 defense measures (for MMPI), 99
 development, 51, 53
 stages of development, 53-54
Ego strength, 82, 166
 global measures of, 112
Einstein, 147, 161
Electroencephalogram, 1, 146
Electroshock, 157
 therapy, 134, 144

Subject Index

Emotional,
  fitness, 34
  insulation, 102
  reaction, 87
  status of clients, 111
Empirical keying, 60, 73, 118
  approaches, 172, 174
  faith in, 150
Empiricism,
  gone mad, 72
Empiricists, 149
Employment selection, 11
  discrimination in, 11
  subjectivism in, 22
Endler-Hunter S-R Inventories, 5
Endogenous depression, 143
Energy level, 139
Engram, 28-29
Environmental factors, 35
Environmental, mould trait, 153
EST, 142
Ethics, code of, 23
Etiology, 134, 152
Euphoria, 112
Evaluation,
  locus of, 4
  personality, 22
  problems in psychological, 23
Evidence,
  anecdotal, 133
  impressionistic, 133
Examiner influences, 3
Excitement, 112
Experience,
  social, 29
Experimental,
  personality research, 7
  psychology, 136
Exploration, psychological, 139
Expressive movements, 39
Externalizing mode, 102

F

Face-valid item content, 162
Facial expression, 135
Factor analysis, 35, 51, 96, 119, 166
  refinement of, 52
Factorial complexities, 81

Faith, scientific, 133
Faking, 8
  detection key, 74
  fake bad-good, 166
False positives, 166
Family attitudes,
  study of, 52
Family ideology, 49, 50, 53
Family life,
  problems of, 47
Family.Problems Scale, 48-51
Family-strain correlations, 152
Family strife,
  teenager with, 170
Fantasy themes, 169
Fear of success, 140
Fee-based friend, 141
Feedback,
  on referrals, 135
Felons, 87
Femininity, 112
Fidelity,
  in personality inventories, 137
Flatness, 141
Folk concepts, 16
Food faddist, 141, 167
Fourier, components, 146
Friend, fee-based, 141
Functional psychiatry,
  disease entities in, 137
Functionalist tradition, 60

G

Gene, mutated, 152-153
General intelligence,
  inheritance of, 132
Generalization, validity, 180
Genetic,
  data, 143
  evidence, 158
  framework, 37
  heritage, 29
  structural entities, 37
  research, 179
Genotypic, 137, 149
Geology, historical, 132
Germ, 152-153
Gull-wing MMPI profile, 141

H

H-scale, 164, 166, 168
$H\text{-}C_H$ scale, 164-165
H_s (Hypochondriasis scale), 156
H_y (Hysteria scale), 156
H_y-0 items, 163
Habitual, 139
Halo effects, 3, 7
Head size, 1
Health, bodily, 68
History, 138, 140
Hit-rates, 144
Homoerotic determiners,
  unconscious, 139
Hostility, 112
Human judgment,
  error in, 133
Human mind,
  the structure of, 162
Human testimony,
  untrustworthiness of, 133
Humans,
  as poor observers, 133
Humor,
  reflex, 143
  sense of, 141
Huntington's Chorea, 152-153
Hypochondriasis, 167, 169
Hypochondriasis scale, 164, *see also*
  Hs scale
Hypochondriacal concerns, 166
Hypomanic, 93
Hypotheses,
  theoretical, 133
Hypothetico-deductive procedure, 5
Hysteria,
  conversion, 3, 16
Hysteria key,
  "characterological" component of,
  163
Hysteria scale, *see also* H_y scale, 163
Hysterical character, 163
Hysterical potential, 163

I

I-E test, 47
IQ, 152, 161
IQ-handling technique, 163
Identity crisis, 170
Implicit personality theories, 32
Impression,
  clinical, 135
Impulse, 169
Incremental information, 149
Individual differences, 48, 132
  in personality, 1
  study of, 1, 52
Indocin, 136
Industrial screening, 13
Inferiority complex, 34, 133
Inferiority feeling, 34
Information-storer, 135
Injustice collectors, 168
Ink blots, 24
Insanity, 29
  fear of, 28
  anxiety over, 29
Insecurity, 88
Insomnia, 89, 93
  amount of, 142
Instability, 88
Instrument design,
  modifying, 62
Integrative neural deficit, 157
Intellect, 132
Intellectual abilities,
  studies of, 79
Intellectual capacities,
  distribution of inherited, 152
Intellectualization, 102-103
Intelligence,
  complex of abilities, 24
  history of measurement, 25
  measurement, 49
  test of, 24, 152
  testing, 40
Intelligence tests,
  Binet, 15
Interest,
  loss of, 140
  measurement of, 69
  SVIB test of, 15
Interests,
  managerial, 68
Internal consistency, 36, 161-162, 165,
  171
  approaches, 174

Subject Index

as a desirable item property, 174
Internal medicine,
    diagnosis in, 136
Interpersonal coolness, 141
Interpersonal integration, 53
Interpersonal relatability, 53
Interpretation,
    automated systems of, 13
    clinical, 22
    by computer, 12-13
    computerized actuarial, 144
    cross validation of, 34
    psychological, 166
    radiologic, 146
    Roche system of, 13
Interpretive systems,
    computer based, 12-13, 86
Interview, 142
    anamnestic, 45
    automated, 136
    data from, 150
    density, 135
    diagnostic, 45-46, 135
    psychodynamic, 157
    tape recordings of, 149
Interviewer, 135
Introversion, 162
    social, 171
Inventories,
    broad-band, 81
    self inventory approach, 27
Inventory items, 61
Involutional melancholia, 144
Item
    clusters of, 52
    format, 46-47
    ideal, 160
    "0," 163
    placements, 145
    selection, 46, 160, 176
    "subtle," 163
    weighting, 36
Item analysis, 140, 169
    "criterion-statistical" view on, 150
Item content, 8
    ambiguous wording, 15
    face valid, 162
    leading questions, 15
    MMPI, 96
    outdated, 15

Item discrimination,
    and demographic factors, 161
Item finding procedures, 155
Item format,
    issues concerning, 151
Item pool,
    construction, 150
    clusters of behavioral items, 29
    deficits in MMPI, 14
    internal structure of, 16
    methods for selecting, 56
    MMPI statements, 26
    Outdated MMPI, 15
    relative stability, 27

J

Jack-knife, law of, 61
Judgment,
    criterion of teachers, 25
    defects in personal, 22
    global, 136
    interviews, 22, 158
    locus of, 4
    personal, 22
    personality, 27
    theory-mediated, 136

K

K-corrections, 76, 165
K-factor, 49, 56
K-scale, 75, 77, 163
Kent-Rosanoff list, 59
Key,
    psychometric, 172
Keying,
    homogeneous, 48, 51
    criterion, 48, 155, 171
    "empirical," 48
    empirical criterion, 55
Keys,
    suppressor, 166
Kraepelin, 64, 157
Kuder-Richardson formula, 172

L

LSD, 104
  immunity, 105
  nonreactors, 105-106
  reactors, 105-106
  repeated usage, 105
  response to, 109
Language,
  communities, 61
  structure of, 29
Latent structure analysis, 46, 151
Law of the jack-knife, 61
Law school, 140
Layman's doctrine, 132
Learning,
  social, 29
  theory, 150
Level,
  of control, 86
  of personality, 6
Life history, 136, 139, 170, 179
Linear scales, 65, 151
Lore, interpretative, 2
Loss of control, 168
Lying, 28, 163

M

Magnan sequence, 167
Major dispositions, 6
Malevolent confluence, 141
Malingering, 61
Managerial interests, 68
Manic-depressive psychosis, 134, 143-144, 158, 179, 183
Manifest anxiety, 88, 112
Manifesto,
  Meehl's 1945, 131
Marital,
  crisis, 98, 103
  problem, 138
  relationship, 4
Masculinity-Femininity
  scale, 16
  variance, 98
Maturity, 4
  global measures of, 112

Measures, 1
  nonreactive and unobtrusive, 9
  physiological, 2
  reactive, 9
Medical,
  evidence, 168
  model, 160
  scholarship, 134
Medicine, 134
Mendelizing genetic syndromes, 152
Mental deficiency, 152
Mental disorders, 30
Mental health,
  budgets, 70
  community, 5
Mental hospitals, 141
  discharge from, 144
Mental status, 140
  methods, 179
Mental status interview,
  semistructured, 136
Mesomorphy, 139
Metatheoretical categories, 137
Meteorology, 147
Methodological bias,
  idiographic versus nomothetic, 148
Method variance, 3
Method factor, 49
Milestone sequence, 54
Miller Analogies Test, 129
Minnesota Counseling Inventory, 119
Minnesota-Hartford Personality Assay, 149, 180
Minnesota Multiphasic Personality Inventory,
  acquiescence and, 16
  atlases for, 33
  changes in, 105
  changes under therapy, 93
  clinical improvement, 96
  cluster scales (TSC), 97
  as commercially viable property, 127
  cost in professional time, 22
  criticisms of, 86
  D-score, 143
  ego defense measures, 99
  Ego Defense scales, 102
  emotional alterations, 104
  fallibility of, 180
  foreign language translations, 13

Subject Index

functioning of, 17
group form, 138
helpful if improved, 170
history of, 23
how to improve, 86
internal structure of, 16
interpretation of, 22, 88
invasion of privacy and, 11
limitations of, 3
and MHPA, 149
main factorial dimensions, 15-16
matrix of items, 96
new MMPI needed?, 146
objections to items, 10
obstacles in revising, 118, 124
pattern, 31, 86, 104
profile, 140-141
profile information, 183
profile validity, 184
purging of, 10
revalidation, 30
revisors of, 123
scale, 8, 155, 163
scale structure, 16
selection in the Peace Corps, 10
standardization normals, 156
t-scores, 106
tests of adequacy, 71
type analysis, 180
use of, 85
variations in content, 73
vocal critics and the, 13
workshop, 23, 31
Minnesota Vocational Interest
Inventory, 129
Model consistency tests, 176
Moderators, 77
Modes,
species personality, 29
Momentary status, 111
Monte Carlo methods, 172, 174-176
Mood,
changes in, 87
depressive, 87
dimensions of, 179
Mooney Problem Checklist, 5, 18
Moral judgment,
stages of, 53
Motivation Research Center, 55
Motives,

long-term, 6
overt and covert levels of, 6
Multiphasic lore, 137
Multiple score tests, 50
Multivariate indicator-space, 154
Multivariate instrument, 149
Mutation, 152
MZ-DZ, 177

N

N-scale, 165
Narcissism,
primary, 139
Negative property analysis, 172
Neurological,
measures, 136
signs, 156
Neurological defect,
gene controlled, 178
Neurology, 136
Neurosis, 12, 23, 66-67, 69, 112
compulsion, 158, 168
Neurotic,
acting out, 138, 170
psychophysiological, 168
triad, 88, 165, 170, 182
work inhibition, 140
Neurotic patient,
discrimination, 173
Neurotic/psychotic distinction, 143
Normality, 165
Normative view, 32
Norms,
age specific, 78
Nosological labels,
strongest evidence for, 158
genetic evidence for meaning of, 158
Nosology, 12, 31
Knaepelinian, 64, 157
standard, 30
Nuisance variables, 160, 162, 169, 171, 173, 175
validity, 164

O

OSS Assessment Staff, 9

Objective measures of personality,
    current status of, 3
Objective inventories, 21-22
Objective measurement, 5
Objective personality tests, 36
    greater validity for, 36
Objective procedures, 137
Observation,
    methods of, 9
Occupational keys, 68, 69
Opiate addicts,
    reformed, 105
Opinion,
    body of, 131
Options, 86
Organ neurosis, 168
Organicity, 66
Orthogonal model, 49
Outcome, long term,
    prediction of, 157

P

Pain
    affective, 143
Paired choice, 47
Paracelsus, 134
Paranoia, 167
Paranoid, 175
    flavor, 168
    irritability, 153
    reactions, 105
    schizophrenia, 167
Parental Attitude Research Instruments, 52
Patellar reflex, 136
Pathognomic response, 46
Pathognomonic signs, 142
Pathology, 66
    general, 82
Patient personality, 135
Peer-rating,
    methods, 74
    variables, 78
Perception, 29
Perceptual-cognitive system, 136
Performance,
    psychomotor, 2
Personal Appearance, 22

Personal Data Sheet, 12
Personality, 1-20
    adolescent, 15
    changeability of, 8
    complexity of, 17, 38
    concept of, 6, 23
    criteria for, 29
    dimensions of, 6, 124
    disruption, 88
    domain, 7
    ephemeral promise of, 30
    experimental research in, 7
    formation of, 29
    general traits of, 2
    genetic framework of, 37
    global description, 5
    human, 132
    individual differences in, 1
    inventory, 12
    judgments, 27, 39
    level of, 6
    in lower animals, 29
    measures of, 1-2, 81, 96, 148
    new theory of, 41
    procedures for assessing, 1-2
    psychopathic, 140
    questionnaires, 6
    reality of, 30
    systems, 27
    test, 11
    total, 5
    unity of, 55
Personality assessment, 1-20
    approaches are outmoded, 6-7
    biasing effects of, 4
    constancy, 28
    current status of, 3
    decisions in, 4
    devices, 4
    history of, 21
    interpretation of profiles, 26
    methods, 2
    modifying, 62
    new horizons for, 3
    objective inventory, 3
    problems in, 1-20
    procedures for, 1
    progress in, 21
    racially sensitive items in, 11
    reactivity of, 9

Subject Index

sources of criticism of, 4-12
state of, 13-14
questionnaires, 6
variance in inventories, 8
Personality pattern, 139
Personality profile, 32
Personality Research Form, 11, 132
Personality research,
   flaws in, 35
   impetus given to, 45
Personaltiy stabilities, 87
Personality style,
   scales of, 87
Personality tests,
   criteria for developing, 35
   empirical emphasis in, 134
   greater validity for, 36
   limitations of validity of, 149
   narrow reference frames, 34
   new items for, 39
   objective, 60
   projective vs. objective, 36
   structured, 146
   task of, 32
   validating against clinical judgment, 149
   what can be measured by?, 51
   why bother with?, 133
Personality Tests and Reviews, 13
Personhood,
   loss of, 4
Personnel,
   decision making, 64
   industrial screening, 13
   screening, 12
   selection, 10, 15
Personological determinants, 61
Personologist, 148
Personology,
   difficulties of psychometric, 149
   limitations of, 147
   substantive, 151
Phenobarbital, 93
Phenomenal, 137
Phenothiazines, 141, 157
Phenotypic, 149
   criteria, 139
   distributions, 153
   hyperspace, 153
   statements, 137
Physical characteristics, 29

assessment of, 1-2
Physiological indices, 2
Physique, 132
Placement,
   actuarial, 145
   decisions, 70
Polar variable, 54
Postpartum, 51
   depression, 90
Potentiators,
   polygenic, 152
Poverty,
   culture of, 51
Pragmatic context, 133
Prediction, actuarial, 12-13, 145-146, 149
Predictions, 39
   accuracy of, 27
   patterned, 23
   valid, 9
Predictive efficiency, 41
Predictor,
   variance in, 76
Prejudice, 22
Primitive, 99
   defense, 99
   level, 103
Prison,
   adjustment to, 87
Privacy, invasion of, 11
Procedures, objective, 137
Process, schizophrenic, 25
Procrustis method, 53
Profile, 88
   analysis, 60, 64, 140
   code type, 12, 23, 31, 64
   coding, 65
   computer interpreted, 125
   constituents, 65
   configural aspects, 12
   cross-validation, 31, 184
   emerging classifications among, 42
   interpretation of, 26
   mixed, 140
Programs, training, 30
Projection, 103
Projections, future, 131

Projective, 146
  format, 56
  methods, 2, 53
  personality tests, greater validity, 36
  technique, 3, 8, 133
  tests, 21, 136
Pseudoneurosis, 169
Pseudometrics, 5
Psyche,
  mystique of human, 38
Psychiatric,
  decompensation, 105
  hospital, 5
  interview, 48
  literature, 134
  population, 144
  rubric, unreliability of, 158
Psychiatry, 134
  dynamic, 158
  dynamic psychological prejudice, 158
Psychoanalysis,
  classical, 135
Psychodelic agent, 109
Psychodiagnosis, 3
Psychodynamic, 139, 153
  causal model, 150
  formulations, 99
  interpretations, 141
  theory, 150
Psychological,
  growth, 4
  diagnosis, 4
  intervention, 5
  similarity, 103
Psychological assessment, *see also*
  Assessment and Personality
  Assessment,
  of future, 136
Psychological clinic, 134
Psychological Corporation, The, 14, 124
Psychological science,
  undergraduate education, 133
Psychological Screening Inventory, 5
Psychological test,
  to measure personality, 132
  problems in revising, 117
Psychological theory,
  sad state of, 149
Psychologists,

educational, 132
  personnel, 132
Psychology,
  subject matter of, 132
Psychomagic, 5
Psychometric,
  considerations, 59
  description of personality, 131
  dimension, 169
  device, 157
  error, 166
  instruments, 40
  key, 172
  methodologies, 49
  patterning, 90
  projections, 134
  properties, 155
  skuldoggery, 153
  strategy, 151
  structural properties, 161
  technology, 56
  tolerance, 184
Psychometrics, 136
  applied, 147
  mission of, 52
Psychomotor performance, 2
Psychoneurotic, 168
Psychopathic personality, 140, 179
Psychopathic deviate scale, 139-140
Psychopathological states, 87
Psychopharmacologist, 134
Psychophysiological,
  measures, 136
  status, 104
Psychosis, 66, 112, 164
  depressive, 183
  discrimination from neurosis, 23
  manic depressive, 143
Psychosomatic, 168
Psychotherapeutic assessment, 33
Psychotherapist, 5, 139, 141, 167
Psychotherapy, 32, 142
  long-term, 138
  rational, 141
Psychotic, 134, 141
  character, 142
  depression, 157, 166
  distortion, 168
  patient, discrimination of, 173
  unipolar depression, 158

Subject Index

Psychotically depressed patients, 144
Psychotropic drugs,
    development of, 134
Pulitzer Prize, 155
Punitiveness—permissiveness, 49

Q

Q-array, 183
Q-correlations, 144-145, 184
Q-sort, 31, 145
Quantitative,
    research, 135, 138
    traits, 56

R

Race differences, 171
Rapport, 168
Rating,
    analysis of, 36
    effects, 3
    flaws, 34
Ratings, by observers, 32
Ratio, 36
Rational-empirical method,
    dependence theory, 151
Reactions, 131
Reactive measure, 9
Reactor (LSD), 109, 111
Reinforcement,
    control of, 47
Reliability, 158
    interjudge, 149, 159, 183
    interpersonal, 25
    test-retest, 159
Religious views, 4
Remission, 96
    evidence of, 93
Report,
    informant, 2
    nonverbal self, 2
    verbal self, 2
Repression, 112
Research, 11
    attitude, 46
    preinventory, 132
Response bias, 46-47, 56

    valid variance in, 48
Response set, 119, 166
Response sets, 3, 8-9, 48, 73
    acquiescence response set
        formulation, 8
    criticisms, 14
    deviant response attitudes, 8
Rigidity, characterological, 163
Roche Interpretative System, 13
Rorschach, 5, 13, 22-24, 40, 60, 146,
    152-153
Revision (MMPI),
    from scratch, 146
Rules, decision, 71
Russell-Whitehead continuum, 137

S

S-R inventories, 5
Sample characteristics,
    demographic, 183
Scale construction, 160, 162, 176
    empirical, 113
    process of, 174
Scale purity, 171
Scale sets,
    personological, 87
    symptomatic, 87
Scales, nonoverlapping, 111
Scales (MMPI),
    criteria for deriving better, 39
    external validity, 16
    high reliability, 27
    high validity, 46
    method of construction, 16
    syndromic, 113
    use of clinical, 16
    typifying, 113
    validational, 113
Scales (MMPI),
    anxiety, 178
    CH-scale, 169
    cluster, 97-99, 109
    depression, 87-88, 93, 98, 109,
        177-178, 182
    ego defense, 102, 109-111
    ego strength, 181
    F, 78, 88
    family problems scale, 48

H, 169
Hs, 93, 98, 105, 182
Hy, 93, 182
introversion (Si), 93, 110, 181
K, 46, 75, 78, 88
L, 78, 88
L_6, 165
M_a, 93, 98, 165, 169, 181
M-F, 16, 93
N, 30, 90
P_a, 30. 90
P_d, 88, 90, 93, 105, 109, 112, 165, 169-170
P_t, 88, 93, 105, 109, 165, 181
S_c, 88, 93, 98, 105, 109, 112, 156, 165, 178
S_t, 171
Scaling, 63
Schizoid type, 165
Schizoidia, 183
Schizophrenia, 118, 155-158, 171
　early, 141
　hysteric, 168
　progress in knowledge of, 39
　pseudoneurotic, 141
Schizophrenic, 25
　process, 167
　reaction, 112
Schizotypal anhedonia, 178
Schizotypes, 135, 157, 175
School, difficulty in, 139
Science, primitive state of, 133
Sciences, physical and biological, 25
Scientism, 36-37
Scoring, 86
　services, 124
Search methods, taxonomic, 176
Selection, employment, 11, 64
　discrimination in, 11
　subjectivism in, 22
Self, 55
　concept, 27, 166
　deception, 166
　denial, 112
Self-report,
　controversy between projective and objective, 41
　distortion in, 73
Semantic dementia, 140
Sentence completion, 53, 155

Sexual attitudes, 16
Sexual deprivation, measure of current, 112
Single-stage assessment, 66
Sixteen Personality Factor Questionnaire (16PF), 132
Situational,
　changes, 33
　contexts, 61
　influences, 7-8
　tasks, 9
　variables, 3
Skills,
　perceptual, 2
Social class, 139
Social desirability, 46, 82, 119
　formation of, 8
Social,
　learning, 29
　living, 27
Sociopathic, 25, 135, 139, 170
Sociopathoid, 138
　personality syndrome, 140
　type, 170
Solitude, Asch type, 146
Somatic,
　compliance, 163
　concern, 167
　conversions, operant based, 168
　items, 56
　preoccupations, 112
Source trait, 97
Sparine, 104
Stability,
　test-retest, 111
Standards for Educational and Psychological Tests and Manuals, 121
Stimulus control, 6
Stochastic processes, 154
Stop items, 113
Strong Vocational Interest Blank, 15, 117, 121, 126, 132, 146, 162
　accident proneness index, 122
　Airforce Officer Scale, 122
　Aviator Scale, 122
　Banker Scale, 122
　Interest Maturity Scale, 122-123
　revision of, 123, 129
Structured personality inventories, 132

Subject Index

Structured personality tests,
    dynamics of, 131
Style of life, 55
Stylistic, 74
    aspects, 74
    tendencies, 75
Styles, individual, 31
Subcultural differences, 11
Suicide,
    attempt, 96
    genuine attempt, 142
    gesture, 99
    MMPI prediction of, 142
    potential assessment, 142
    prediction scales, 144
    risk, 144, 157
Superego, constraints, 139
Suppressor, 74
    items, 164
    key, 164, 166
    variables, 75-76
Symptom,
    descriptions, 72
    status measures, 109
Symptomatic status,
    alteration in, 103
Symptomatology, 86
Symptoms, 145
Syndromes,
    disease, 29
    genetic, 152
Syndromic set, 112
Syphilis, 168
System, defensive, 166

T

T-S-C,
    scales, 7-9, 109
    set, 103
Taxonomic,
    analysis, 137
    constructs, 151
    entities, 143
    model, 178
    problems, 174
    search methods, 176
    sortings, 145
    typological problems, 174
Taxonomy, 132

Temperament, 12, 138
Tension, 88
    level of, 99
Test,
    booklet, portable, 85
    building, 132
    construction, 144, 155, 162
    development, 62
    how good, 132
    hidden hand in, 48
    variance, 76
    validation, 162
Testing,
    cost of, 70
    technology, 119
Tests,
    achievement, 146
    advances in construction of, 12
    how to beat personality tests, 10
    indirect and objective, 6
    industrial use, 10
    intelligence, 15, 24, 146
    interest, 15, 146
    morality of, 10
    multiple score test, 50
    personality, 11, 146
    racially sensitive content in, 11-12
    special ability, 146
Thematic Apperception Test, 5, 55, 146
Theory, 56
Theory construction, 60
    models for, 35
Therapist, 135
Therapy, 11, 70
    interpretation of, 142
    protocols, 135
    psychoanalytic, 135
    rational, 135
    uncovering, 135
Thought disorder, 161
Total personality, 5
Trait,
    assessed from history, 145
    assessed from interview, 145
    attributions, 145
    critical, 145
    genetic, 183
    pattern, 145
    phenotypic, 183
    putative, 51

source, 97
theory, 150
Traits, 1, 63, 72
   of anxiety, 87
   being assessed, 16
   general personality, 1
   putative, 51
   robust, 53
   stable domain of, 52
Transference, 168
Translations,
   foreign language, MMPI, 13
Treatment, 70
   art of, 133
   nonchemical, 134
Trips, bad,
   absence of, 105
Tuberculosis, 152-153
Type, 152
   asocial, 146
   extreme political, 160
   ideal, 107
Typological analysis, 137

U

Underachievement, 140
Unity of personality, 55
University of Minnesota Hospitals, 167, 181
User acceptance, 120

V

Values,
   study of, 129
Valid variance,
   response bias in, 49
Validation,
   of actuarial descriptions, 144
   construct, 155
   cross, 161
   of inferences, 149
   of measuring devices, 148
   of personality tests, 149
   processes, 132
   psychologists attitudes toward, 133
   spending time and money on, 132
Validity,
   convergent, 162
   external, 16
   increase in, 76
   of personality tests, 31
   profiles in cross-validation, 31
   Rorschach, 182
   scales, 74
Variables,
   dimensional, 152
   moderator, 161
   nuisance, 160, 169, 171, 173, 175
   unidimensional, 176
Variance,
   nonrandom, 76
Vectors of the mind, 80
Verbal,
   cleverness, 141
   cynicism, 141
   knowledge, measured by achievement test, 153
Vertigo, 157
Vocational aims, 4
Vocational Interest Blank,
   occupational keys for, 68

W

WAC, 127
WAVE, 127
Wechsler, 78
Weight loss, 142
Will, 12
World War I, 12

Y

Yea-sayers versus nay-sayers, 8
Youth subculture, 141